CORSICAN FRAGMENTS

NEW ANTHROPOLOGIES OF EUROPE

Daphne Berdahl, Matti Bunzl, and Michael Herzfeld, founding editors

CORSICAN
FRAGMENTS

Difference, Knowledge, and Fieldwork

Matei Candea

INDIANA UNIVERSITY PRESS
Bloomington and Indianapolis

This book is a publication of

Indiana University Press
601 North Morton Street
Bloomington, Indiana 47404-3797 USA

www.iupress.indiana.edu

Telephone orders	800-842-6796
Fax orders	812-855-7931
Orders by e-mail	iuporder@indiana.edu

Manufactured in the United States of America
Library of Congress Cataloging-in-Publication Data

Candea, Matei.
  Corsican fragments : difference, knowledge, and fieldwork / Matei Candea.
      p. cm.
  Includes bibliographical references and index.
  ISBN 978-0-253-35474-7 (cl : alk. paper) — ISBN 978-0-253-22193-3 (pb : alk. paper) 1. Ethnology—France—Corsica. 2. Kinship—France—Corsica. 3. National characteristics, French. 4. Corsica (France)—Social life and customs. I. Title.
  DC611.C818C36 2010
  944'.99—dc22
                            2009051157

1 2 3 4 5 15 14 13 12 11 10

Contents

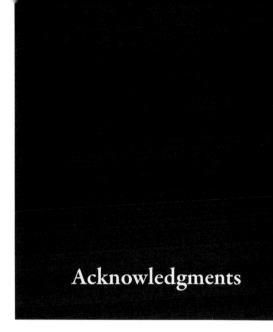

Acknowledgments

My first thanks go to my neighbors and friends in "Crucetta", both Corsican and Continental, for their kindness during my stay there in 2002–2003. As an anthropologist, I learnt much from them about the challenges and rewards of living together in one place that is also many places—and this I have tried to set down in this book. But as a disorientated 22-year old, I learned much more from them of friendship and hospitality than I could contain in these pages—this I carry with me. I also owe a profound debt to the bilingual schoolteachers who not only introduced me to the Corsican language, but also infused me with the energy of a project which they share with anthropologists: the difficult task of conjoining difference and similarity, of maintaining both a plurality of perspectives and a mutual communicability.

My next thanks go to four anthropologists without whom this book would never have seen the light of day. First is Maryon McDonald, to whom this work is indebted in a way which is not exhausted by the language of referencing. The same is true of Marilyn Strathern, whose comments and discussions in the course of the writing-up seminar in Cambridge were more influential than a bibliography can tell. Michael Herzfeld's close reading, encouragement, and advice have been invaluable; in particular, I thank him for encouraging me to write *ethnographically*. Finally, James Laidlaw's keenness of vision and critical acumen have saved me from many an intellectual blunder over the years, while his friendship, infallible advice, and ever-inspiring conversation have been a constant reminder of the value, both academic and human, of the examined life. I also owe profound debts to the following colleagues and friends: Tom Yarrow for his invitation to see archaeologically and for countless other seeds of thought; Alexandra Jaffe for her detailed comments on chapter 6 and for her encouragement and intellectual generosity since the days of my fieldwork; Barbara Bodenhorn for her comments on the section on kinship and for her friendship and guidance ever since our first supervisions on Marx; Christina Toren for giving me that final salutary nudge out of postmodernism at the St. Andrews senior seminar; Martin Holbraad for pointing my way into the maze of the one and the many; Caroline Humphrey for patiently navigating through it over many lunches in the King's College SCR; and Basim Musallam for his thoughts on hospitality and scale and for much else besides. I also owe thanks to Matteo Mameli, Alexander Scheckochihin, and Stefan Uhlig, who perhaps did not suspect that our heated arguments about citizenship and multiculturalism would help to refine this work. The late Susan Benson's close reading and helpful comments on early versions of this work were as inspirational as her earlier guidance during my undergraduate days. I also wish to thank Andrew Barry, Susan Bayly, Ozlem Biner, Michael Carrithers, Jo Cook, Alberto Corsin-Jimenez, Giovanni Da Col, Jeanette Edwards, Mark Elliott, Harri Englund, Mark-Anthony Falzon, Paola Filippucci, Sarah Green, Dave Gullette, Penny Harvey, Laura Jeffery, Sian Lazar, James Leach, David Leitner, Nick Long, Martha de Magalhaes, Chloe Nahum-Claudel, Yael Navaro-Yashin, Morten Pedersen, Adam Reed, Joel Robbins, Michael Scott, Nikolai Ssorin-Chaikov, Rupert Stasch, Catherine Trundle, Soumhya Venkatesan, Piers Vitebsky, Eduardo Viveiros De Castro, Gwyn Williams, Lee Wilson, and all my former colleagues at King's College and the Department of Social Anthropology in Cambridge, where this book was written under the aegis of the Sigrid Rausing Lectureship in Collaborative Anthropology. My gratitude goes also to Miki Bird, Daniel Pyle, Merryl Sloane, Rebecca Tolen, and all at Indiana University Press whose fantastic editorial work have made this book possible.

An earlier version of chapter 3 appeared in *Anthropological Theory* (Candea 2008; SAGE Publications, Inc. ©), while parts of chapters 7 and 8 appeared in the *Journal of the Royal Anthropological Institute* (Candea 2010B; Blackwell Publishing, inc. ©). I am grateful to both for allowing the partial reproduction of this work here.

Last but not least, I want to thank my family: Alexandru Papilian, Victor I. Stoichita, Victor A. Stoichita, and Pedro and Maria Stoichita, for their direct and indirect roles over the years in shaping not just this book, but the person who wrote it; Catherine Candea, for her close reading of many versions of this work and for her strength, wisdom, and unerring judgment; and finally, Katherine Sturgess, for her curiosity and insight on the good writing days, her forbearance and patience on the bad, and for her love and friendship throughout.

CORSICAN FRAGMENTS

Prologue: Roadmap

The theoretical conclusions will then be found to
be implicit in an exact and detailed description.

—EVANS-PRITCHARD 1976

I'd say that if your description needs an explanation, it's not a good description, that's all.

—LATOUR 2005

There is a venerable tradition in British social anthropology which requires that
theoretical argument be woven implicitly into descriptive writing. This does not boil
down merely to the rhetorical pursuit of an "empirical style": instead, an argument
emerges slowly at the pace at which one reads a careful description and gets infused
with the complexity of detail through which it is filtered. Somewhat unexpectedly,
perhaps, this rather unfashionable tradition dovetails with some influential recent
pronouncements on social scientific method.[1] These have tended to emphasize the
slow unfolding of connections and tracing of flows, at the expense of the powerful shortcuts of theory, which so suddenly and effortlessly zoom out to reveal "the
whole picture."

This book partakes of these sensibilities. It is an account of society, language, and the power of place on the island of Corsica from the profoundly limited perspective of one—fairly young and initially quite inexperienced—ethnographer who spent over a year there in 2002–2003. Corsica, which first became a part of France in 1769, has long been a popular destination for travelers in search of the European exotic. Since the late eighteenth century, it has also been a prime locus of French concerns about the meaning of "Frenchness" and about national unity, compounded by the revival of regionalism in 1960s France and the appearance of armed Corsican nationalist groups in the 1970s. But Corsica was also caught up, in complex ways, in the French colonial project and is now intricately enmeshed in a vibrant and contested Franco-Mediterranean assemblage of histories, peoples, and tensions. The lives of Corsican pastoralists and engaged intellectuals, Moroccan labor migrants, continental French holiday makers, and civil servants interweave, mingle, and intersect, claiming space between rootedness and disconnection, between stillness and flow.

Many books on Corsica have attempted a panoramic survey, identified "problems" and offered "solutions." By contrast, this book suggests that insight into the themes which exercise Corsicans and non-Corsicans, such as place, identity, difference, and society, can be garnered not so much despite ethnography's necessary limitations but through them. By tracking the gradual and progressive "enfielding" of one anthropologist, with all its attendant blunders and awkwardness, the book suggests that this process can mirror and yield valuable insights into the similar predicaments of others who are only ever partially "local." As a result, while each chapter is in some measure thematically focused, the book as a whole is not structured like a reference work, with chapters on history, identity, language, and so forth building up a total composite picture. Rather, the argument proceeds primarily by means of a narrative traced and shaped through a sequence of partial positions which do not add up to a whole but to a journey. The rest of the prologue breaks with this commitment to implicit argument in order to provide a synthetic roadmap to the chapters.

[handwritten margin note: WHY WE TRUST NAIVE ?]

At the heart of this book is a question about the place of difference in Corsica and in anthropological analysis. Anthropologists working in Europe, and particularly those working in the Mediterranean, have often found difficulties with the widely held conviction that anthropology is, at heart, a science of difference or, to quote Adams, "the systematic study of the Other, whereas all of the other social disciplines are, in one sense or another, studies of the self" (Adams 1998, p. 1). In this particular division of labor, the Mediterranean, as Michael Herzfeld once noted, adapting

Douglas, is matter out of place: neither quite Other, nor quite self (Herzfeld 1989, p. 7), and the same goes for Europe, that constantly shifting terrain of differences and similarities, which can in no straightforward sense play the role of a stable "us" against which the anthropological account of a "them" can be deployed.

In turn, this has left Europeanist anthropology itself somewhat "out of place," as the embattled 1980s debates around "anthropology at home" testify. In the best cases, this liminality has been an asset, forcing Europeanist anthropologists, more urgently perhaps than others, not to take difference for granted—which in turn has led to some extremely sophisticated analyses of the processes whereby difference is socially constructed, an outcome of certain processes, rather than the starting point of the anthropological account (Chapman 1978; Herzfeld 1989; McDonald 1989). This interest in the construction of difference, however, came under serious critical fire from those who felt that "anti-essentialism had gone too far" (Werbner 1997) in disregarding people's affective investment in their own identities, or in disempowering members of dominated communities which relied on identity politics (Briggs 1996). In the twenty-first century, there was a powerful return toward taking difference seriously in anthropology, as Said's (1979) and Fabian's (1983) critiques of Othering lost some of their impact and the whole 1980s "crisis of representation" (Clifford and Marcus 1986; Marcus and Fischer 1986) increasingly came to seem somewhat old-fashioned and overblown. The mark of this return to difference has been a shift away from postmodernism in what has been called an "ontological turn" (Viveiros de Castro 2003; Henare et al. 2006), marked by calls to move beyond mere cultural difference (which still implies natural sameness) into real ontological alterity (Henare et al. 2006). For one of the main theorists of this new turn, anthropology's vocation is to become "the science of the ontological self-determination of the world's peoples" (Viveiros de Castro 2003, p. 18).

This is not just a story about theoretical trends. We have here a dilemma which goes to the very core of the anthropological endeavor: is difference or sameness the ground against which analysis should proceed? If traditional anthropology was taken to task for "Othering" its object (cf. Said 1979), is social constructivism in danger of "saming" it (Viveiros de Castro 2003)? Corsica in and of itself forces the analyst to reconsider this alternative, for the foremost issue in debates around Corsica, ethnographically speaking, is precisely the question of Corsican difference from the French: to what extent does it obtain, and of what kind is it? Thus, one is likely to write past much of the action if one begins either with the assumption that this difference is the basic datum from which the analysis should proceed, or with the assumption that this difference is a mere social construct. Somehow, we must keep in view two seemingly incompatible realities. In the first, entities whole and meaningful are an explanatory asset, a starting point, as when the political scientist Bernabéu-Casanova states: "we consider that there is a Corsican people, which shares a language, a culture, a territory. To say this is already to take a position" (Bernabéu-Casanova 1997, p. 13). In the second, such entities (people, language, culture, territory) are an effect, a contingent selection from a teeming multiplicity of other possibilities for contextualization. In order to address these apparently incompatible realities, the book proposes a double theoretical move.

First, it aims to introduce a disturbance into debates about the social construction of identity. Theorists working in the field of science and technology studies have repeatedly claimed that the distinction between essence and social construction is something of a red herring. Construction, after all, is key to actually bringing things into being—as long as we drop the qualifying word "social" (Latour 2005, pp. 88–93). To claim that things are constructed is not to somehow negate their reality, any more than seeing a building site negates the reality of the building which later comes to stand there. Applied to the subject of this book, this real constructivism would not insist condescendingly upon the emotional importance of identities to participants, nor would it praise them as a fake but politically useful "strategic essentialism," nor even insist that their being socially constructed is fine because everything is socially constructed (i.e., unreal). Rather, it would take seriously the ways in which the solidity of (id)entities emerges not through the magic of social fiat, nor from the collective imagination of people, but from real, historical, traceable assemblages of people, things, places, and ideas held together by links and relations of different kinds. In this vein, the questions I will be asking of the entities which undergird people's accounts of difference—such as the village community, the French nation, or Corsican culture—are not "are they real?" or "are they made up?" but rather "have they been realized?" and "of what are they made up"?

Second, the book aims to counterbalance the previous move by tempering the recent push to ground alterity in ontology. Indeed the particular field of identity, ethnicity, and nationalism presents some tricky terrains to navigate for the would-be real constructivist. In a context in which the French state has gone so far as to decree that legal mention of the notion of "the Corsican people" is in and of itself anticonstitutional, I cannot but share Viveiros de Castro's concern for the dangers of saming. However, as an ethnographer working in Europe at a time of increasingly virulent neo-nationalisms, which turn on grounding difference in being (Stolcke 1995; Holmes 2000), I am also slightly worried about the thought of anthropology as "the science of the ontological self-determination of the world's peoples." This proposal, by an Amazonianist anthropologist, is premised on a distinction between Euro-American mono-naturalism and Amazonian multi-naturalism. The thought is perhaps that non-Euro-American ontologies, unlike Euro-American ones, inherently obviate the mirage of holism and ethnicized closure. But in that view, what are ethnographers of Europe or America supposed to do? Either we take the implication that anthropology has no place studying Euro-American ontologies (which would seem a rather problematic step backward, to say the least), or we risk extending the program of ontological self-determination to precisely the kinds of ontological projects of mono-naturalist ethnicizing closure of which everyone in this anthropological debate is equally wary. As Viveiros de Castro points out:

> The image of Being is obviously a dangerous analogic soil for thinking about non-western conceptual imaginations, and the notion of ontology is not without its own risks. Perhaps Gabriel Tarde's bold suggestion that we should abandon the irremediably solipsist concept of Being and relaunch metaphysics on the basis of Having (Avoir)—with the latter's implication of intrinsic transitivity and an originary opening towards an exteriority—is a more enticing prospect in many cases. (2003, p. 17)

This book follows the trail of Viveiros de Castro's "perhaps." As a result, the analysis here remains always *in media res*, located in between purportedly different groups of people. It does not take one such group and its difference from others as the self-evident starting point of the account—as is common in much anthropological exegesis about the culture or ontology of the X. In this respect, it retains the central insight of 1970s and 1980s works on the construction of difference (Chapman 1978; Handler 1984; McDonald 1989): for better or worse, difference and sameness are only ever partial achievements.

In sum, the first argument is about the achieved reality of differences among people, places, languages, and so on: *there is nothing "mere" about construction.* The second argument is about the always contingent, partial, and incomplete nature of such differences and samenesses: whether ontologically or analytically, *difference does not come before sameness, nor sameness before difference.*

Luckily—and here I am giving away the ending—achieving this balance between alterity and a common world, between difference and open-endedness, is not just an anthropological concern, but also concerns many of the people with whom I lived and worked in Corsica. Thus, one solution to this theoretical problem is already there, ethnographically, in Crucetta and in other such places where people deal with relationships and differences on a daily basis. The book's narrative progresses from this theoretical problem to its ethnographic resolution.

The first chapter sets the scene of the account in the village of Crucetta, in which a number of people with diverse trajectories and backgrounds live in some respects together and in some respects past one another. The methodological figure of the field-site as an "arbitrary location" (Candea 2007) is introduced to argue that the distinctive value of ethnography might occasionally lie precisely in its limitations and incompleteness. Having thus shown where the account will take place and having reflected on what such "taking place" might involve, chapter 2 introduces

Corsica. However, Corsica here is not, as one might initially expect, the broader context or background to our account of the village. Rather, the island is introduced as an object of concern and debate which inhabits, rather than frames, the daily lives of people in Crucetta. The chapter examines the *mise en discours* of Corsica over the past two centuries or so, as an inherently problematic object of knowledge, one which is ineffably mysterious and definitionally unknowable to outsiders. This detour through the genealogy of Corsica thus folds back into the ethnographic landscape painted in the first chapter, fleshing out the ways in which distinctions between Corsicans and non-Corsicans in Crucetta bring up assumptions about different kinds of knowledge and insight.

But there is more than one way of thinking about knowledge. With the help of theories of distributed cognition, chapter 3 examines the actual connections among different people, places, and objects which are mobilized when "locals" in Crucetta come together to watch, track, and attempt to fight a fire which creeps toward the village. Emplacement emerges in this chapter as the result of particular traceable relations, far more substantial than metaphor, far less fixed than essence. Tourists' comparative distance from the phenomenon of fires is thus recast not as a difference in kind (indexing something profound about Corsicans or non-Corsicans as such), but rather as a difference in the quantity and nature of relations with other people, places, and things which the tourists are able to mobilize when the crisis of a fire hits. Chapter 3 thus introduces a theme which will become increasingly central to the account: there is a thick web of relations among people, places, and things, which gives substance and conviction to the kind of accounts of essence and mystery examined in chapter 2. These empirically traceable relations "fill up" with recognizable, real stuff, the otherwise abstract claims about the reality of Corsican difference from the continental French, or the patently romantic portrayals of the island and its people as an organic whole. At the same time, the chapter introduces a key paradox: these clear categories and these thick webs of relations in practice do not quite match up; after all, there are non-Corsican inhabitants of Crucetta who are profoundly connected in the above-mentioned sense, just as there are Corsicans who may just be passing through.

This paradox is further unpacked in the next three chapters, which together trace the powerful interplay of ambiguity and certainty at the heart of people's everyday management of differences among things (chapter 4), people (chapter 5), and languages (chapter 6). Together, they articulate a broader argument about the interplay of freedom, definition, and ambiguity. Anthropologists have often contrasted the rigid, state-imposed ways of categorizing people with the generative multiplicity and fine contextuality of local ways of negotiating multiple identities. This contrast usually implies a distinction between an oppressive essentialist imposition of bounded categories and inherently critical, anti-essentialist local practices which give subjects more freedom. The situation in Crucetta is, on the face of it, quite the opposite. On the one hand, the French state's official refusal to recognize the Corsican people is justified through an argument about the negation of essentialist, fixed categories of identity, in the name of an abstract citizenship which in principle allows each individual to juggle multiple forms of identity and belonging. In response, Corsican nationalists in Crucetta and elsewhere are engaged in a definitional battle over the nature of Corsicanness: can it be cast in the same terms in which the French state casts Frenchness, as an abstract, voluntary, non-essentialist framework for citizenship? Or must it rely, as French models themselves do (albeit in an often covert or disavowed way), on a more substantive account of cultural or ethnic rootedness? Thus, explicit political debate, precisely because it seeks to define and redefine clear-cut categories, is the space in which such categories can be challenged, manipulated, and remade. This is also the arena in which, painstakingly, entities such as the Corsican people or the Corsican language can be assembled, a project in which some people in Crucetta are engaged.

When we turn by contrast to the day-to-day ways in which people "do identity" in Crucetta, we move from abstract discussions of the nature of Frenchness and Corsicanness to the myriad ways in which people map minute differences in accents, looks, behaviors, and other such clues, in order to be able—often nearly instantly and almost always without asking—to "tell who is what." What emerges is the paradoxical "thingness" of identity examined in the previous chapter: the fact that seemingly clear-cut distinctions among different "kinds of people" (Continentals, Corsicans, Arabs), while they are seldom explicitly defined and in practice trail off into infinitesimal micro-distinctions, nevertheless emerge as self-evident and binding aspects of reality. It is their very lack of (ultimate) definition which, paradoxically, makes such distinctions so irrevocable and non-negotiably real.

Chapter 7 ties together the discussion of knowledge and relationality and the discussion of difference, inclusion, and exclusion by examining a local idiom: *knowing* (*connaître*), which is used intransitively to denote an open-ended relationality which attaches persons to other persons, places, and things. Discussions of "knowing" and "being known" in Crucetta articulate a concern with the daily management of relationships and connections of various kinds. The polysemy of knowing allows it to shift situationally from being expansively inclusive to mapping an impenetrable interiority, something which binds Corsicans to one another and to the island in a way which Others can only contemplate from the outside. This chapter thus draws together a related set of questions which runs throughout the rest of the book: is there an insider's view of Crucetta (chapter 1)? Can a Continental ever "really understand" Corsica (chapter 2)? Can someone become local (chapter 3)? What makes something Corsican (chapter 4)? Can someone become Corsican (chapter 5)? Can someone become a Corsican-speaker (chapter 6)? These questions now all emerge as refractions of the same question: can one become a part of the kind of assemblage delineated by the word *connaître?*

Finally, chapter 8 suggests that one partial answer to this question is already present, ethnographically, in Crucetta—if one only looks in the right way. It focuses on a tiny, evanescent bit of ethnographic imponderabilia: a tendency for people in Crucetta to avoid asking or giving each other's names at a first meeting. One could add this "anonymous introduction" to the long list of instances of Corsican "reticence," "secrecy," or "closedness," or one could find in it, paradoxically, the very principle of initial open-endedness which allows one to start knowing and becoming known, to enter into what otherwise seems an impenetrable interiority. This requires us to think beyond the familiar self/Other dualism which animates the anthropology of identity in order to ask questions about becoming, beginning to relate, and "introduction" in the sense of the entry of one object into another— here, of a person into an already existing relational assemblage. That this "way in" takes the form of a negativity, a question unasked, a holding-in-abeyance, is highly significant. In this way, the ethnographic occurrence of the anonymous introduction parallels the methodological fiction of the arbitrary location, with which the account begins.

A Note on the Text

The names of persons, villages, and hamlets in this book are fictitious. All translations from French and Corsican, unless otherwise stated, are my own.

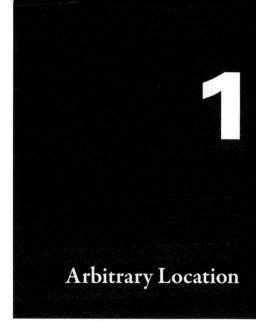

Arbitrary Location

Anthropologists don't study villages
(tribes, towns, neighborhoods . . .);
they study *in* villages.

—GEERTZ 1973

The village is a thousand shards
of broken mirrors.

—GALIBERT 2004A

Crucetta

The house known as "the Englishwoman's house" (*la maison de l'anglaise*) stands empty. "The Englishwoman," *l'anglaise,* died two years before my arrival in the Corsican village I will call "Crucetta," and the ocher house with blistered light-green shutters has recently acquired new owners: the Viltanés, a family from the Continent, who plan to spend their summer holidays here once they have "done the place up." Next summer, the shutters will be painted bright blue, and the vines will be luxuriant and neat over the metal pergola. Two brothers and two sisters, holding nets for crabs and salt-encrusted snorkels, will be chasing each other up and down the stone staircase. But for now, the house is empty, save for the last remnants of a solitary life. *L'anglaise,* unlike the Viltanés, had lived in this house all year 'round, for over twenty years. She had been a painter of some local fame, and when her son came to take away her canvases, some in the neighborhood felt that he was plundering the cultural heritage of Crucetta. His action certainly left people with no compunction when it came to claiming what he did discard.

Which brings me to the reason for my visit. My neighbor Petru, who since my arrival in the neighborhood has taken me under his wing, has decided that I am doubly qualified, as a bookish type and one hailing from England, to take my pick of the leftover jumble of reading materials which has been unceremoniously dumped in a mildewed, shelf-less bookcase in what was once a living room.

Petru is a young man of eighty-three, with twinkling eyes and wispy white hair escaping from under his trademark cloth cap. He is one of the last active shepherds in a village which was once a flourishing agricultural center at the heart of the lush Balagne region—"the granary of Corsica." Petru is the last shepherd in Crucetta to use a donkey for travel and transport, day in, day out; others long ago abandoned the heavy wooden saddle for a pickup truck or the iconic Citroen C15 minivan. Increasingly, however, Petru's donkeys' primary use seems to be to give rides to the children of summer residents, among whom the shepherd is something of a celebrity. For those who have invested in a summer house at the heart of this Corsican village, Petru is the perfect mix of rugged authenticity and knowing humor. His body speaks of his trade: short, dense, and still surprisingly powerful, matured with age into a careful slowness which contrasts starkly with the fragile hesitancy of elderly city-dwellers. Petru's hands are brown, coarse, and careful, hands that can still milk a ewe or dig a ditch at an age when others find it hard to hold a remote control. The middle finger of his left hand was bent out of shape by some unmentioned accident. When he stops to wipe the sweat from his brow, the skin of his forehead above the line of his ever-present cap is startlingly white. Petru's voice, too, captivates the seekers of authenticity. Its peculiar timbre is noticeable first, deep like whispering gravel. And then the language itself—for Petru is one of the last old men whose French is clearly a somewhat forced second to his Corsican; his French grammar and pronunciation are like borrowed clothes stretched over an uncompliant body. Petru thus embodies a certain ideal of Corsican autochthony which pleases tourists no less than cultural activists.

But real authenticity can be slightly dry fare when it is unseasoned by some ironic twist. And the holiday makers clearly enjoy the fact that Petru sees straight through their romantic foibles, the fact that he can, with one comically exaggerated expression of astonishment and admiration (slack jaw, raised eyebrows), pour gentle scorn on their keenness to hang rusty sheep shears on their whitewashed walls or rest their aperitifs on an old threshing stone. *L'anglaise* too, despite her long-term, full-time residence, seems to have gone in for this sort of thing, and her walls are decorated with traditional farming implements in various states of disrepair. And indeed, hearing Petru talk about her, it seems that for all their erstwhile closeness, they, too, had lived past each other in some important ways. The painter used to walk every morning along a dirt track which led away from the village. I, too, came to walk that path. After picking through some brambles and sheep droppings, the path suddenly opens up onto a little ridge from which one is hit, all at once, by the formidable expanse of the valley below and, beyond it, a forbidding mountain range. Dusty greens and pale ochers, sharp grey peaks and the gentle froth of trees in the distance; the smell of myrtle, rosemary, and rockrose; and the occasional bells and barks of unseen dogs and their flocks, carried uncannily close by some unfelt breeze. A bench had been placed there, beside the thin metal cross, ensconced in a stone base, which gives this spot its name: *a crucetta,* the little cross. The English painter had loved *a crucetta* so much that she had asked for her ashes to be scattered from that spot into the valley below.

For Petru, by contrast, *a crucetta* is first and foremost a sheepfold, which stands some yards up the hill from the little ridge: a low dry-stone double arch with a solid wooden pen attached, a place one reaches not by the little path, but by walking through dry, dusty olive groves behind scattering sheep. Petru has about as little use for the bench as the painter had for the pungent sheepfold: *a crucetta,* in sum, was two very different places, and the difference between them was stark. When he described the painter's last wishes, Petru explained with somewhat amused disdain that she had asked to be "burned and thrown away, over there, at the cross." A strange thing to wish for, indeed, to a man whose vision of death involves orderly and impressive white vaults collating over generations the dust of entire families down in the "little village" by the church. Over time, I became a regular at both of those places, the sheepfold and the bench; both together, and the difference between them, motivated my choice of pseudonym for the village of "Crucetta."

In Crucetta, the mirage of a holistic account for a whole village dissipates and we are left with something rather different: Petru and *l'anglaise* lived side by side, lived together, in a place that was also two places, their realities splitting off from each other in subtle but profound ways. Nor were they alone: the village in which *l'anglaise* lived did not quite map onto the village the Viltanés were about to move into—and neither of those corresponded particularly well to the village in which a number of migrants from North Africa eked out a discreet and fleeting existence for some months of the year. As Petru led me through the *maison de l'anglaise* and his various memories of her, I began to glimpse the multiplicity of disjunctive lives and understandings which brushed past each other in the neighborhood in which

FIGURE I.I. A *crucetta*

I had just settled. I started to think of my uneasy trawling through the dead woman's castaway books as in some ways a disturbingly apt metaphor for the work of ethnography in Crucetta: here I was, collecting fragments of intimacy.

> On the one hand English villages are imagined as centers that remain fixed. They form a focus for long-term attachment, containing folk intermeshed in an intricate web of connections, each place a discrete unit looking outward. On the other hand they appear to be vanishing institutions. They vanish either because they are left behind, with people moving out to worlds that have nothing to do with the village, or because they are submerged, invaded by people moving in from elsewhere who turn it into a different kind of place, creating a radical fragmentation between a communal then and an anonymous now. (Strathern 2004, p. 23; cf. Strathern 1981)

My opening vignette could seem a straightforward instance of this familiar story, of the fragmentation introduced into a previously whole place by accelerated movement. The contrast between Petru and *l'anglaise* seems to bring up the classic opposition between rooted insiders, who are shaped and molded by their local knowledge, and more or less ephemeral outsiders, strangers, add-ons, whose link to landscape (rather than land) is romantic and superficial. But look again, and the account separates itself from itself: the ashes of the English painter fly over the valley from the little cross and mingle—infinitesimal, dispersed—with the land, the dust, the trees, the river. In the most literal and physical of ways, *l'anglaise* has become a part of the place, complicating easy distinctions between insiders and outsiders, persons and places, metaphorical and real connections. Such distinctions clean up and hierarchize, they allow one to specify what the story is about. But by the same token, they fail to capture the things in between, complications upon complications which are of necessity edited out of seemingly complete and meaningful accounts.

And yet there were some overarching coherences to Crucetta. For the view of villages described by Strathern is one which inhabitants of Crucetta themselves articulated on more than one occasion, as they reflected on the past and present of the village in which they lived. I am including in this generalizing category ("inhabitants of Crucetta") people such as Petru, for whom this "communal then" was an intimate memory, as well as people such as the Viltanés, for whom this past was a romantic horizon which they themselves had never experienced. As Strathern noted, people "share their villages" even when they seem to be living different, indeed incommensurable, lives. That is to say, these different people, with their different attachments and relationships to place, share their ideas about what a village is, and this in turn makes them similar. "But those similar ideas disguise themselves by appearing as ideas about dissimilarity: they are ideas about how different everyone is from one another, how different places are" (2004, p. 25).

One could scale up this insight to talk about another kind of similarity and difference: "cultural difference," too, is a shared trope among inhabitants of Crucetta, particularly when they feel it divides them from one another. One difference in particular is salient here, that between Corsicans and the continental French, a constant topic of discussion and implicit reference in the village. Yet, at the very moment at which people stress their cultural differences, they are still living together in a world in which there are cultural differences. At the moment at which they articulate their different—indeed, perhaps irreconcilable—attachments to the island of Corsica, they are living together in a world in which Corsica is a common point of reference, a unitary object, a salient entity.

This book is an attempt to find an anthropological footing in this rather destabilizing situation, in which differences are similarities and similarities are differences. The problem, put simply, is this: how can one produce an account which keeps in view both the fact that there are real differences among people and places, that intimacies, even in a small village, are multiple and fragmented, and the fact that these differences are bridged by shared, conventional ways of thinking about difference? Or, to put the problem conversely: how can one produce an account which acknowledges the fact that entities which are daily brought up to explain differences and similarities among people, such as "(being from) the village," "Corsicanness," or "French culture," are enacted constructions rather than timeless essences, while still taking difference seriously? This problem echoes an ambiguity at the heart of the anthropological endeavor, which constantly oscillates between difference and similarity as philosophical, heuristic, and ethical frames of reference, but which also derives in part from the location of my ethnography.

A Multi-Sited Research Project Capsizes

This account is not the one I had originally set out to write. I had arrived in Crucetta in September 2002 with the aim of studying bilingual (Corsican-French) education, a recently established educational practice which had been pioneered in a number of local primary schools. I chose Crucetta as the central base for my research as I was told that its bilingual school had a very high profile on the island. This was due to the sterling efforts of its schoolmaster, Pascal, a man who had been an impassioned advocate of Corsican language and culture since his youth in the 1970s. Pascal, when I first met him, was an energetic fifty-something with a cropped beard and an infectious laugh. He sported wire half-moon glasses which spent most of the time either hanging from a string around his neck or tucked up onto his balding pate. With his gruff kindness and meticulous elocution, he reminded me of some of my own favorite schoolmasters, those stalwarts of the Éducation Nationale who, in a primary school near Paris, helped to shape this Romanian immigrant into a fluent French-speaker. Like them, Pascal loved the French singer Georges Brassens, with his impeccable use of the subjunctive and irreverent sallies against all forms of established order. Like them, he instilled in his pupils an eagerness to learn as much as knowledge itself. Unlike my own schoolmasters, however, Pascal did this in two languages.

Bilingual education was the latest outcome of a complex tango between the French state and local cultural activists, which had over the past thirty years progressively introduced "regional languages and cultures" into the national educational curriculum in a number of French regions (Jaffe 1999, 2005, 2007; McDonald 1989). The government's increasingly liberal policies on regional language and culture provided the legal structure and the empty forms which teachers such as Pascal filled in with inventive teaching materials and curriculum elements. These teaching materials were often devised ad hoc by teachers and shared as photocopies or electronic files with colleagues from a few valleys away. This interface of formal and informal, state and non-state, nation and region, has long been a feature of French regionalist education (McDonald 1989).

In Corsica, however, the question of regional language and culture has taken on a rather more urgent note than in other French regions. Since the 1970s, Corsica has been in the forefront of the French news and of the government's preoccupations in part due to a number of well-equipped and extremely determined paramilitary organizations which regularly apply plastic explosives to public buildings and the second homes of continental French residents; machine-gun the facades of town halls, courts, and police stations; and issue emphatic statements denouncing what they term the "French colonial state." Alongside these and in a complex relationship with them, official Corsican nationalist parties take part in local elections on platforms ranging from hardline demands for independence to softer calls for greater autonomy within France (Hossay 2004; Loughlin 1989). Beyond nationalism proper, there is a broader circle of regionalist enthusiasts and activists promoting Corsican language and culture (McKechnie 1993; Jaffe 1999) who have an often ambivalent relationship to the frankly independentist, let alone the explicitly violent sections of Corsican nationalism. Hence, the rather complex position of bilingual schoolteachers, who are often located in some way within or on the margins of this extended (and, internally, very diverse) regionalist/nationalist universe—and yet are employees of the French state (Candea, forthcoming A).

Within this complex and contested situation, my original plan was to study the ethical self-formation of both teachers and pupils in a bilingual schooling context. I had envisaged this as a multi-sited study (Marcus 1995; Candea 2007). Crucetta's primary school was one of a number of such institutions across the island, which were linked by thick networks of bilingual schoolteachers such as Pascal, who met periodically at training seminars and network meetings; by contrast, the kinds of spaces within which educational policy was made, contested, and applied mapped other trajectories, from Crucetta to the regional administrative headquarters and all the way to the Parisian headquarters of the National Education Ministry. I had come prepared to "follow" (cf. Marcus 1995) these complex assemblages and trajectories through various sites, of which Crucetta's primary school was only one. Within this framework, I had thought of the village of Crucetta—rather summarily, in retrospect—as one more "site," another place in which these processes and trajectories played themselves out. I had come prepared to ask (among other things) how and to what extent technologies of the self, linguistic forms, and definitions of culture which were promoted in a school setting converged with or diverged from those promoted at home "in the village" (for an excellent study in this vein, see Reed-Danahay 1996).

I had certainly not come to Corsica, in other words, to do a village study. Fresh from my theoretical pre-fieldwork preparation, I shared Gupta and Ferguson's slight suspicion of what they call the "common sense of the discipline," according to which "an anthropological dissertation would normally involve an ethnographic study of a *local community* (however 'linked' it might be with a wider system), and . . . such a study would make use of the usual fieldwork methodology (stereotypically, 'twelve months in a village'), appropriately supplemented with historical 'background'" (Gupta and Ferguson 1997, p. 25). Stereotypically, twelve months in a village? Not for me, I thought. Since I had to live somewhere, I rented a one-bedroom flat fashioned out of the vaulted cellars of an old house at the center of the village. But the village, I vowed, would just be one site among many in a methodologically sophisticated, multi-strand account.

As it happens, I had rather misjudged the difficulty. Increasingly, it became obvious that the hard thing here was not to break out of the village, but to keep it in view. The difficult thing was not so much to be multi-sited, as to be "sited" at all.

The Village Multiple

To begin with, it is somewhat unclear where to begin: where would a description of "the village of Crucetta" start? "While places have centres . . . ," writes Tim Ingold, "they have no boundaries" (1993, pp. 155–156), and Crucetta was no exception. Or rather, which adds up to the same, it had a multiplicity of conflicting boundaries. An account of going to Crucetta from the nearby town of Ile Rousse, for instance, makes this unboundedness palpable.

The large Place Paoli in Ile Rousse, with its impressive double row of palm trees and its statue of the "father of the Corsican nation," Pascal Paoli, who was also the founder of this small coastal town, is lined with cafés and restaurants, which spill out onto the square their color-coded sets of chairs and tables. Here, those who are familiar with the place know that they are already to some extent in Crucetta. Crucettacci own some of these cafés, others work in them, many are sitting at the tables drinking coffee and reading newspapers. On opposite sides of the square are the two pharmacies and behind, in another street, the two bookstores, none of which need any qualifier when mentioned "up in the village." Ile Rousse is where most Crucettacci work: in 1999, according to the National Institute of Statistics and Economic Studies (INSEE), only 29.2 percent of the active population of Crucetta worked within the *commune* (a designation I will elaborate below); this figure fell to 24.3 percent in 2006. Ile Rousse is also where many of them socialize, where all of them go if they need a doctor, a vet, the post office, or a cash machine; where they do their weekly shopping; where children over primary-school age go to school; and where young people go for a night out in the various bars and clubs—most of which, however, are closed out of season.

The "road to Crucetta," as it is usually known, starts a few streets away from the Place Paoli, down a wide and dusty avenue bordered by tall trees. One drives past a tall block of flats with a supermarket on the first floor and a number of hardware stores, until the view opens up onto a wide grey-green plain with the ever-present mountainous backdrop. As the road rises steeply, the first outlying villas start to appear against the background of *maquis* and olive trees, anything from expensive architectural wonders of dry-stone walling and wood, to standard pink "bricks" and unfinished concrete skeletons. After a long stretch of narrow winding road, Ile Rousse and the sea recede into the distance, and a sign announces that you are entering Crucetta. Throughout France, such road signs signal that you are entering an *agglomération,* an inhabited area, and they automatically imply a speed limit of fifty kilometers per hour. Their exact location is therefore often fixed according to practical concerns of road safety, and they do not necessarily mark a spot which is either locally or administratively meaningful as an inner/outer boundary. By this point, in fact, one has already been driving for a while on the land of the *commune* of Crucetta.

La commune is a term which will return throughout the account and needs some elaboration: it is the smallest unit in French administrative geography; while it is centered on a town or village, its territory encompasses the surrounding land. The entire territory of metropolitan France is comprehensively subdivided into 36,772 *communes.* The political representatives of the *commune* are the mayor, his deputy (*le premier adjoint*), and the council, often referred to collectively as *la municipalité.*

In Crucetta, *la commune* was used contextually to refer to the village, to its population, to the entire territory, or to *la municipalité*. Thus, one might say, "Crucetta is a *commune* of 850 inhabitants," but also "the supermarket isn't on our *commune*, it's on the *commune* of Sole," or "the *commune* has built a covered bus stop which is really popular with the elderly inhabitants."

A few kilometers farther up the road, past more villas, the road snakes past a small hamlet of beautiful huddled stone houses, cradling in its tarmac bend a short, squat chapel. Up another steep incline and around a few more curves, one reaches yet another sign announcing the name Crucetta, this time placed to coincide with the village's main hamlet. We have thus reached Crucetta, but the moment at which we entered it remains uncertain. Indeed, the decision to start in Ile Rousse appears, in retrospect, totally arbitrary. Like most Corsican villages, Crucetta has a sizable population of "weekend migrants" who work in the much larger town of Bastia but commute back to the village every weekend. It also partakes of the broader Corsican trend toward what the anthropologist Isac Chiva has termed "attached emigration" (*émigration a attaches;* Chiva 1958): a diasporic population living on the French mainland and farther afield, which returns to the village every summer and at major holidays and is continuously, although sometimes remotely, involved in the sociality, economy, and general life of the village. As Charlie Galibert has noted and indeed demonstrated in his beautifully evocative ethnographies of the village of Sarrola Carcopino (Galibert 2004b; Galibert 2004a), any account which aims to encompass a Corsican village as an anthropologically coherent place, a center in Ingold's sense, will have to become in practice multi-sited, since the village extends indefinitely through time and space, along with the peregrinations and imaginations of its inhabitants.

Setting aside for now the question of boundaries, the inner multiplicity of the village was no less of a hindrance to the isolation of a single site. This multiplicity was, first, visual. While the consistent palette of grey, cream, pink, and ocher and the invariably red-tiled roofs present a surface conformity, this dissolves, as soon as one looks more carefully, into a motley assortment of building types, from old, crooked, tightly packed stone houses, through imposing two- and three-story villas, to the low, modernist architecture of the new school complex and the two blocs of council flats. To the informed eye of one who does not come to Crucetta as a ready-made thing, but who has lived there since before the 1960s, this apparent confusion is mediated by time. And when the complex and subtle time frames attached to these buildings are sifted down and flattened out for the benefit of an interested newcomer, the landscape falls into the following "archaeological" shape.

The first layer of this simultaneous archaeology, the old village, linked to the imposing parish church below by a long straight stone path known simply as "the cobbled (way)" (*a chjappata*) and, below the church, the cemetery with its neat agglomeration of shining white family vaults make the common designation "the little village" visually obvious. The old village, otherwise known as the hamlet of Pietra, is the largest and most central of the three or four (depending on whom you ask) hamlets which together form the village of Crucetta: Pietra, Santa-Croce, Casale, and L'Olmu. This village/hamlet distinction and orderly subdivision was rather unstable, however. L'Olmu, which was effectively a continuation of Pietra, was sometimes characterized as a neighborhood of the latter, especially when, as often happened, Pietra was conflated with Crucetta as a whole (as "the old village"). By contrast, the larger hamlets of Santa-Croce and Casale, which were physically separated from Pietra by tracts of scrubland, tended toward being treated as villages in their own right—which were described as on or in the *commune* of Crucetta. Some older inhabitants of Pietra went so far as to say that those from Casale had always been more involved with the neighboring village of Murettu than with Crucetta. Such characterizations of hamlet inhabitants—others being that those from Casale were rich and those from Santa-Croce were very religious, for instance—seemed to be more common among older inhabitants and were usually framed in the past, rather than the present, tense. The archives of Crucetta council meetings also attest to an earlier time when the hamlets/villages were periodically locked in political and economic struggles over their respective centrality and peripherality to the entity Crucetta.[1]

In the course of my fieldwork, however, inter-hamlet debates hardly featured, and issues of center/periphery seemed to have been mostly settled in favor of Pietra. The village's butcher, its baker, and its grocery store were all concentrated there, as were the four bars, two of which doubled as restaurants and hotels, and its town hall, situated in a rented house in the center of the hamlet. But increasingly and more to the point, the whole of Crucetta tended to be on the periphery of the nearby town of Ile Rousse. Added to this was a gradual yet fairly drastic change in the actual shape of the place, a second "layer" produced by the appearance, since the 1960s, of the villas. One of the first of these belonged to the headmaster Pascal's uncle, who built a lone house nearly a mile from the center of the largest hamlet. Pascal recounted that when his uncle first built his lone villa outside the village, many in Crucetta said he was mad. Soon enough, however, other Crucettacci followed his example, including in time the headmaster himself. To me, he explained his decision in terms of his need for freedom and independence, the desire to get away from the close neighborhood of the village center, where everyone knows everyone's business, and one's neighbors are constantly "breathing down one's neck" (cf. Jaffe 1999, p. 43).

Since the 1960s, many more villas have been built around the old hamlets, introducing a dramatic change in the landscape, which is common to most Corsican villages and which is sometimes referred to disdainfully as *mitage,* "moth-eating":

the image is of the green fabric of the countryside being slowly filled with tiny, white villa-shaped holes—an image which resonates more widely with metaphors of decay from an original state of completeness and unity. Judging by people's attitudes at the time of my fieldwork, it did not take very long for the fact of building a house on the outskirts of the village to shift from being an eccentricity to being a fairly conventional sign of social success, referred to positively as "making one's house" (in Corsican: *fà a so casa*). As a result, the space between the once clearly delimited hamlets is increasingly being filled with new constructions, folding the built environment into one increasingly continuous if heterogeneous shape. Standing at the approximate center of this built environment, an unprepossessing complex of concrete buildings, which included the village school, the events hall (*salle polyvalente*), and a block of council flats (Habitations à Loyer Modéré; HLM), had emerged in the 1980s.

As I have begun to suggest, a diverse and mobile population inhabited this multiple space. To interrupt the all-seeing, panoramic description which has been creeping into my account, however, let me introduce this topic through its treatment by Pascal, the schoolmaster. This makes the point that Crucetta, like most places, already comes with its embedded sociologies; it already contains accounts of itself and its own local panoramas (see Latour 2005) which add layers to its already teeming complexity. Every three years, all French primary schools must present a school project (*projet d'école*), in which they outline a plan for a new activity which they propose to implement during the next three years. Each school project must be headed with a report on the school and its environment, which outlines a problem to which the project is a response. In 1999, the schoolmaster wrote, in a rounded, even hand on faintly lined paper, the following assessment of the village of Crucetta:[2]

I. 1) Geographic, cultural and social data
. . . The population of [Crucetta] is spread over 3 types of habitat:

A) Old traditional habitat (centre of the village). Relatively sparsely populated. Many empty houses during the winter (little or no modern amenities). These houses are often inhabited by Maghrebi immigrants.

B) Social housing, HLM type, located near the school. . . . Inhabited by many families, often with a large number of children, but economically weak: high level of unemployment or temporary work. These people are often coming from outside to seek work in Corsica. . . .

C) Around the village: many individual villas, comfortable, inhabited in the great majority by people of [Crucetta] origin.

Note: If one considers the Maghrebi population more specifically (around 25% of the schoolchildren in these last few years) one may note that they inhabit either the old village (rented houses), or the HLMs. This population, due to the precarious nature of work, is highly unstable: many 5–6 children families only stay for a few years, or even a few months before leaving the village. . . . Only the autochthonous population, living in type C) housing is really stable.

Since the headmaster's tripartite sociology was school-centric, it left out the fluctuating and mobile population of tourists and part-time residents whose children were not studying in Crucetta and whose intermittent presence turned certain neighborhoods of the old village into bustling communities for select periods of the year. This obvious blind spot aside, however, his account was reflective of local discourses, in which the center of the village stood for tradition, but also for comparative poverty, old age, emptiness, and paradoxically, a certain form of marginality. And although the progressive emptying out of this marginal center was collectively deplored by many who considered themselves locals (whether they in fact lived there or not), the movement had its own momentum: the marginality of the center was in itself an incentive for people to move out to the periphery and "make their house."

At cross-purposes both temporally and geographically with the trajectories of tourists, of the elderly inhabitants of the old village, and of Franco-Maghrebi labor migrants, the daily trajectories of most of those who lived in the villas rarely included the old village center. As the teacher's report suggests, however, they, rather than the inhabitants of the center, were usually identified as the autochthonous, stable population of Crucetta. Of course, the elderly (Corsican: *i vechji*) were often considered keepers of a form of super-autochthony, as it were, and were identified as the living embodiments of tradition. But this did not come without some ambivalence; and however central it made them to certain imaginings of Corsica and villageness, this centering was in itself a form of marginalization, in which they became the somewhat distanced objects of admiration and ethnography (McKechnie 1993). These complex attitudes toward the old center were interestingly brought out in relation to my own presence in the village. Educated middle-class inhabitants of Crucetta thought it particularly fitting that I should be renting a flat in the old village. It was obviously the right place for a social scientist, both *qua* anthropologist concerned with tradition and, in a different sense, *qua* sociologist concerned with marginality and social problems. I was not expected to do much research in the villas, on the other hand, and my incursion into those spaces was, I came to realize, tacitly treated as an indication of my taking a break from "the field" and retreating into "real life." People would offer me coffee and biscuits and eagerly ask for my anthropological impressions and comments. On a few occasions, I became a mediator between the marginal center and its central periphery, such as when the schoolteacher asked me to inquire whether my neighbor the shepherd would allow his pupils to come witness the milking of the ewes, or when his wife asked me to make sure that my neighbor would set aside a lamb for her that Christmas.

Crucetta was thus not simply internally diverse: the exact makeup of this diversity, the built environment and its semantic density, the population, its origins and trajectories, formed a complex and perpetually shifting mass which had little to recommend it as a single field-site. By contrast, there were no lack of leads to follow here for a multi-sited account. Some spaces, like my own neighborhood in the old village during high tourist season, could be thought of fondly as communities of face-to-face interactions (although one would have to follow their fleeting inhabitants to their winter retreats on the French mainland); others, such as the villas taken together with the nearby town, might perhaps be imagined to form socioeconomic aggregates; the networks and traces left across the island by Corsican-language activists, or by the dwindling number of active shepherds, or indeed by the steely web of French educational administration could be prime candidates for mobile analysis. In fact, of all these potential sites, Crucetta itself is perhaps one of the least obvious choices, since it seems to be held together by very little beyond an administrative boundary and a romanticized imaginary of an originally unitary, organic state.

Intimacy, Interrupted

The ethnographic counterpart of this problem was a constant interruption of intimacy. Ethnography, be it in one site or in many, usually draws its power and relevance from "the experiences of people the ethnographer has known under conditions of relative intimacy" (Herzfeld 1997, p. 90). And intimacy there was: over time, various people let me into their everyday lives and allowed me to share in their realities. And yet, very often, this intimacy was fragmented, interrupted, or deferred. Not only because of the necessary partial disconnection of any ethnographer, but also because people in Crucetta, like Petru and *l'anglaise,* often lived past each other. The problem of incomplete ethnography suddenly appeared as a problem inherent to the field itself: how is one to build a thick description of a group of people when *their* descriptions and understandings of each other are so often, it turns out, thin? How is one to ground one's knowledge in intimacy, when people's intimacies only stretch so far?

One Sunday evening, around the end of my fieldwork, Madame Viltané, the woman who eventually moved with her family into the *maison de l'anglaise,* invited me over for a drink and a chat. I had often spoken to one or another of the Viltanés as we bumped into each other in the neighborhood, but had never had a chance to have an extended conversation, and I had asked whether she would mind a sort of unstructured interview. She was quite taken by the idea and made some time to talk to me, while her husband and their two sons were down by the sea, fishing for crabs with a Corsican neighbor. This was only my second time inside that house and there was no recognizing the place. As Madame Viltané walked me through the pristine rooms with their white walls and new curtains, I tried to recapture and superimpose memories of the dark, dusty shell of a home I had seen nearly a year before. As she recounted the intricate history of the purchase—the English woman's son, she felt, had made things unnecessarily difficult—I understood that my last visit had in fact been somewhat illicit. Petru had not thought it necessary to tell me that the house, back then, already belonged to the Viltanés. I, in turn, didn't feel like telling her that I had already seen the inside of her home.

We leaned on the balustrade of the outside landing, sipping Muscat wine and looking down at the garden and beyond, at the crooked alleys and terra-cotta rooftops of the eastern side of the village. Madame Viltané's daughters were playing quietly somewhere in the house. The setting sun turned clothes lines into reddish bunting, swaying gently in the summer breeze. Our conversation eventually fell, as conversations between continental French inhabitants of Corsica often do, upon the question of danger. Madame Viltané expressed the opinion, which I had heard countless times before, that buying a house at the center of an old village is far safer than buying or building a stand-alone, modern villa nearer the shore. The countless news reports of blown-up villas haunt the imagination of many Continental residents—particularly those for whom Corsican nationalism is an opaque and poorly understood specter, a tangled and confusing skein of underground militants in balaclavas and outspoken nationalists on the eight o'clock news. Why do villas get blown up? Is it resentment, prejudice, politics, or business? Opinions are many among the Continental residents, hard facts rather fewer. But many feel that a nice old house in the center of a village is unlikely to attract the plastic-explosive treatment. Yet, in all fairness, for Madame Viltané, as for most of the Continentals I came to know, such concerns were only one of many which made village houses seem preferable. Fears blend imperceptibly with the more commonplace yearnings for local community, traditional architecture, and cultural authenticity which inform urban-to-rural migration throughout Europe (see, for instance, Waldren 1996).

But there is more than one kind of fear. Thoughtfully tucking some stray blonde curls behind her ear, Madame Viltané ventures to explain that she was initially rather wary of some people, like the son of one of our Corsican neighbors, Jean. She pauses and looks at me briefly. "Not just people like him," she adds, emboldened by my inquisitive nod, but as a matter of fact, *him,* Jean. "Do you know him?" she asks. "What is he like?" I tell her that Jean, whom I have come to know quite well, has always seemed a straightforward, trustworthy man, laconic to the point of curtness, perhaps, but overall a good sort. She is less than convinced. To her mind, there is something worrying about Jean. Dark fears creep into the conversation. I ask her, "Why these suspicions, why the uneasiness?" "Well, a number of things," she says, but chiefly, she tells me of the time Jean's father took her around his house, showing her the various rooms. Jean's room, she said, was bare of all decoration, nothing, no posters on the walls—a bed, a bedside table, an alarm clock, and that was it. "Now, that just isn't normal, is it?" For her, that just couldn't be the dwelling of a psychologically balanced individual.

People living past each other, fragments of intimacy: the Englishwoman's last wishes and the walls in Jean's bedroom stand for two among many moments of disjuncture and misunderstanding. They reveal the thinness of people's ethnographies of each other, the limits and revocability of intimacies. How is one to build an ethnographic account in these conditions?

This experiential problem of intimacy interrupted and deferred, underscores the conceptual difficulty: to what extent could this village be *a* site? Wherever I looked for "the village," multiplicity appeared. I would have a heartfelt and intimate conversation with a continental French neighbor about her fears concerning Corsican nationalism, and five minutes later, three streets down, bump into Thomas, who would kiss me noisily on both cheeks, wrapping around my shoulders a forearm tattooed with the acronym of the main nationalist paramilitary group. Other, very different gaps opened between the little cross and Petru's sheepfold, rifts of disjuncture and incomprehension which were far more convoluted, intricate, and difficult to map than the simple divides I had come prepared to study (divides between the French state and local practices, between the Corsican and French languages, between "the school" and "the village"). Unlike such familiar dualisms, disjunctures such as that between Petru and *l'anglaise,* between Madame Viltané and Jean, constantly opened up where I least expected them, eluded easy categorization, and faded back into insignificance before I had time to systematize or attempt anthropological explanation. At which of these moments was I doing an ethnography of the village, one site in a multi-sited project? How was I to connect these instances? Surely, each pointed toward different connections, different trajectories which, if I were to investigate them properly, would lead me out of Crucetta, in very different directions. The "multi-," in other words, was not a problem, but the "-site" was.

Holism

Although it is tempting to see this as a problem resulting from (post)modernity, the mark of a change from a communal then to a fragmented now, it turns out that the problem, in one sense, was much older than this. As Charlie Galibert (2005) has noted, anthropologists who have approached Corsican villages from a monographic angle long ago found that they had to rethink their unit of study: even before they took into account in-migration or other flows of population, notions of the local and the community were poor framing devices for a reality which involved intricate and overlapping patterns of land possession and use (De Francheschi 1986; cf. Wilson 1988), kinship (Lenclud 1979), political allegiance (Ravis-Giordani 1983), and so on, which did not coincide or map in any straight-forward way onto a single geographic space. In addition, transhumant pastoralism had long produced crisscrossing traces which punctured any imagined coherence of local units. Some anthropologists and historians chose to take as a basic unit of study the district or the valley; others left the question open. As Galibert notes, "there is a certain plasticity of the basic significant unit in Corsica, a variety of spatial 'inserts' within and without the bounds of the *commune;* approaches are thus a question of scale, continuous variations (*des variations dans la permanence*)" (2005, n.p.).

But this problem is not simply a Corsican one, either. This challenge to the monographic imagination emerged in the very first attempt at bringing social anthropology "part way home" (cf. Cole 1977), namely, Julian Pitt-Rivers' Spanish ethnography *People of the Sierra* in 1954. If the village is a system, notes Pitt-Rivers, so are Andalusia, Spain, and Europe: the limits of the analysis are not to be found in the material itself; they must be defined by the anthropologist (Pitt-Rivers 1954, pp. 208–209). It bears mention that anthropologists working in Europe were the first to question and criticize the paradigm of community studies (Boissevain 1975; Cole 1977; Grillo 1980; for a retrospective overview, see MacDonald 1993), in terms which in many ways prefigured the more radical critique of bounded field-sites in anthropology as a whole (e.g., Gupta and Ferguson 1997). This suggests that, as Marilyn Strathern points out, it is not a de facto difference between simple and complex societies which made holistic monographs meaningful "over there" and incomplete "over here"; rather, the holistic form of explanation itself has ceased to convince (Strathern 2004, pp. 21ff.).

The problem, in other words, is principally with anthropological ways of seeing (see Green 2005), not with the kind of places that Crucetta, or Corsica, or indeed the Mediterranean or Europe are: these places come to seem messy, disintegrated, or difficult to study not because they are, but because of the assumptions we have about what they *should* be like. The question then is no longer "why does Crucetta (or Corsica) not behave as an integrated whole?" but rather, "why did we think it might in the first place?" One answer to that question is to be found in the history of the discipline and the image of the lone fieldworker working in a village field-site, producing a holistic, integrated account of the village which then would stand as the microcosm of a broader, macrocosmic entity, the culture or society under study (Strathern 2004, p. 9). These anthropological assumptions have, of course, been thoroughly excoriated by critics from the 1980s onward and have, at least in part, ceased to convince.

But another answer is that, in the Corsican case as in the English one, the people who live there themselves think in these terms much of the time. Corsica is often treated, by its inhabitants (be they Corsican or not) and by external commentators, as a self-evidently meaningful unit, an integrated whole—at least ideally, since such depictions tend to come with caveats about the recent disintegration of the island. Within this logic of integrated wholes, what goes for the island also goes for the village, which therefore becomes the island's microcosm (see Herzfeld 1987). The next section examines the underpinnings of this depiction of Corsica as a geographic, human, and historical whole.

A Corsican Whole

The island of Corsica lies just north of Sardinia and 50 miles west of the coast of Tuscany. Its surface of over 3,300 square miles makes it the fourth largest Mediterranean island after Sicily, Sardinia, and Cyprus. While it is part of the same geological formation as Sardinia, Corsica's landscape is rather more striking, with a profusion of high peaks, the highest—Monte Cinto—towering at nearly 9,000 feet. Indeed, Corsica is the most mountainous of the Mediterranean islands, with more than half of its surface above 1,300 feet and one-fifth above 3,300 feet (Willis 1980, p. 333). An imposing granitic mountainous spine runs in a rough diagonal across the center of the island, sprouting secondary ranges on both sides. These run down to the coast on the south and west of the island, separating a series of roughly parallel valleys, each opening onto the sea. The northeast of the island sports a lower schistose massif which extends into the thin northern peninsula of the Cap Corse. An alluvial plain runs along the east coast of the island; this oriental plain is 87 miles long but only 6 miles at its widest point, and it represents the largest continuously flat expanse on the island.

This topography has climatic repercussions, with notable differences between the climate of, on the one hand, the relatively open valleys, fronting onto the sea, and the broader expanses, such as the oriental plain and the Balagne in the northwest—the region in which Crucetta is located—and, on the other, the higher and more enclosed valleys of the center. While the former are characterized by a typical Mediterranean climate (relatively warm winters with irregular and often violent rain, hot and dry summers), the latter are characterized by colder winters, sharper diurnal/nocturnal differences in temperature, and spring frost. Above 400 feet, the climate has been described as nearly alpine, with persistent snow throughout half the year and extremely high winds (Ravis-Giordani 1983; see also Simi 1963; Simi 1979, pp. 213–287).

It has been common among historians to regard geography as destiny in the Corsican case, and the striking layout of the island does indeed expose one to this

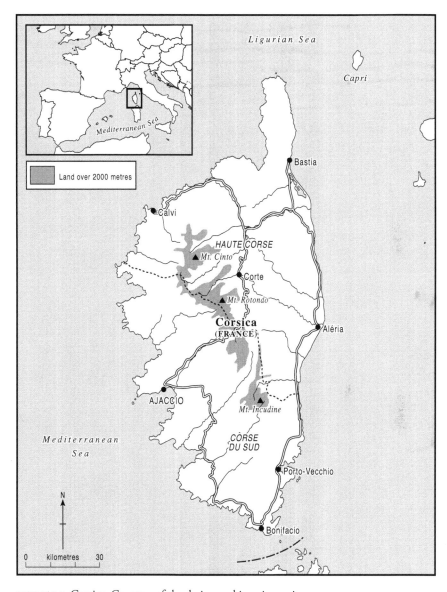

FIGURE 1.2. Corsica. Courtesy of the design and imaging unit,
Department of Geography, University of Durham.

temptation. The high elevation, the lack of obvious internal axes of communication, and the subdivision of most of the island into deep, self-contained valleys have all been pointed to as encouraging if not determining a certain set of outcomes, some socioeconomic (pastoralism rather than extensive agriculture, small-scale settlement rather than urban development), others cultural. The historian F. Roy Willis, for example, argues, "The Corsican thus developed an autarkic way of life, based upon the extended family, the clan, the village and to some extent the natural region in which he lived" (Willis 1980, p. 334).

As Willis's statement already begins to suggest, however, the topography of Corsica was at least as influential as an anchor for moral and metaphorical constructs of interiority and identity as it was as a material determinant of socioeconomic outcomes. Indeed, representations of Corsicans as a closed people on a closed island have taken on a life of their own as powerful organizing tropes. The ease with which altitude, rocks, frugality, autarky, and timelessness can be combined into a potent metaphorical complex is evident, for instance, in the French traveler Auguste Blanqui's comment in 1838:

> [I]t is a strange and deplorable curiosity that in Corsica all villages, without exception, are located on heights, where they appear from afar, grey shapes, like eagles' nests clinging to the rocks. Most are truly inaccessible. . . . Sooner or later, the Corsicans will have to climb down into the plains, if they wish to profit from the benefits of civilisation and the sacrifices of the Motherland [*la mère patrie*]: their current location is incompatible with the progress of wealth. As long as the inhabitants refuse to forsake their observatories, they will remain contemplative, and will be forced to live off dairy and chestnuts as their fathers have done for over a thousand years. (Blanqui 1995[1838], p. 470)

More recently, the Corsican historian Pierre Antonetti has mooted the hypothesis that Corsicans' very psychology has been marked by the stark opposition between mountain and sea, claiming:

> [N]o insular people was less prone to follow the call of the sea. . . . It is from the mountain that "homo Corsicanus" has taken and expected everything. And, first, a refuge against the ever-repeated onslaughts of invaders to whom he soon abandoned his shores. Corsican civilisation is not coastal. Rome tried it. Aléria [a Roman and pre-Roman archaeological site on the east coast] bears witness to this. But during the great darkness of barbarian invasions, Corsican man withdraws once more into the interior. Then came the rule of Pisa, ephemeral yet sufficient to bring life back to the marinas of the Cap Corse, in some ports of the Eastern plain and on the southernmost tip of the island. But it is above all Genoa which implanted the littoral towns and ensnared Corsica in a net of seafaring colonists. Isn't the great, the tenacious misunderstanding between

these sea-borne colonisers and this terrestrial people, in part due to their different profound vocations? If the Corsicans, in the end, refused the "Genoese peace," might it not be because, unbeknownst to themselves, their profound, unconscious psychology rejected an urban civilisation, and a maritime one? (Antonetti 1973, p. 14)

Both Blanqui's and Antonetti's statements map, from different positions, a powerful discursive space in which Corsica's geography is made to stand for interiority and possibly even incarceration, the mountain versus the sea, a people surrounded but never truly "penetrated" or changed by foreign invaders. A redux version of this history has become something of a commonplace, as in Willis's claim: "After the final destruction of their first few city-ports in the ninth century by the Saracens, the Corsicans withdrew to their mountains for the next thousand years and abandoned the coast to their colonizers from Pisa (eleventh to thirteenth centuries) and from Genoa (thirteenth to eighteenth centuries)" (Willis 1980, p. 333). The macro-figure of the Corsican stalking through his mountains and through the millennia is the thread which runs through these various accounts, giving narrative coherence to the extremely complex and rich history of the island. Reciprocally, this historical narrative, wrapped around a striking landscape, gives form and conviction to the essential transhistorical continuity of Corsicanness, mooted by Antonetti above, but also by the archaeologist Olivier Jehasse (1986) and the president of the Corsican University of Corte, Jacques-Henri Balbi, who noted more broadly that "while they have been touched by all the great impulsions of history—for instance, in our case, the Greco-Latin, Germanic, Islamic, and Occidental layers—the essential core of island societies has not been modified. It is likely that the way of life, the mentality of neolithic islanders was almost integrally transmitted until the last century" (Balbi 1989, p. 116; quoted in Galibert 2004b, p. 41).

At the risk of stating the obvious, such narratives of transhistorical continuity are here presented as part of my ethnography, not as part of my own description of Corsica. This being said, it is worth pausing for a moment to consider, as David Sutton has argued of similar narratives on the Greek island of Kalymnos, that there is little sense in simply dismissing such accounts out of hand as obviously naïve distortions (Sutton 1998, p. 144). Sutton argues, following Handler and Linnekin (1984), that taken to the philosophical limit, any account of continuity through time glosses over the fact of change, including those of detailed academic history no less than the seemingly less rigorous generalizations of other ways of engaging with the past. With this argument, Sutton aims to temper the debunking tendencies of the social scientific literature on the modernity of nationalism (Anderson 1991; Gellner 1983; Hobsbawm 1983), noting that to trace current nationalist accounts of multi-millennial permanence to the nineteenth century is just as much of a claim to historical continuity as the nationalist claim itself, simply on a different scale. By contrast, Sutton proposes that we take Kalymnians' specific (cultural) ways of engaging with history as seriously as our own (equally cultural) Western academic history.

I would not follow Sutton quite so far into relativism. Rather than start from the primacy of cultural difference, I would take up Sutton's claim that "there is nothing *structurally* different about a claim to continuity of thirty years or of 3,000 years" (Sutton 1998, p. 144; emphasis added). All of these claims to historical continuity are structurally similar because they are impositions of sense upon contingent accounts of history, and as such they necessarily select certain elements and forget others. That is to say, there is an irreducible antinomy between accounts of historical contingencies and attempts to impose, find, or elicit meaning from them or, in other words, between description and explanation. Grandiose essentialist accounts of a people or nation moving through time unchanged are, in this view, only an extreme version of the kind of narrative emplotment of contingent history which one finds in the most minutely detailed, empirically grounded, and modestly circumscribed forms of historical explanation (as opposed to description). In this respect, claims to historical continuity operate in an analogous way to claims to cultural similarity, such as the claim that one can isolate, among the myriad differences and variations of Euro-American intellectual landscapes, "Kalymnian" versus "Western" cultural approaches to history (Sutton 1998). Making sense of culture and making sense of history are similar processes of necessarily selective entity building—at whatever scale they operate.[3] The question is how one might keep both this necessary—indeed, inevitable—entity building and the radical contingency upon which it operates in view at the same time.

This figure of Corsica as self-evident meaningful unit is answered by the figure of the Corsican village, part and microcosm of the whole following a familiar segmentary logic. Evans-Pritchard pointed out the fact that "home" in English and *cieng* in Nuer refer to entities of different sizes depending on the context: "home" may be England to an Englishman in Germany, and Oxford to the same person when in London (Evans-Pritchard 1940). Michael Herzfeld (1987) finds the same correspondences in various Mediterranean contexts. Thus, he notes (by reference to Pitt-Rivers 1954) that the Spanish word *pueblo* refers both to the village and the district—just as in the south of France, *pays* is still sometimes used to refer contextually to the village, the region, and the country, while the modern Greek word *kseni* refers both to outsiders from other villages and to "foreigners." In all of these cases, "the moral boundary between insiders and outsiders . . . seems to be formally similar at several quite distinct levels of social identity" (Herzfeld 1987, p. 76). Or, as he puts it more forcefully, there is an "essential homology between several levels of collective identity—village, ethnic group, district, nation. What goes for the family home also goes, at least by metaphorical extension, for the national territory" (Herzfeld 1987, p. 76). Galibert (2004b, p. 201) has evocatively shown the salience of these micro/macro connections in the Corsican case, through a logic which is both segmentary and analogical. He quotes, for instance, Renucci's statement that "[a] Corsican belongs to his family, to his village, to his district, to his region, to his island: a set of successive shells to which he adheres through a kind of umbilical cord" (Renucci, quoted in Galibert 2004b, p. 201). A vivid illustration of the common and ubiquitous nature of this principle (beyond the theoretical constructions of anthropologists) comes from the logo of the Corsican chestnut-flavored beer Pietra. It shows the outline of the island filled with what to an eye attuned to Corsican imagery is the immediately recognizable pattern of interlocked houses of a Corsican mountainside village. This is Corsica, literally, as a village.

It is against the background of such expectations of organic completeness, such neat correspondence between the nested levels of collective identity, that Crucetta came to seem problematic and full of gaps (cf. Green 2005)—not just from the perspective of an ethnographer, but also from that of its inhabitants. It is against this background that the schoolteacher's report self-evidently outlined a problem: social disintegration, rural exodus, empty houses, unstable populations. He was not alone in fearing a breakdown of the "social fabric" (*le tissu social*) of the village. Many middle-class inhabitants of Crucetta voiced concerns about the rise in violence and incivility, the aging of the population, the poor integration of immigrants—all themes which scaled up neatly into worries about the island as a whole (or rather, increasingly, not a whole).

In this vein, J.-M. Andreani, editor of the French journal *Le Monde* and author of a book on Corsica, writes: "No one . . . has been able to check the slow and inexorable drift of Corsican society, gangrened as it is by endemic violence, confused by the loss of any opportunity or perspective, of its traditional landmarks and frameworks" (Andreani 1999, p. vii). These concerns are grounded in an understanding of society as an organic, holistic, and yet threatened and disaggregating entity, an unraveling tapestry. The invention of society in the nineteenth century was already, from the start, accompanied with worries (Karsenti 2006), the social fabric apprehended from the start through its problematic thinness in the modern world (Durkheim 1984). Maryon McDonald has suggested that, in the process of European nation-building, the figures of "majority and minority were born together, and the minority born as disappearing" (McDonald 1993, p. 227). Similarly, the social fabric, one might say, was born unraveling.

To say this is not to reduce such expectations of the completeness of the village or the island to mere erroneous accounts of things as they are; rather, these are horizons (past or future) in view of which action is taken in places like Crucetta. For instance, Pascal's depiction of the problematic state of the village was the background for his proposal to extend the remit of Corsican language and culture in the school. This was in accordance with a more general consensus within the French educational ministry, according to which "[t]eaching regional languages and cultures encourages the continuity between the social and family environment and the educational system, thus contributing to everyone's integration into the local social fabric" (Éducation Nationale 2001, n.p.). This was a project he often expounded to me and in which he was a firm believer, noting specifically that the most disenfranchised inhabitants of Crucetta, the Franco-Maghrebians, stood to gain the most from this increasing integration into the local social fabric. Other upshots of such visions of completeness were less benign. One elderly Corsican man, with whom I had been discussing the village's past at some length, concluded wistfully: "Before, the houses were full. Now," he added with a belligerent nod, "there's Arabs in them!" In this way of seeing, the presence of "Arabs" is effectively an absence, a gap, since they are not counted among the proper elements of the holistic entity that Crucetta was/should be.

As Bruno Latour notes, "The question is not to fight against categories but rather to ask: 'is the category subjecting or subjectifying you?'" (Latour 2005, p. 230). Similarly, the issue here is not, from an anthropological point of view, to fight against wholes per se, but rather to ask what kind of whole it is that is being imagined and strived for. Holistic projects can be imaginative projects of social inclusion, crafting new, unexpected entities, networks of heterogeneous elements, or they can promote "integralisms" born of violent "ruptures in the experience of belonging" (Holmes 2000, p. 5). In order to be able to ask this question, however, we need to have somewhere to stand, ethnographically, from where these wholes, their making and unmaking, become visible.

Holism, Reloaded

What we need, then, is an anthropological method which helps us to interrupt the taken-for-granted coherence of holistic accounts, in order to see more clearly the process of their making, but also what they leave out. Surely, however, this brings us full circle, and we are back where we started: isn't multi-sitedness the method which allows anthropologists to leave behind the mirage that their field-sites are bounded wholes and therefore to get a much better angle on the way different sites, times, and persons are involved in the crafting of entities? As George Marcus notes approvingly, the multi-sited imagination has punctured the illusions of sited holism, the classic wellspring of ethnographic authority:

> The intellectual environment surrounding contemporary ethnographic study makes it seem incomplete or even trivial if it does not encompass within its

own research design a full mapping of a cultural formation, the contours of which cannot be presumed but are themselves a key discovery of ethnographic inquiry. The sense of the object of study being "here and there" has begun to wreak productive havoc on the "being there" of classic ethnographic authority. (Marcus 1999, p. 117)

And yet, this is not so much a rejection of holism as its reconfiguration on a much larger scale, leaving behind the holism of the bounded field-site or the local community in favor of the much grander holism of a multi-sited "cultural formation," as I have argued more extensively elsewhere (Candea 2007, 2009). If postmodern ethnography posited wholes by showing their fragments, multi-sited ethnography tries to follow and encompass these wholes themselves.

The appearance of multi-sitedness has been one of the most productive methodological advances in anthropology since the 1990s. It has allowed anthropologists to thoroughly rethink place and to pursue ever more complex objects of study in new and exciting ways. It is unambiguously a good thing. Its one potential drawback, however, is that its new, reconfigured holism collapses what was previously a very productive tension at the heart of anthropology: that between the site and the object of research. With the expansion of anthropological method, the sites of research can multiply until they correspond with the object itself, the cultural formation one is attempting to research. This is particularly clear when the object of study is a diasporic population or its cultural identity where the focus is often on the totality of a diasporic community, rather than on the incoherence of a local area, on the minutiae of daily cohabitation in a neighborhood where people don't know each other (see for instance Smith 2006; cf. Candea 2009).

The same selection of sense over space is evident in Galibert's historical ethnography of the Corsican village of Sarrola Carcopino, researched through the letters and writings of one of its inhabitants turned colonial soldier (whom Galibert evocatively describes as by turn a "Ulysses" and a "Robinson Crusoe"). Galibert beautifully captures the coherence of the village as it extends beyond the local: "The village, object, of our research, thus appears bounded neither in space nor in time. It cannot be reduced to its geographic area (since our Ulysses shows its extension to the ends of the world), nor to its historical place (since our Robinson shows it is finite neither in the past—active memory—nor the future nor the present, redoubled as it is by imagination)" (Galibert 2004b, p. 45). Later, he notes, "The *paese* (the village) becomes a complete world, englobing within this single word, the village itself, natural birth-place of the family, and the *pays,* the island, intermingling different lived experiences, constituting a centre whose meaning [*sens*] expresses itself beyond, or even at the expense of geographic and/or historical continuities [*solidarités*]" (ibid., p. 51).[4]

I propose the complementary and inverse move—a selection of space over sense. To bound off the merely geographical entity "Crucetta" as my field-site, to hold it together for the purpose of analysis, is precisely to highlight its necessary fractures and incompleteness; it is to resist dissolving and resolving it into parts of wider holistic entities, be they of the old holism (as a local community) or the new (as a cultural formation). To hold on to Crucetta as what I have termed an "arbitrary location" (Candea 2007), one with no overarching meaning or coherence, is to remember that all these heterogeneous people, things, and processes are "thrown" together. Crucetta in this sense is not an object to be explained, but a contingent window into complexity.

Anthropological critiques often attempt to shatter previous approaches in order to establish their own novelty (see Bashkow 2004), but this is not the aim here. Rather, we can imagine, alongside multi-sitedness, another instrument of inquiry: arbitrary locations whose role is precisely to interrupt the assumed coherence of translocal cultural formations. This notion of an arbitrary location is itself a partial return to an older feature of anthropological method. The kind of traditional anthropological field-site, of which proponents of multi-sitedness are often suspicious, could be described as a double entity: it was, on the one hand, understood as a found object: a really existing feature of the world out there, a discrete spatial or human entity, a local community which was supposed to have its own consistency and meaning, the kind of entity which could become the subject of an exhaustive and comprehensive monograph. On the other hand, it was also to some extent an arbitrary location defined by the researcher as a framework for a study of something else. Thus, Evans-Pritchard remade political theory in Nuerland, and Malinowski challenged Freud in the Trobriands.

As a heuristic-device, then, an arbitrary location is perhaps best understood as the symmetrical inversion of the Weberian ideal type. The ideal type was an abstracted notion, nowhere existing and for that very reason easily definable, a notion which served as a control for the comparative analysis of actually existing instances (Gerth and Mills 1948, pp. 59ff.). It allowed, in other words, a researcher to connect separate localized instances, usually in different places, in view of their meaningful similarities. The arbitrary location, by contrast, is the actually existing instance, whose messiness, contingency, and lack of an overarching coherence or meaning serve as a control for a broader abstract object of study. It is arbitrary insofar as it bears no necessary relation to the wider object of study (Nuerland to politics, the Trobriand islands to the Oedipus complex). While the ideal type allows one to connect and compare separate instances, the arbitrary location allows one to reflect on and rethink conceptual entities, to challenge their coherence and their totalizing aspirations. The distinction I wish to recapture is that between the coherence of a model and the contingency of a location. If the ideal type is meaning which cuts through space, the arbitrary location is space which cuts through meaning.

With the advent of multi-sitedness, the demise of the first aspect of fieldwork (the field-site as a naturally bounded entity or local community) is to be celebrated unreservedly, and I am far from urging a return to former conceptualizations of fieldwork. By contrast, the second aspect of fieldwork (the field-site as arbitrary location) has given anthropologists a place to stand, from which they can examine the assumed coherence and shape of big models. Similarly, to keep in view Crucetta not as a (necessarily translocal and transhistorical) meaningful anthropological place, but as a (necessarily partial, incomplete, and in its mere geographic contiguity, meaningless) arbitrary location, enables us to examine the shape, the making and unmaking of the wider holistic entities which brush past each other there.

Crucetta as Arbitrary Location

Let us now return to Geertz's claim that "[a]nthropologists don't study villages (tribes, towns, neighborhoods . . .); they study *in* villages" (Geertz 1973, p. 22). What this chapter has tried to provide, besides an introduction to Crucetta, where much of this account is going to take place, is a reflection on what such "taking place" might involve. This can be seen as a gloss on this Geertzian claim—albeit one which is probably quite different from what Geertz himself had in mind.

This book is not an ethnography of the Corsican village of Crucetta. In a world which is already, and has always been, inherently multi-sited, such a project (to study a village) would necessarily take us far beyond the village's geographic location, toward the ineffable whole of a part-local, part-diasporic, symbolic-material-historical-emotive entity, a cultural formation stretching out over time and space. This is an important story to tell (I refer readers to Galibert 2004a and 2004b), but it is not, in the main, the story I shall be telling here.

Rather, this is an ethnography in the village of Crucetta, conceived in the most myopic and purposefully unimaginative sense as an area of geographically contiguous space—and nothing more. This Crucetta, for all its "mereness" (Herzfeld 1997, pp. 91, 94), is a location in postcolonial Europe and, more specifically, in that particularly vibrant and contested Franco-Mediterranean assemblage of histories, peoples, and tensions which had remained somewhat unexplored since Rabinow's seminal *French Modern* (1989) and which has recently returned to the anthropological limelight through ethnographies mapping Berber transpolitics in Algeria and France (Silverstein 2004) and the colonial memory of diasporic Maltese *pieds-noirs* (Smith 2006). The themes which crop up in Crucetta are precisely those which inform these twenty-first-century works: they concern diverse attachments to memory and place; contests over culture, language, and authenticity; integralism and violent "ruptures in the experience of belonging" (Holmes 2000, p. 5)—all fought in the uneasy spaces left by a deafening French and international debate over nation and citizenship, Europeanness, race, and the purported "clash of civilisations" (Huntington 1993). Ethnographically, however, this account makes the opposite move, a rather surprising choice in the current climate—the choice to stay put. To stay put, not because people or processes are in some sense local or bounded, and thus deserve a local or bounded analysis; on the contrary, the account stays put precisely because places themselves (even in the "merest" of Corsican villages) are already, as I have argued above, shifting and multi-sited, because people's presences are already trajectories, and their histories and identities always already hark to wider wholes, elsewhens, elsewheres. Crucetta is thus not the object of study, but the site of study. It is not a microcosmic representative of a wider macrocosm or a local site attached to or in a dialectic with global phenomena. It is a methodological fiction, a fixed camera which records aspects of these diverse traces.

This purposefully myopic approach is a way of revisiting the perennial question of what anthropology, with its investment in ethnography, can bring to subjects which one could just as easily approach through the frames of other disciplines (sociology, political science, history, cultural studies, etc.). The notion of an arbitrary location is, in one sense, a return to the specific implantation in particular locations which has been at the core of anthropological knowledge practices, but it is emphatically not a restatement of the division of labor between local ethnographic work and the grander, synthetic view of the political scientist—quite the opposite. For the big entities endorsed by states or sociologists are not, when all is said and done, very big at all. Bruno Latour noted that "the big picture," the "whole of society" so favored by sociologists, usually boils down to a hand gesture about the size of a pumpkin (Latour 2002). Similarly, "Corsican culture," "the French language," or "European society" are, after all, small enough to fit onto the TV screen and the printed page, to drop into conversation over a cup of coffee or a glass of wine. In other words, while these entities may well travel far and gain currency from Paris all the way to Crucetta and back again, they do not exist in some ethereal sphere above the local or in some theoretical demimonde; they only come into being at the points of their articulation, and these points are always places which, like Crucetta, are amenable to ethnography.

Paradoxically, then, ethnography's greatest strength and advantage might take the form of a lack or a gap: the ethnographer's incapacity to see everything in one all-encompassing vista; ethnography's way of forcing one to rub up against the limits of one's understanding of one's closest neighbors, and the limits of their understanding and knowledge of each other; its myopic attention to the way big pictures and big processes are always built, shaped, and molded on the ground.

The methodological tool of an arbitrary location keeps this particular virtue of ethnography sharp. It enables me in the rest of this book to bring into view the always contingently situated formation of entities such as Corsica, France, competing languages, cultural differences, and enduring senses of place, to highlight both their achieved coherence and their necessary incompleteness. I do this by purposefully leaving one question unasked: the question of Crucetta itself as a coherent entity. This book is therefore the opposite of a village ethnography.

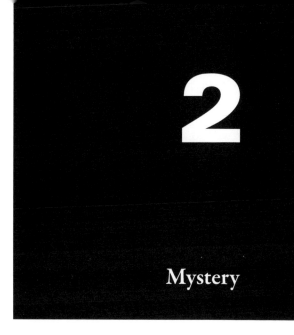

2

Mystery

For what, indeed, is a thing? A thing, as opposed to
an idea, is that which we know from the outside, as
opposed to that which we know from the inside.

—DURKHEIM 1988

[President Charles] de Gaulle had his mystery, just as we
have Corsica. . . . within him was a domain on which we
knew light could never be shed. That is what I call Corsica.

—ANDRÉ MALRAUX, QUOTED IN ANDREANI 1999

Getting There/Being There

March 2002. The waiting room dedicated to Corsican flights in the Parisian airport
of Orly is an unprepossessing sight. Spaces devoted to domestic flights are always
something of a poor relation in large international airports, and this is no exception:
the seats are shabby and the floor has not been swept for some time. Moving from
the brightly lit bustle of the main airport hall into this quiet room, where a mere
sprinkling of passengers wait somewhat despondently for a liberating announcement, one is reminded that this is an evening in March. The sun has set unnoticed

on a greying Paris and a cigarette sputters out in sympathy in one of the passengers' fingers—soon to join the collection of butts on the floor which suggests that the no-smoking sign is more by way of an adornment. The main sound in the room comes from a television in one corner, which is broadcasting the evening news. Coincidentally, the national news features an item on Corsica. Police sirens, palm trees swaying in the night, camera flashes in a darkened hallway. A grave voice-over announces that an explosive device has been discovered on the doorstep of the mayor of the Corsican town of Bastia. This is the second attempt . . . suspected nationalist involvement . . . the mayor's support for politician Jean-Pierre Chevène-ment. As I focus in, the image jump-cuts to the tearful face of the mayor's wife, crying about "them," about death and danger, about "this island" and the choice to stay or leave. Watching the broadcast, it dawns on me how little I know about Corsica, as I prepare to set off on my first pre-fieldwork trip. And yet, at the same time, these images and tropes are familiar. Death, politics, nationalism, sirens in the night, and mysterious explosive packages: these images of Corsica are familiar in a background kind of way, banal almost, for anyone who has grown up in the pale light of French newscasts. My fellow passengers too seem unruffled. The one or two who had bothered to raise their eyes to the broadcast calmly let their attention wander as the next item comes on: football. A sharp burst of static, then the television set is drowned out by a tinny voice announcing that boarding has commenced.

Over a year later, I know just as little about who may or may not have wanted to blow up the mayor of Bastia's apartment, and the Corsica of newscasts, sirens, and mysterious packages in the night is still as distant and impenetrable. I am sitting at a wooden table in the courtyard of a small log-cabin restaurant, which is perched atop a mountain pass nearly 4,000 feet above sea level. Behind me, I can just make out the white blur of Crucetta in the crook of a much smaller mountain pass far, far below. And behind that, the painfully sharp blue of the Mediterranean. Ahead of me, a tenuous road snakes down into the deep wooded expanse of the Giunssani valley, and it is up this road that my interlocutor has come, his car straining as much as mine, although he likely had less anxiety at sharp bends over steep precipices than I had. The man across the table from me is in his sixties, wearing chinos and a thin sweater over a polo shirt; his white beard is on the restrained side of bushy. His assured manner and slightly pedagogical tone speak of a career in education, a life spent teaching in the once-flourishing and now nearly extinct schools of the Giunssani micro-region. My friend the schoolmaster Pascal arranged for me to meet Mr. Filetta, describing him as a cultural activist of the old school, one of the generation of teachers who incorporated their passion for Corsican speech and the Corsican past into their teaching long before the educational/academic nexus had even begun to elaborate and format these into the teachable subjects of Corsican language and history. When Mr. Filetta speaks of Corsica, his sentences are festooned with a wealth of local erudition, of times, places, and accents. We are speaking in Corsican and he picks up on some particularities in my pronunciation which he describes as setting those from Crucetta apart from even their closest neighbors. For a moment, we are united in the camaraderie of micro-knowledge, and he seems to treat me as quite simply someone from Crucetta—perhaps because sustaining this particular kind of linguistic intimacy with a Romanian-French-English Ph.D. student would just be too anomalous. But soon he remembers our respective roles and returns to telling me a story about Corsica; the story he tells is one of progressive disenchantment. It is about fields being eaten by scrubland and children forgetting the names of their great-grandfathers, about rural schools closing, and about a young generation of people who are struggling to imbue their lives with the substantive core of Corsicanness. It is an essentialist story, in which history, people, place, and words are rolled into one. Pointing to the Giunssani valley below, he notes that the name of the forest which covers much of it, the *tartagine,* comes from the Indo-European root *tar,* meaning "deep valley." The root does not relate to any word in present-day Corsican or French. And yet, "when one says that word," he notes enthusiastically, "one remembers without knowing it the primitive language of the Corsicans who were here."

This chapter inquires into the specific knowledge practices which leave Corsica hovering between mystery and essence. It looks at the Corsica of national newscasts, with its familiar mysteries; its disturbing, unplumbed depths; its machinations, implicit connections, hidden dangers. This Corsica does not simply float in the ether, it is quite palpably present to many inhabitants of Crucetta. But the chapter also looks at Mr. Filetta's Corsica, essential and bound up with a deeper, immanent knowledge, a language before language, a people stretching back to prehistory; this Corsica will always elude the definitionally superficial gaze of the foreign visitor. In his excellent review of anthropological literature on Corsica, Charlie Galibert has noted this double tendency: toward distanced objectivity, on the one hand, and on the other, toward claims to quasi-immanent, culturally rooted understanding (2005). This chapter tracks the roots of this knowledge binary in eighteenth- and nineteenth-century French representations of Corsica, which resurface potently in the everyday lives of Corsican and non-Corsican inhabitants of Crucetta today.

These two Corsicas, the mysterious and the essential are, I will argue, two sides of the same coin. The coin is Corsica as a "thing" in the Durkheimian sense: something essential, existing and unknown, something out there. The emergence of Corsica as a thing in this sense delineates two subject positions—that of mystified outsider, that of knowing insider—which are themselves reflections of one another. These couples, mystery/essence and insider/outsider, reinforce each other and together constitute a powerful discursive mechanism which limits and delineates how Corsica can and should be known. This chapter, in other words, tracks a partial history of the *mise en discours* of Corsica (Foucault 1976).

A Domain on Which Light Could Never Be Shed

There is a striking paradox at the heart of French accounts of Corsica. On the one hand, the island, as many commentators have noted, is persistently described as mysterious and unknowable, impenetrable to an outside gaze. On the other hand, it is among the most persistently documented and repeatedly investigated parts of the French territory. Malraux's quote, above, speaks to a pervasive sense of Corsica's constitutional lack of clarity: news reports, tourist brochures, and popular literature on the subject of the island are replete with accounts of concealment, romantic mystery, and sheer impenetrable complexity. Corsica in the nineteenth century was a familiar topic for French novelists such as Dumas, Maupassant, and Mérimée, who inserted into French popular culture the description of the island as a place of violence, poverty, and passion, lonely isolated villages, women in mourning, bandits—and, above all, mystery: dark, seething secrets, hidden purposes, and stiletto blades flashing in the night. Insofar as we accept Benedict Anderson's claim about the constitutive role of novels in the production of national consciousness (Anderson 1991, p. 25), we can conclude that French national consciousness has been intimately bound up with Corsica as an internal Other, a mystery within. Some of the spirit of this literary genre lives on in a new, nonfiction literature which has cropped up since the 1980s, in which the political and economic intricacies of Corsican nationalist movements, their dealings with the French state and with organized crime, form the subject of revelatory accounts by investigative journalists and nationalist insiders. These authors draw aside the thick veil of mystery and secrecy which hides these goings-on and reveal the naked truth to their suddenly demystified readership (see, for instance, Poggioli 1999; Laville 1999; Follorou 1999). But for all these unveilings, the mystery of Corsica somehow remains intact.

Continentals living in Crucetta were often enmeshed in this mysterious Corsica. Two weeks after I first moved in, a local Continental friend invited me over for lunch. After coffee, most of the family having dispersed, my friend's mother, Françoise, her ex-husband, Pierre, and I were still in the kitchen. Suddenly, without any introduction, Françoise said with some glee: "I don't know if you knew, but this place is a hotbed of nationalism." She proceeded to tell me that the area was home to an underground nationalist group whose leaders had not long ago been assassinated. Pierre cut in and said, knowingly, that here, you shouldn't say anything. If the house next door explodes in the night, you haven't heard anything: "here, if they ask you something, there's three answers: yes, no, I don't know. . . . Because life, around here, it's cheap." In this, my friends were not very far from the oft-repeated anthropological wisdom which has sought to ground mystery in the very fabric of Corsican society, culture, or psychology:

> A veritable rhetoric of the unsaid rules over important questions in Corsica. *'In bocca chjosa ùn c'entre mosche'* (no flies get into a closed mouth). To say too much is harmful, one must not say what one knows, betray secrets; but also: one should not ask. The saying says the risk of death which is linked to speech, it links the risk of death to speech. (Galibert 2004a, p. 7)

Certainties about Corsican secrecy, in other words, proliferate across different domains: through literature and anthropology, through newspapers, and in the assumptions of many Continentals and Corsicans. "Corsican secrecy" is not, in other words, a mere representation. Rather, it is a framing device woven into the very fabric of what it means to describe Corsicans as a cultural unit.

Françoise and Pierre proceeded to substantiate their claim, recounting in detail a number of murders which had happened in the region. Around the long wooden table, in the cool vaulted room, a world of mystery and danger was being summoned, which seemed rather out of keeping with the lazy, sunny afternoon. But this world was out there too, if one knew where to look: Françoise pointed out the spray-painted graffiti which could be seen on various walls and signposts in Crucetta, as in the rest of Corsica. "I.F.F.," she explained, means "*I Francesi Fora:* French Out." Other graffiti expressed support for Yvan Colonna, the fugitive who was suspected (and since, convicted) of murdering a French prefect in 1997 and had since been in hiding—some said on the island itself, others claimed in Latin America—eluding the best efforts of the French police to track him down. Colonna had been a regular feature of newscasts, and so here, in Crucetta, was a trace of national news, painted on the wall one walks past on the way to buy a loaf of bread. Other graffiti, however, retained their mystery: we puzzled together over one example we had all seen on the wall of the church, which seemed to read, in Corsican, "Freedom for Turks" (*Libertà per Turchi*). We threw this one backward and forward, wondering which Turks were meant and who was keen to free them. Many weeks later, the schoolteacher Pascal enlightened me on that particular graffito: Turchi is the name of a Corsican nationalist.

"Freedom for Turks" stands as a potent exemplar of the multiple economies of knowledge that coexisted in Crucetta. What to Pascal and others was a set of traceable connections, involving named individuals, places, and events, some legal and some illegal, some politically motivated and others not, some known and some unknown, became for Continentals such as Françoise a tangled skein of mystery, danger, and titillation, something to be uncovered and revealed. As she picked up the empty coffee cups and cleared the crumbs off the table, Françoise gave me the address of a website, www.amnistia.net, which would tell me "what really goes on in Corsica, what no one says." She went upstairs to her office and brought back a handful of print-outs of various articles. These, and the website more generally, were of a piece with the investigative literary genre described above: scandals uncovered, illegal activities brought into public view, embarrassing connections of prominent politicians revealed.

In parallel to this popular investigative journalism, a less sensationalist literature similarly promises to give the confused reader the key to the island, in a dispassionate, factual sort of way. For instance, a short book by Jean-Louis Andreani, the editor of the newspaper *Le Monde,* is simply entitled *Understanding Corsica* (*Comprendre la Corse;* Andreani 1999). Similarly, a late 1990s government report starts from the premise that Corsica is unknown and in need of unveiling: "we felt that our work should begin with . . . the search for truth . . . [s]o that our fellow citizens may come to a better knowledge of the reality of Corsica, this integral part of the republic" (Glavany 1998, n.p.). I myself found that, upon hearing I had spent a year living in Corsica, French acquaintances would enthusiastically ask me to "explain" Corsica or to tell them "what was really going on," what the problem really was—and possibly, what I thought the solution might be. It is as if Corsica is, in and of itself, intrinsically, an open question: the truth of Corsica is out there and has yet to be uncovered.

And yet—here is the paradox—Corsica is among the French regions which have received the most extensive factual coverage and geographic, economic, historical, and sociological description. As early as 1770, two years after Corsica became a part of France, Louis XV commissioned two royal military geographers, Testevuide and Bedigis, to draw up a land survey of the island: when the survey, known as the *plan terrier,* was completed twenty-five years later, it covered thirty-seven rolls of topographical maps and included seventeen folio volumes detailing the physical geography, fauna and flora, patterns of production and consumption, land tenure arrangements, health, climate, and demographics. We can believe the historian F. Roy Willis's claim that, by that point, "no province of France was more thoroughly documented" (Willis 1980, p. 346). Nor did the fact-finding stop there: in the two and a half centuries since Corsica's entry into France, the French government alone has produced twenty-five official reports on the topic of the island (Culioli 1999; cf. Biggi and Meisterheim 1997), and a significant number of reports were commissioned by other bodies or simply offered to the public by journalists and travelers. So why is Corsica still so persistently shrouded in mystery? Rather than short-circuit the question by finding its answer in the ineffable essence of the island itself, its constitutive mystery, one might attempt to question the question itself: what is mystery an effect of? The answer to that question may in part be found in the reports themselves.

Corsica Becomes French

One key feature of the long succession of French reports on Corsica is that they are invariably cast as responses to a problem. Built into the instructions given to the two geographers for drawing up the *plan terrier*, for instance, was an assessment of the problematic situation of the island: "Corsica is a devastated, depopulated country that must be regenerated. . . . To regenerate a country is to give it the full existence of which it is capable in its population, its agriculture, and its commerce. The Survey makes known these three things, not only in what they have been and what they are, but also in what they can become" (quoted in Willis 1980, p. 331). The geographers duly built into the survey both this problem and an extremely detailed scheme for improvement, to which I will return below. The sense that Corsica was problematic and in need of improvement was pervasive at the time: eight years before the *plan terrier* was completed, a priest, the Abbé Gaudin, published an account of his travels in Corsica that were prefaced by his "political views towards its betterment" (Abbé Gaudin 1997[1787]). The author presented his work, of which the second part is mostly in verse, as not primarily a literary endeavor, but rather as a "truthful" and "useful" account of the island and also as "an act of patriotism" (ibid., pp. v–ix).

As Willis makes clear, a number of circumstances conspired to make Corsica (and its betterment) a pressing problem for the French monarchy. At the time of Corsica's annexation to France, the island had, for over fourteen years, been proclaiming its independence as a republic, under the leadership of Corsican general Pascal Paoli, from its former Genoese masters. Paoli's independent Corsica had been hailed by the likes of Rousseau, Voltaire (see Hall 1968), and Boswell in England as the promise of a new era of self-determination and enlightened republican government. In the preamble of an unfinished constitutional project for Paoli's Corsica, Rousseau famously wrote:

> [W]orthy Corsicans, who knows better than you how much can be done alone? Without friends, without support, without money, without armies, enslaved by formidable masters, single handed you have thrown off the yoke. You have seen them ally against you, one by one, the most redoubtable potentates of Europe and flood your island with foreign armies; all this you have surmounted. Your fortitude alone has accomplished what money could never have done. (Rousseau 1953, p. 280)

Paoli's regime was crushed, however, by French troops at the battle of Ponte Novo in 1769, and Paoli fled to England. Genoa, which continued throughout Paoli's rule to claim de jure if not de facto possession of the island, had agreed to cede Corsica to France in a treaty the previous year, while France agreed to pay a sizable sum in return. This prompted Voltaire to comment wryly, "It remains to be seen whether men are entitled to sell other men: but that is a question no treaty will ever examine" (quoted in Antonetti 1973, p. 370). Corsica thus became a French province, under the special administrative status reserved for previously feudal or princely states, such as Brittany or Languedoc (Colombani 1973), which included a nominal local level of government, although as historians such as Roy Willis have shown, the French state's attitude to Corsica during the ancien régime oscillated between top-down developmentalism and simple neglect (Willis 1980).

This complex and contested incorporation of the island into France sets the scene for the particular concerns which led to the *plan terrier*. While some French voices in the aftermath of Corsica's annexation deplored the event on Corsicans' account, others deplored the expenses, both in payments to Genoa and in military campaigns, to conquer, as one critic put it, "this miserable land, which is in general neither cultivated nor barely cultivable . . . this kingdom of poverty" (Aiguillon, quoted in Willis 1980, p. 329). To show that Corsica was in a state of poverty as a result of determinate causes, which enlightened French governance could remedy, would have silenced both lines of criticism.

By the time the *plan terrier* was completed in 1795, however, these concerns had been swept away along with the French monarchy itself. With the French Revolution, Corsica's status shifted and the island was declared "an integral part of the French Empire, . . . [whose] inhabitants must be ruled by the same constitution as other Frenchmen" (quoted in Antonetti 1973, p. 400). "Freedom" being the order of the day, Paoli's Corsica received a new, retrospective shine. The new French Assemblée Nationale voted in favor of the return of "Corsicans who, after fighting for freedom, have exiled themselves," including Pascal Paoli himself who, writing from London in 1789, had declared himself in favor of Corsica's part in the French Revolution: "it seems that everywhere the populace wants to be free, and perhaps we too shall be, at least as French people" (quoted in Graziani and Taddei 2002, p. 155). Paoli returned to Corsica (now a French department) in July 1790 via Paris, where he was acclaimed by the National Assembly and met the king. The former ruler of the Corsican nation was promptly elected president of the department. Reputedly, Paoli declared upon setting foot on the island: "O my fatherland, I left you enslaved, I now find you free" (Graziani and Taddei 2002, p. 156). This harmonious fusion of Corsican and French aspirations to "freedom" remains a trope for some Corsican commentators today, such as Gaston Casanova, who claimed that "the XVIIIth century Corsican revolution . . . can only escape ultimate failure by being absorbed into the French revolutionary stream" (Casanova 1980, p. 39).

Paoli's *engouement* for the French Revolution was not to last, however. Soon, the radicalization of the revolution in Paris had repercussions in terms of internecine struggles on the island between the more moderate Paoli, faced with increasing threats to religion and property, and his more radical local rivals. In the end, Paoli turned to the English for support and broke with France, constituting a short-lived Anglo-Corsican kingdom (1794–1796), of which he was not however awarded the viceroyship, which went to Sir Gilbert Elliot. At this point, Paoli's position on the possibility of freedom within/without France changed again: "The king [of England] . . . will be king of Corsica: but Corsica will be able to correct any faults in the English constitution through its own constitution, so as to ensure its happiness and freedom. And, most importantly, we will not lose the name of Nation. Corsica, united to France, was no longer Corsica. The kingdom of Corsica will now be as free as that of England" (letter from Paoli to Galleazi 1794, quoted in Antonetti 1973, p. 423).

After the French retrieval of Corsica in 1796, in part under the political and military impulsion of Napoleon Bonaparte, Paoli fled to London once more, where he would die a decade later, leaving behind the trace of another change of mind concerning Frenchness and freedom: "Freedom was the object of our revolutions; we now enjoy it on our island; what matters it from which hands it comes?" (letter, 6 September 1802, quoted in Antonetti 1973, p. 423). The reconquest of Corsica in 1796 marked the beginning of an uninterrupted administrative inclusion of the island into France as a formal entity. It also marked the beginning of administrative, economic, educational, and legislative attempts to make this inclusion into an effective integration, attempts which would continue—with various intensities and through various permutations—until the late twentieth century.

The original inclusion of Corsica into France was thus itself a complex and contested process, made in fits and starts. The debates which surrounded it show the mutual implications of claims to difference (the Corsican nation as a discrete entity whose sovereignty must be recognized) and claims to similarity (the sovereignty of Corsica as a universal enlightenment value, the Corsican fight for freedom as a subset of all people's fight for freedom, embodied in the French Revolution). It shows, in other words, the extent to which Corsica was, from the start, implicated in the complex dialectic between universality and particularism which so many scholars have seen as characteristic of post-revolutionary France.

This eventful history also suggests that the original questions and issues which prompted the commission of the *plan terrier* were thoroughly out of date by the time the plan itself came out. Corsica had come to live a very different life in the French political imagination: from annexed republic, to enlightened precursor of the French Revolution, it would soon return to the limelight as the birthplace of the great emperor himself. And yet, the image of Corsica as problematic persisted and came to live a life of its own, which one can trace through the spate of reports running from the late eighteenth century through the late twentieth.

The Corsican Problem

In 1997, the *préfet* of Corsica, Claude Érignac, was shot dead in the streets of Ajaccio. The *préfet* is the highest representative of the French state on the island. Officially, he "is in charge of the national interest, is responsible for public order and sees to the respect of the law" (Préfecture de Corse 2003). In response to what they described as a "terrible blow to a symbol of the Republic, and therefore, to the Republic itself" (Glavany 1998, n.p.), the French National Assembly appointed a commission to investigate the state of public service in Corsica. The commission produced a report, known as the Glavany Report (from the name of the leader of the commission). History, however, failed to stand still and wait for the report's results. Barely a month after the commission was instituted, a group of police officers, under the new prefect's orders, burned down a makeshift bar. The bar had been built illegally, but illegal too was its destruction. The prefect was demoted and put on trial. The National Assembly appointed a new commission to investigate the workings of the police force in Corsica; the commission produced a new report (Forni 1999). In other words, the exact shape and specific instantiation of the so-called Corsican problem (*le problème Corse*) vary with the historical and political context, but the format (problem—investigation—report) remains, enshrining the notion that the heart of the matter is a lack of accurate or sufficient knowledge.

There are, naturally, many differences in style, purpose, tone, and concerns among these reports on Corsica, spanning two centuries. And yet, read against one another, a set of similarities and continuities appears. These continuities are less surprising if one considers the extent to which the various reports draw upon each other, with or without acknowledgment (Culioli 1999). Thus, Mottet, an attorney presenting an official parliamentary report to King Louis Philippe in 1836, cites a report by one Colmont from two years before; the journalist Paul Bourde in his account of the island in 1887 comments on a commission appointed by the Ministry of the Interior in the same year; Georges Clémenceau, president of the council and minister of the interior writes a parliamentary report on Corsica in 1908 which quotes a report presented to the Academy of Moral and Political Sciences in 1838 by Auguste Blanqui. The aforementioned Glavany, ninety years later, quotes both Mottet and Clémenceau. The accumulation of cross-referenced (but also, in some cases, plagiarized) reports both reflects and helps to establish the increasing formalization of *le problème Corse*. As early as 1887, the structure of Bourde's report, entitled "In Corsica: Clanism, Political Mores, Vendetta, Banditry," stands as a striking testimony to the widespread understanding of Corsica as self-evidently problematic: the first eleven chapters (1999[1887], pp. 57–211) give an account of various aspects of Corsica (ranging from criminality to traditional poetry), and the twelfth is simply called "the cures" (*les remèdes*). By that point already, in other words,

Corsica had implicitly become the Corsican problem, something to be revealed, understood, and solved. And indeed, since the nineteenth century, with surprising consistency, one finds the word "Corsica" associated with the word "problem" or, more euphemistically, "question" in political speeches, in newspaper articles, in conversations, in books of all shapes and kinds (Labro 1977; Lefevre 2000). The constant representation of the island as problematic is an important way in which Corsica is constituted as a locus for action, merging into the very definition of the island the suggestion that something should be done about it.

And there are other continuities. With surprisingly few exceptions, the reports follow the same pattern. They oppose the enormous potential of the island and its current derelict state. They then assign causes and provide solutions. Two main problems emerge from these reports with surprising consistency. One asks: why, being similarly endowed by nature as the richest parts of Italy or southern France, is Corsica not productive?[1] The other asks: why, being a part of France, does it not follow French laws and mores?[2]

In framing the question of Corsica's unproductive state, a number of the reports present the reader with a cornucopian inventory of the riches which the island's climate and soil would in theory allow: wheat, wines, cotton, silkworms, raisins, figs, olive oil, soap, mulberries, flax, chestnuts, oranges and other citrus, wood, tar, honey, wax, marble, granite, jasper, anchovies, oysters. To this basic list, Réalier-Dumas, a French civil servant on the island reporting in 1819, rather hopefully adds hemp, tobacco, sugarcane, copper, silver, and gold (Mottet 1980[1836]; Abbé Gaudin 1997[1787]; Réalier-Dumas 2000[1819]). Properly "cultivated," Corsica could even yield *human* resources: the writers of the *plan terrier* laid out a meticulous plan for increasing the population of the island from 150,658 in 1794 to 598,914 at an unspecified future date. This plan involved setting up three agricultural colonies on the eastern plain, run by 1,800 families, as well as three spas run by 18 further families. With surreal arithmetic seriousness, the authors attribute five children to each of the 1,818 families, leading to a population increase of 9,090 in the first instance and thence incrementally to reach not only the planned 598,914, but hopefully a full million—all the while providing a combined annual revenue of 1,650,000 *livres* (Willis 1980, pp. 334–335, 339).

It is not just the quantity, but also the quality of Corsica's population upon which these reports comment. The "natives," claims the Abbé Gaudin, are well disposed and "almost new" (1997[1787], p. xviii); their children are astonishingly "precocious, . . . attentive . . . , serious . . . , curious. They are a truly elite race" (Blanqui 1995[1838], p. 471). Blanqui's conclusion is an instance of the moral and metaphorical construction of French culture/cultivation as process: "With such children and such soil, Corsica must become one of the most beautiful French *départements;* we need only to sow with intelligence, and shield the land from heather and the youth from idleness" (ibid.). Similar formulations were present in French nineteenth-century discourse on both "the Arab" and "the Kabyle"[3] (Silverstein 2004, pp. 49, 55), pointing to the often-noted continuity of nineteenth-century government policies and concerns about French colonies and about remote regions or the lower social orders of metropolitan France (Colonna 1997; Rabinow 1989).

In the second set of reports, this concern with productivity is subordinated to a concern with administration, political behavior, law and order. The cornucopian shopping lists tend to be replaced by detailed accounts of electoral fraud, of uncontrollable feuds, of self-appointed bandit kings, and of the corruption of administrative functioning. However, both kinds of report show a strong concern, common to many contemporary colonial settings, with "sanitation and seeing" (Thomas 1990). For some reports, this means building roads, draining the pestilential marshes, and cutting back the wild vegetation. For others, it is a case of establishing clear administrative procedures, flushing out hidden bandits, and cutting back the wild networks of fraud and nepotism.

In fact, through its claim of investigative rigor, a report itself functions as the first step in the "French action upon Corsica" for which it calls. Time after time, we find the same concern with painstaking and truthful detail, making Corsica legible and understandable, opening it up to the scrutiny of the (French) reader. The report categorizes, lists, exhibits, establishes causalities and responsibilities (the climate's, the natives', the state's, etc.). As in Timothy Mitchell's analysis of the colonization of Egypt, the report enframes: "the same technologies of order created both a disciplinary power and a seemingly separate realm of meaning or truth" (Mitchell 1988, p. xv). And yet, however much it draws on previous works, each report seems to find the same confusion unclarified, the same preoccupying mystery, the same enduring problems.

In part, of course, this is a feature of the lack of action taken by the French state on the basis of these reports. As Willis points out, the detailed development plans proposed in the *plan terrier* were never implemented; the wars of the *directoire* and, later, the Napoleonic Wars put the Corsican problem on the back burner, and on the back burner, effectively, it remained. The economic crisis of the island endured and was attributed in report after report to essentially similar causes: poor infrastructure, hydrographic imbalances, over-fragmentation of land ownership, small size, and the supposed indolence of the population. Astonishingly, the diagnoses and the proposals of the agricultural development plan implemented by the French state in 1957 were to all extents and purposes the same as those proposed nearly two centuries earlier by the authors of the *plan terrier* (Willis 1980, pp. 346–348).

This failure of the French state to develop Corsica has often been held up as the self-evident reason for the endurance of *le problème Corse*. Yet, to leave it at this is to miss the equally salient fact that the very accumulation of reports in and of itself has produced a discourse about the nature of the island as inherently problematic. This is not to say that the infrastructure was not poor or the water balance unhelpful for cultivation, but just that the form in which the island was problematized took on a life of its own. It produced certain familiar discursive objects, entities which endure today and which have effects independent of the actual rivers, roads, and land rights of the island itself: the "timelessness" of Corsica (in which the same problems constantly recur), the inherent "complexity" of the reality of the island, and the sense that accurate knowledge about the place is crucially missing.

Reports as Proto-Ethnography

To probe into this ever-renewed mystery of Corsica, I will perform a reverse operation to that proposed by Mary Louise Pratt in her contribution to *Writing Culture* (Pratt 1986). Pratt suggested that the classic rhetorical device whereby ethnographic writers defined themselves in opposition to older and less specialized genres of writing—travel books, personal memoirs, journalism, and accounts by missionaries, settlers, colonial officials, and the like—made it difficult for them to reflect upon the conventions of their own genre. She proceeds to recover some of the suppressed continuities between the narratives of travel writers and those of twentieth-century anthropologists. One of these continuities is the role of the ubiquitous opening personal narrative, in which the ethnographer's entrance into the field is dramatized. Pratt sees in this direct inheritance of earlier travel literature the central but disavowed linchpin of ethnographic authority, on which hinges the difficult balance of objectivity and subjectivity characteristic of much twentieth-century anthropology. As Clifford Geertz later put it, "being there" was central to the way ethnographic texts were "author-ized" (Geertz 1988, pp. 1–24; cf. Foucault 1979).

In Pratt's account, travel literature is not the explanandum, but merely the touchstone by which ethnography is made aware of itself. I propose we now attempt the reverse and use Pratt's and Geertz's insights to consider the author-izing of the reports described in the previous section. If one analyzes the report writers' authorial personas and their truth-claims, it appears that these reports did indeed prefigure the balance of erudition and documentary research, on the one hand, and personal experience, on the other, which would later characterize anthropological literature. As a general rule, the authors speak explicitly from personal experience of the island, often opening with an arrival account, detailing the time they spent in Corsica, and backing up their general claims with personal impressions and quotes from the "natives."

This immediately raises one question, which Pratt does not spell out, regarding the value of personal experience: why is it that personal experience is such a powerful legitimating trope? This question has broad epistemological implications to which I will return. However, there is a partial and circumscribed answer which can already be given at this stage: in the Corsican case at least, following the model of the first-contact account, the value of the author's personal experience is framed against everyone else's ignorance of the island. This may seem a paradoxical statement; after all, although most of the reports' prospective audiences had probably not been to Corsica themselves, the island was certainly not unknown and had been involved in Mediterranean political and economic networks since antiquity. But exoticism is relational (cf. Herzfeld 1989), and distance can be an emergent property. With striking consistency across two centuries, the authors of reports on Corsica insisted on the unknown, mysterious quality of this nearby island:

> I believed that the curiosity which makes us so eager to read . . . the relation of foreign travels, should find no less interest in the description of one of our own provinces, which may be even less known to us. (Abbé Gaudin 1997[1787], p. xii)

> The Tahitians are better known to us than the inhabitants of Sardinia or Corsica. (Precis de la geographie universelle, quoted in Réalier-Dumas 2000[1819], p. 1)

> Corsica is so unknown and so far. (Bourde 1999[1887], p. 223)

> [W]e felt that our work should begin with . . . the search for truth . . . [s]o that our fellow citizens may come to a better knowledge of the reality of Corsica, this integral part of the republic. (Glavany 1998, n.p.)

The sheer repetition of this concern, from 1787 to 1998, suggests that Corsica is unknown as a matter of essence rather than due to a lack of information; that Corsica, like Levinas's Other, is not merely unknown, but unknowable. Partly, this has been a result of the succession of reports and the repetitive act of discovery itself. If Corsica is permanently being discovered, it must be permanently unknown.

But even in the details, these reports, while presenting themselves as true, simultaneously produced the mystery in which Corsica was shrouded. I have described the effort of exhibition and clarification which went into these works, sorting causes from consequences and the mutual influences of different phenomena. Yet mystery, in these accounts, remains multi-leveled and multiply problematic. It is the impenetrability of the mountainous Corsican interior, where the lack of roads and the fear of outlaws impedes commerce and agriculture; it is the isolation of high-perched villages, foreign and hostile to one another, impervious to civilization and the passing of time; it is the thick Corsican vegetation, untamed, unmapped, uncultivated, a haven for criminals and impenetrable to the law; it is the knife and the gun hidden in a secret pocket of the shepherd's coat and the dark passion of the Corsican man, boiling away beneath a stony exterior, ready to erupt into a vicious murder. To quote Blanqui once more: "[Corsica] rises out of the Mediterranean as a volcanic mass, and the character of its inhabitants is similar to the geological makeup of the land" (1995, p. 466).

So, for all of the reports' attempts to organize, explain, and establish causalities, the multiple instances of the unknown (geological, vegetal, social, psychological) boil over into one another, fusing at the symbolic and metaphorical levels. Here, between causality and metaphor, between reality and fiction, are the makings of what Taussig has termed an "epistemic murk" (Taussig 1992). What the reports discover and convey to the reader is what they started from: the mystery that is Corsica.

Again, we find a phenomenon which has been described for ethnographic writing. James Clifford has noted the paradoxical underside of ethnographic writing, whose implicit surrealism challenges its explicit ordering of the world into distinct cultures (Clifford 1981, pp. 563ff.; 1988, p. 147). Marilyn Strathern has reframed Clifford's analysis in terms of Bruno Latour's opposition between the twin processes of separation and mixing, "purification" and "translation" (Strathern 1999, p. 119; Latour 1993). In positing these intertwined processes as the characteristic hallmark of modernity, Latour suggests that the power of "the moderns" rested precisely in the explicit "purification" of nature from society and humans from nonhumans, which covered (and thereby allowed) an implicit "translation" resulting in new "hybrids": "The moderns . . . succeeded in such an expansion only because they have carefully separated Nature and Society . . . , whereas they have succeeded only because they have mixed together much greater masses of humans and nonhumans, without bracketing anything and without ruling out any combination!" (Latour 1993, p. 41). The reports on Corsica could be framed in similar terms. As Clifford argued about ethnographic writing, nineteenth-century reports on Corsica present an ordered account while simultaneously producing Corsica-as-mystery, a world in which individuals, villages, and volcanic rocks all partake of the same mysterious essence. One could extend Latour's comments on the efficacy of modernity to the efficacy of these reports: the legitimacy of the report comes from its purification of the mysterious and entangled reality of Corsica into discrete objects of knowledge, while it simultaneously and illicitly fuses these discrete instances back into a darkly rich epistemic murk. This murky mystery of Corsica, then, becomes the framing device against which the reporter presents his revelatory truth. As such, it is not likely to be dispelled by the report, since it is its very condition of possibility.

Prejudice and Method

Let us return to the question of personal experience. I have argued that the value of personal experience was framed against the trope of first contact with a mysterious, unknown location. Some reporters, however, also wrote against another kind of unknown, located this time in their audience: "prejudices" (*les préjugés*). As early as 1787, Gaudin denounces French prejudices, which impede the proper government of the island and a real understanding of its problems (Abbé Gaudin 1997[1787]). Negative opinions on Corsica are denounced thirty-two years later by Réalier-Dumas as the mark of imperfect understanding (Réalier-Dumas 2000[1819]). In 1838, Blanqui proposes to disprove the French prejudice that there are many thieves in Corsica (Blanqui 1995[1838]). The theme of French prejudice about Corsica remains an extremely prominent issue in contemporary writing and everyday life even in the twenty-first century.

A concern with a non-Corsican manner of perceiving Corsica is, in one form or another, the starting point of a great number of otherwise disparate books written about Corsica since the 1970s. Thus, for instance, the anthropologist Ravis-Giordani's excellent and exhaustive opus on Corsican shepherds devotes a chapter to "the image of Corsica and Corsicans" in non-Corsican writings from antiquity to the nineteenth century (Ravis-Giordani 1983, pp. 31–39). In conclusion, he notes:

> The picture of Corsican mentality and mores is ultimately so complex and contrasted, that even those who draw it give up trying to account for it. Doubtless we need to pursue the analysis of the objective conditions of existence of the Corsican people in order to understand these appraisals of it, those at least which can be supposed to have been formulated in good faith. (Ravis-Giordani 1983, p. 39)

Similarly, the historian Robert Colonna d'Istria opens his introduction with an outline of three forms of Continental prejudice: that which accuses without knowing, that which romanticizes the island as unknowable, and that which strives to be more Corsican than Corsicans themselves. In response to such positions, Colonna d'Istria states, "The purpose of this book is not to make Corsica intelligible, but rather more modestly, to explain what took place there during the 20th Century" (Colonna d'Istria 1997, p. 17). Sanguinetti, author of a more explicitly political critique of the French state's policies in Corsica, puts the point rather more brutally:

> Before we enter into the heart of the matter, it will be necessary to provide a summary introduction to the container and the contents, namely Corsica and Corsicans, for the benefit of those who are approaching the insular problem for the first time, or those whose opinions are little more than superficial prejudices or tendentious and insulting ideas. (Sanguinetti 1979, p. 13)

Corsica's image and continental French prejudices (*préjugés*) are not only tropes for writers' introductions. They also play a strong part in everyday definitions of Corsican/Continental difference. One of the first things which many people in Crucetta asked me upon hearing that I had never before set foot on the island was whether I had any *préjugés* on the topic of Corsica. Although I remember feeling a slight surprise at the eagerness and benign tone of the question, my instant reaction was to deny any such prejudices: I had come to Corsica with an open mind, to discover reality on the terrain. My response seemed to be only partly satisfying, and looking back, I would suggest that I had misread the import of the exchange. Although I attempted to counter what I took to be a suspicion of bias, what was actually at stake in such exchanges was the rehearsal of a common narrative in which the Continental outsider, arriving on the island, rectifies his preconceived views through firsthand experience. This is a trajectory I later heard in countless forms during my stay in Crucetta. Given the visibility of the island in the national media, the possibility that a Continental has not heard of and thus has no preconceived ideas at all about Corsica is not considered seriously. At best, the general assumption often seems to be that the Continental can arrive with an awareness of his preconceptions. At worst, he brings with him a deeply ingrained and uninformed negative image of Corsicans which he then offensively bandies about. In this context, someone who claims to have no prejudices is more than likely to be part of the second category.

Narratives of the misapprehensions, arrogance, and presumption of the latter kind of visitors are rife in Corsica, and the storytellers' reactions range from benign amusement to real annoyance. A friend who lives in Bastia, who defines herself as a Continental of Italian descent married to a Corsican man, told me of Continental tourists who struck up a conversation on the train and (assuming she was Corsican) expressed their surprise at the fact that her husband "let her go out by herself." On another occasion, at a public meeting of Corsican schoolteachers, one participant told, with outrage and amusement, of the head of a Continental school with whom she had organized an exchange, who nearly broke off the arrangement on account of the "lack of safety" (*insécurité*) of Corsica. Everyone agreed that this was typical behavior on the part of Continentals. Pascal, on whose invitation I was present at the meeting, asked me, for everyone's benefit: "See, what the image [of Corsica] is like? Lack of safety! Do you feel unsafe here?"

Some Corsicans drew a considerable amount of amusement from stories of outrageous Continental fears. One friend told me of a Corsican friend of his who was being pestered by Continental acquaintances wanting to camp in his field. In the end, the Corsican told them very seriously that they were free to do so, if they were prepared to take the risk of nationalists blowing up their tent. Reportedly, the Continentals believed him and desisted. My friend followed this story up with an account of seeing, on the eight o'clock news, a couple of Continental tourists who were asked by a reporter whether they felt scared on the island. "Not at all," they replied. "But of course, we don't go out at night." Corsican amusement is mixed, however, with concern and disbelief at stories of Continentals having panic attacks upon setting foot on the island and other such embodiments of the Corsican/ Continental divide. Continentals who have firsthand experience of Corsica, such as my neighbor Cécile, a schoolteacher in Paris, also frequently mocked the outrageous fears of those who only know the island from news reports. One of our first discussions concerned precisely that topic, and we bonded over accounts of the overblown fears which our respective sojourns in Corsica had prompted among family and friends in Paris.

This concern with Corsica's image in Continentals' eyes is also regularly reflected in the public statements of local politicians and officials. The summer of 2003 saw a sudden increase in nationalist attacks on public buildings and Continentals' homes; when the Corsican Assembly reopened after its summer break, its then-president spoke very strongly against "the current climate" of violence, which "gives Corsica a detestable image" (Radio Corsica Frequenza Mora 2003). That this was the politician's main stated gripe against the destruction of public buildings and private homes suggests the importance of image in this context. That the audience remained wholly implicit (i.e., no mention needed to be made of who will see this image—who else could it be but those in continental France?) is revelatory of the extent to which Corsica remains conceptualized as an object of French knowledge—albeit incomplete or erroneous knowledge. The very next day, the new French prefect of the island concluded his first public speech, in which he had stressed his desire to get to know Corsica on the ground by visiting and talking to people, with the phrase: "I have no prejudices about Corsica." As an interesting thought experiment, one might try to imagine the same statement made by an incoming official about another place, such as Paris or the Bourgogne. What, in the case of Corsica, passed without comment would be considered in most other situations an absurd and impossibly patronizing statement.

The persistence of "French prejudice" has often been described as an inherent feature of relations between Corsica and the rest of France. Alexandra Jaffe, for instance, notes that "during the three-month strike of 1989, in which Corsican civil servants protested the lack of compensation for the high cost of living on the island, some of the intensity and duration and extent of popular support for the strike among Corsicans was a response to reactions from the French government and press that Corsicans identified as part of a history of prejudice" (Jaffe 1997, p. 154). But we may well ask, given the fact that French reports on Corsica proposed to dispel prejudice as early as 1787, why this "French prejudice," like the island's mystery, seems to be impervious to the succession of reports and accounts which seek to dispel it?

In his work on racism, Pierre-André Taguieff has located the rejection of prejudice in nineteenth-century France within a specific intellectual tradition, which he traces from Montaigne, through Descartes, Voltaire, and the "Lumières" (Taguieff 1987, pp. 183–223). Taguieff's genealogy finds an etymological echo in the progressive disappearance in French of a previous meaning of *préjugé:* the word also used to mean an index or sign (Rey 1993, p. 1614). In current parlance, it means merely a mistaken pre-notion. Like the later concept of stereotype, analyzed by Maryon McDonald, *le préjugé* is commonly defined in these discourses as an unsatisfactory representation partly because it is not based on a *direct experience* of reality (McDonald 1993, p. 221). Its very definition, therefore, is bound up with the methodological empiricism of truth-claims based on personal experience, precisely the kind of claims to "being there" made by the reporters.

As anthropologists, we need not look very far for traces of this empiricism in our own intellectual genealogy. After all, Emile Durkheim devotes an entire chapter of *Rules of Sociological Method* to the need for sociologists to reject *prejudice*—preformed ideas (1964). This was, Durkheim claims in the second preface to that much-criticized book, the meaning of his famous injunction to treat social facts as things—to treat them as new objects, experienced from the outside, not in terms of the preexisting internal conceptions we have of them:

> For what, indeed, is a thing? A thing is opposed to an idea as that which we know from the outside, to that which we know from the inside. . . . To treat certain order[s] of facts as things, is not therefore to class them within this or that category of reality. It means observing a certain mental attitude with respect to them. It is to approach their study with the principle that we absolutely ignore what they are. (Durkheim 1988, p. 77)[4]

In this sense, one might agree with Taguieff when he notes that, in its most extreme form, this rejection of prejudice as a methodological principle implies a suspicion and critique of all dated knowledge (Taguieff 1987, p. 194). Once Corsica is posited as a thing out there, unknown by definition, each report can redefine previous accounts of Corsica as prejudices. And indeed, following this principle, these very same reports are held by many today as paradigmatic examples of Continental prejudice. Out of the nine reports mentioned above, eight were available for purchase in bookshops on the island during the period of my fieldwork. Several thousand copies of the Glavany Report have been sold on the island since its publication in 1998 (Culioli 1999, p. 11). Older reports, some dating back to the seventeenth century, have been re-edited in inexpensive formats and are laid out on racks outside the doors of bookshops in the Corsican towns of Bastia, Corte, Ajaccio, and Calvi. Cécile brought another of them to my attention, which she had discovered in an obscure edited volume on French travel accounts. Clearly, the framing of Corsica-as-subject-matter, in which these nonfiction works once participated, has been successful to the extent that these writings are still understandable, recognizable, and even interesting to a fairly nonspecialist public today.

Our aging reports have now been given a new lease on life as historical documents. They are fairly routinely used as historical sources about nineteenth-century Corsica (with varying degrees of earnestness and irony; see, for instance, Glavany 1998; Lefevre 2000). For others, they are not so much documents about Corsica as documents about French prejudices about Corsica. This is certainly the spirit in which the Corsican historian Culioli presents his own edited volume, *La Corse aux rapports* (1999), in which he reproduces two official reports and two journalistic accounts of the island. In his introduction to these documents, Culioli emplots the reports into a history of the French domination of Corsica. Of the journalist Piobb's account, while he notes it is detailed and well documented, Culioli remarks: "his book is the exact expression of France's perception of Corsica and its people. . . . Piobb remains very French in his manner of perceiving Corsica, which is a tad colonial. But at least he does it with a relative generosity" (Culioli 1999, p. 41).

In other words, I would argue that "French prejudice," like "Corsican mystery," has taken on a life of its own. Each tends to be presented as a merely remediable lack of accurate knowledge about the island. But the knowledge is there, and still they persist. This suggests that these discursive entities have become entwined with the kind of thing Corsica is. Corsica is (that is, has become) unknown by definition, and hence the French are prejudiced about it as a matter of course. And this very same discursive formation opens up space for another subject position, that of the insider.

Immanent Knowledge

> [A] new figure has entered the scene, the "indigenous eth-
> nographer." . . . Insiders studying their own cultures offer
> new angles of vision and depths of understanding. Their
> accounts are empowered and restricted in unique ways.
> —CLIFFORD 1986

The anthropological concern with ethnographic authority in the 1980s sparked a reconsideration of the politics of knowledge implied in the category "indigenous ethnographer" or "native anthropologist" (Abu-Lughod 1991; Narayan 1993). Narayan in particular offered a critique of the category on both conceptual and political grounds. Conceptually, she aimed to destabilize the sense of boundedness and completeness implied by the notion of the native ethnographer through an account of her own not-quite-at-home fieldwork. Politically, Narayan problematized academic representations of the native anthropologist *qua* challenger of Western intellectual hegemony by pointing to the roots of the category itself in older, exclusionary, colonial knowledge practices (Narayan 1993, pp. 672ff.).

These arguments fed into wider debates about nativism and cosmopolitanism (Kuper 1994; Friedman 1997; Kahn 2003). While critics of nativism pointed to the sinister horizons of claims to knowledge based on essential rootedness, other authors pointed to the sinister horizons of constructivist challenges to the authority of native scholars and spokespeople (Briggs 1996; Fischer 1999). As Clifford Geertz once noted of a related debate, "we are being offered a choice of worries" (Geertz 1984).

What does emerge from this unresolved and occasionally aporetic debate, however, is a clear sense that "the notion of the native is not an innocent concept, and neither is a native positionality" (Navaro-Yashin 2002, p. 14)—and the same, of course, goes for the cosmopolitan. Rather, claims to knowledge based on rootedness and nativeness—just like claims to knowledge based on objectivity and distance (Daston and Galison 2007; Anderson 2001)—are the product of particular histories and the allies of particular politics. As I have done throughout this chapter, I will take this insight born of anthropological reflexivity and bring it in contact with the history of nonfiction accounts of Corsica. What this history shows is that, at least in the case of Corsica, the kind of authority derived from rootedness and the kind of authority derived from distance share both historical roots and logical assumptions. In effect, as anthropologist Charlie Galibert (2005) has noted, they are mirror images of each other. They can even be combined in surprising ways.

One seemingly major break between nineteenth-century and late twentieth-century accounts is the appearance, in the latter, of implicitly or explicitly native positionalities. Many post-1960s authors of nonfiction work on Corsica make explicit reference to the fact that they are themselves Corsican or have Corsican "roots." For instance, on the back cover of a collection of Corsican folklore, a book held in very high esteem by those involved in the study and promotion of Corsican language and culture on the island, the two editors are described as "Claire Tiévant, ethnologist, [and] Lucie Desideri, *Corsican* ethnologist" (Tiévant and Desideri 1986; emphasis added).

As Galibert (2005) has noted, an internal, immanent positionality has emerged in Corsican anthropological and ethnological writing which eschews the figure of objectivity together with that of externality and distance (see, for instance, Salini 1996; Verdoni 1999). In such cases, Galibert notes, the project of a scientific rationalization of alterity is negated by "[t]he affirmation that the full and total reality of the island is knowable directly by those who are in (and of) it. . . . This mirroring strategy inverts . . . the temptation of losing oneself in order to become other, into the temptation to remain oneself without going through the other" (Galibert 2005, n.p.).

In fact, however, only a handful of authors explicitly ground their authority in their Corsicanness. However justified Kuper's fears of nativism may be for certain contexts, mainstream Francophone nonfiction literature remains so far broadly dominated by the same discourse of universalism which underpins Kuper's own position. In the main, truth-claims in post-1960s literature on Corsica are explicitly premised—as in the nineteenth-century reports—on scientific rigor, research, scholarship, and experience. Yet the authors' Corsicanness often appears in the introductions, prefaces, or back covers of these works. When the authors might be reticent to frame themselves in such a way, the publisher does it for them. This suggests that, if not the author, at least the editors and, presumably, the reading public are sensitive to something akin to a nativist theory of knowledge, according to which roots (however defined) give one a privileged insight into a place, an insight which is not reducible to scientific inquiry and personal experience.

This notion of rooted knowledge is not a new, post-1960s development in nonfiction discourse about Corsica; rather, it is the necessary counterpart of earlier depictions of Corsica as mystery, as unknowable thing. The entire positivist drive of the nineteenth-century reporters, constantly moving on from prejudice, ever probing into mystery, postulated the truth of Corsica as out there, as the counterpart, the desired target, and ultimate justification of their work. This truth, holistic and mute, present and patiently awaiting discovery and exhibition, was lodged in the people and the land and in the essential ties that bound them. The post-1960s novelty (although occasionally anticipated, as we shall see) is the suggestion that this essential truth might speak directly, through the mouths of its bearers.

The problem of such a suggestion for the creation of an authoritative text is obvious. The more Corsican roots become entangled in an author's truth-claim, the more she will be led to justify what she can provide for her Corsican readership. And indeed this question does arise with great regularity. In many prefaces of late twentieth-century nonfiction books about Corsica, the author explicitly states what Corsicans and non-Corsicans, respectively, may expect to get from the book. Thus, Colonna d'Istria comments:

> The following pages are addressed not only to Corsicans, to those who, from near or from afar, have lived through the events of the century which is about to expire (for them, these pages will constitute a kind of memory; they will find here, in perspective, all that they already know), but also to all the others who may perhaps find here some keys for understanding the present situation. (Colonna d'Istria 1997, p. 15; see also Antonetti 1973; Masson-Maret 1991; Sanguinetti 1979; Tiévant and Desideri 1986)

Yet this authorial position, from which a writer is enabled to speak (about different things) to both Corsicans and Continentals, is not a direct correlate of a nativist theory of immanent knowledge. Rather, it draws its power from the boundary, present in the nineteenth-century reports, between the observer (assumed to be external) and the native (assumed to be representative). Post-1960s authors who address this double audience are themselves attempting to balance science and essence, observation and roots, the signifier and the signified. For most of the eighteenth- and nineteenth-century reporters who denounced French prejudice, this didn't lead to a statement of Corsicans' self-knowledge. Corsicans were part of the matter under study and were usually left out of the equation either as potential authors or as potential readers: the question was not of Corsicans' access to the truth, but of others' access to the truth about Corsicans. As in pre-1970s anthropology, there was a fairly strict division of labor between the external observer and the representative native in the production of a text for the consumption of a third party, "back home" (Geertz 1988, p. 132; Appadurai 1988; Narayan 1993).

One of the most interesting examples of this division of labor can be found in a seeming exception: James Boswell's *An Account of Corsica* (1768). Boswell, the famous English biographer, visited the island shortly before the French conquest, when Paoli ruled over an independent Corsican republic. Boswell's sympathy for the Corsican cause is clearly stated. As the historian Brady puts it, "Boswell saw Corsica in classical terms: Paoli was a hero from Plutarch, and the Corsican government resembled Sparta in its form and spirit" (Brady 1965, p. 39).[5]

This might seem a far cry from the reports on *le problème Corse* examined above. And yet Boswell's account shares a number of common themes, tropes, and concerns. Most important, Boswell clearly enunciates the division of labor between the observer and the native. Consider his introduction to *An Account of Corsica:*

> I would not take upon me to [write this account], till I consulted with the General of the nation. I therefore informed him of my design. His answer is perhaps too flattering for me to publish: but I must beg leave to give it as the license and sanction of this work. Paoli was pleased to write to me thus; . . . "Nothing can be more generous than your design to publish the observations which you have made upon Corsica. You have seen its natural situation, you have been able to study the manners of its inhabitants, and to see intimately the maxims of their government, of which you know the constitution. This people with an enthusiasm of gratitude, will unite their applause with that of undeceived Europe." (Boswell 1768, pp. ix–x)

Paoli's answer interweaves the various themes described earlier. Paoli (to whom *An Account* is dedicated) outlines Boswell's credentials for being there (cf. Geertz

1988), acknowledging his detailed observation of the natural, social, and legal realities of Corsica. As in the later French reports, there is a political and ethical problem (albeit a very different one). Finally, we see the theme of non-Corsicans' prejudice outlined in the hope of an "undeceived Europe."

Boswell himself covers this author-izing ground again in the course of his work, but the interesting thing here is that it is Paoli who seals Boswell's authority with his own stamp of approval. The Corsicans whose manners Boswell has observed lend Boswell their representativity, explicitly articulated and reinscribed by Paoli, the most representative of Corsicans. Through Paoli's mouth, the immanent truth of Corsica has spoken—and it has spoken for Boswell. In the final instance, however, neither Paoli nor the Corsicans write the account, any more than they are expected to read it, since it is explicitly aimed at the people back home.

This division of labor between the representative native and the objective observer persisted broadly throughout the nineteenth-century reports, despite the fact that a number of Corsicans were in fact writing accounts of the island in the nineteenth century. One of these was Jean De La Rocca, who produced a 500-page report, "Corsica and Its Future" (De La Rocca 1857). In the main, his analyses and his proposed policies for the betterment of the island were similar to those of the Continental reporters of the time—to the extent that he even carried over the image of first contact, but from an imaginary native's point of view:

> The Corsican, standing atop his cliffs, can see the industry he is begging for, steaming by his shores and heading far away, towards less hospitable lands, bearing movement, life, fecundity, prosperity, happiness. By God! yes, the first ship which, carrying a great capitalist and a clever industrialist, will land on our shores, will have discovered Corsica! (De La Rocca 1857, p. 496)

Like other reporters, De La Rocca stigmatized previous accounts: "There is no lack of works on Corsica . . . but apart from some rare exceptions, all are more or less inexact" (De La Rocca 1857, p. 3). And like them, he based his authority on long residence on the island and firsthand experience of the phenomena he wanted to describe, although a tinge of romantic access to the very heart of things seeps into the account:

> Many times we have travelled the length and breadth of Corsica, we have scaled its mountains, penetrated its deep forests, visited its smallest localities. We have complemented through study the observations made on the site itself, and called to our aid the lights of statistic[s]. (De La Rocca 1857, p. 4)

Insider knowledge could, however, create the opportunity for an accusation of partiality. The missionary De Lemps, one French nineteenth-century reporter who does mention accounts of the island by Corsicans, claims that "the love for the land of their birth has been detrimental to the truth of their accounts" (De Lemps 1843, p. 17). This suggestion of the unsatisfactory partiality of Corsicans writing about Corsica is echoed 157 years later in the opening lines of Marianne Lefèvre's *Géopolitique de la Corse:* "Analysing the Corsican . . . 'problem,' the Corsican 'question' appears an arduous task, insofar as neutrality seems to be excluded from the terminology of book titles, . . . written mostly by islander academics and journalists" (Lefevre 2000, p. 1). Here, the mention of the authors' origins is made to stand against them.

To return to 1843, De Lemps also stigmatizes, as all reporters tended to do, the inexact and unfair judgments of the island by foreign sources. He thus conveniently sets himself up as the only valid source of truth about Corsica: "For us, whom a holy mission has kept for many years among this people; who have studied without preconception their habits and mores, we trust we may avoid those two traps most dangerous to the honour of history: flattery and detraction" (De Lemps 1843, p. 17).[6] This was written in 1843. In 1973, the historian Antonetti takes up exactly the same authorial position of impartiality and objectivity by placing his book "[a] s far from the naive exaltation in which too many islanders wallow, as it is from the systematic denigration which is the joy of too many 'Continentals'" (Antonetti 1973, p. 11). Thus, while claims to objectivity premised on detachment might at first glance seem diametrically opposed to the engagement rhetoric of rooted knowledge, the two can be combined and in practice often are (cf. Anderson 2001; Candea forthcoming B). Impartiality and in-betweenness can be read through the prism of a form of nativism, as in the following statement from the ethnopsychologist Masson-Maret:

> Although I am deeply attached to [Corsica], and have roots there, it is as an ethnopsychologist, using a method of rigorous investigation which eschews the intuitive and the irrational, that I have set out to discover the Corsican personality. . . . Many are the books on the subject of Corsica . . . , but they are often the work of Corsicans directly implicated in the cultural and emotional problems linked to the island, or of "foreigners" . . . whose approach is often superficial and "uninitiated." (Masson-Maret 1991, p. 7)

In other words, one might say that the very way in which Corsica has been "put into discourse" (*mise en discours*) through the coupled mystery/essence forces authors who would produce accounts of Corsica into a reflexive engagement with the sources of their own authority and, in the best cases, into extremely productive epistemological experimentation, as for instance in Galibert's "interstitial" approach to anthropology, written from the perspective of a Continental anthropologist who was also a part-time resident of the village he describes for over twenty-five years: "Neither a technical and neutral relationship—the exteriority to the object as an intrinsic guarantee of objectivity—nor a sympathetic fusion with the object—being internal to the object as an intrinsic guarantee of authenticity—ethno-anthropological knowledge must be a work of mediating difference and distance" (Galibert 2004b, p. 225).

Beyond Othering

BANG! As the noise subsides, it dawns on me that I have never before heard an actual gunshot. It is louder than I had imagined, and I make an effort to keep smiling and soothe my jangled nerves. This is not going to be the last gunshot of the morning, and I am painfully aware that the man directly to my left must be suppressing giggles at my obvious jumpiness when he shot his small black handgun behind my back. People always shoot, I was told, at these processions, as indeed at weddings and to celebrate electoral victories. Not that everyone in Crucetta finds this particularly nice, however: the elderly men shooting their rifles from balconies as the effigy of Saint Anthony is borne through the village are rarely the object of much censure, although people do worry, in a general sense, that what goes up must come down. But they are "shooting for the village," the women sitting in front of the church had told me earlier that morning, with a shrug: what are you going to do? "It's the others, though," one of them leaned in, confidentially, while her companions nodded, straight-backed, arms crossed, severe. The younger Crucettacci who "think they're all that," shooting fancy weapons like they're in some movie. "They're pimps, those ones," another woman cuts in, using an idiom which I had often heard in Crucetta to refer to ostentatious displayers ("Look at that, what a pimp's shirt you're wearing!" Petru would occasionally jibe with mock admiration when I donned a button-down shirt, instead of my usual T-shirts). In this case, however, the undertone of illegality is crucial. "They" are the people of whom it is known or rumored that they belong to underground nationalist groups, or those who are suspected of involvement with drugs or racketeering.

I am rather glad a few hours later as the procession sets off that I have never probed into that aspect of people's lives and thus cannot gauge the level of illegality involved, if any, when my companion in the procession discreetly nips off to his scooter from the trunk of which he gets a small handgun. He is certainly not keen to be seen shooting it, that much is clear, which is why he shoots from behind my back. Although he may well be hiding it from a disapproving aunt, the police are not infrequently present at such events, keen to catch people in the act of firing unregistered weapons, a small misdemeanor which can lead to uncovering more serious ones. For all its mereness, Crucetta is not without its share of serious police attention, and I was repeatedly told by reliable people of phone taps, arrests, and discovered gun caches. These various thoughts go through my mind as the procession slowly snakes up the tarmac road into the heart of the old village to the tune of gunshots: the boom of rifles, the short sharp shock of handguns, and occasionally the rat-a-tat-tat of something automatic—which, unsurprisingly, is nowhere to be seen. At any rate, this train of thought replaces my initial awkwardness at playing a role in the procession. Planning to spectate rather than participate, I had been won over by an elderly friend's insistence that I join in the procession and indeed wear the white habit of the village's "brotherhood" (*cunfraterna*), as he foresaw a lack of willing young men this year. Despite my protests, he insisted that I was well known enough by this point to do it and that no one would mind. Worries about the incongruity of my position and doubts as to the accuracy of my friend's prediction were banished however, as much by the sight of many smiling familiar faces in the crowd of onlookers as by the sheer indescribable loudness of the whole thing, along with the smells of incense and gunpowder in the blazing late morning sun.

As we turn out of a narrow alleyway into the large Place de la Mairie, my marching companions mutter and point out, with the barest of nods, a person standing not far from us taking photos. People had been taking photos throughout the procession, on small cameras and mobile phones, but this was different. An unknown man, alone, with a sophisticated SLR camera: a plainclothes policeman. Handguns disappear within the folds of habits as the procession heads back toward the church.

A few days later, I met an extremely kind couple of British tourists who had been renting a house in the center of the old village. It turns out they had witnessed the procession, and we exchange opinions on the event over a lemonade on their verandah. Amused by the incongruity of finding out that a Cambridge-trained anthropologist had been in the middle of what they took to be a traditional Corsican event, they promise to send me their photos. When the thick envelope arrives a few months later, the identity of the "undercover policeman" becomes clear: it was, of course, the British tourist himself. Looking at his photos of the procession, I wonder what the couple made of the way in which, throughout this series of photos, men on the sidelines are staring intently and suspiciously at the camera.

This chapter has examined how written nonfiction accounts of Corsica in the past two and a half centuries have established a number of enduring framings, which are part of the way in which Corsica has been produced as a "thing" in Durkheim's sense, a subject matter, a distinct locus for interpretation and intervention. Notwithstanding the political and epistemic ruptures of the 1970s, much current Francophone writing on Corsica exhibits a number of discursive features common to earlier reports and to travel literature. Among these features are the introductory reference to prejudice, stereotype, and bias as a framing device for the author's truth-claim; and the delimitation of the island as a space of privileged knowledge, a mystery to outsiders, but essentially linked in some way to the consciousness of its natives. This is a history of how Corsica was split into two entities: a thing and an idea, a mysterious essence out there and a necessarily imperfect representation.

As the above vignette suggests, however, the lines between knowledge and nescience in Crucetta were rather more complex and involved than any simple distinction between insiders and outsiders could account for. In other words, the coupled mystery/essence needs to be studied as an entity in itself, a framing device which accompanies Corsica as it careens through the French (and Corsican) public imagination: the very figure of the unknowable, Corsica excites and incites questioning and probing. Corsica, in this framing, is always already the Corsican question, the Corsican problem, and every study on the subject seems to propose a solution, an unveiling, an unmasking. And yet the problem, the mystery, persists, partly because it is a function of the questions asked. Corsica will never be answered because it is not a question. Failure is already, from the start, built into the ever-repeated attempts at explaining or understanding the island, and it is this failure which prompts further attempts. What is enshrined through this self-perpetuating epistemic dance is the ineffable entity and wholeness of the island, its unity as a thing in Durkheim's sense, the thing that predates and resists analysis. What is also produced is the sense of some ineffable intimacy on the other side of that veil of mystery, which binds Corsicans to the island and to each other in unbreakable bonds of immanent knowledge.

This is, of course, only one strand of a broader story. Anthropologists working in Europe have documented the ways in which certain areas become discursively overdetermined as internal Others of broader political entities: Brittany in France (McDonald 1989), the south in Italy (Schneider 1998), Crete in Greece, and Greece for Europe as a whole (Herzfeld 1985, 1989). This process is often described as an essentialization of the margins by the center, a use of internal Others as foils for defining the self. In the process of European nation-building, Maryon McDonald argues, "Perception was loaded with theories dividing the civilized and uncivilized, rational and irrational, reason and emotions, modern and traditional, knowledge and folklore, science and belief, logic and intuition, and other dichotomies making up the context and rhetoric of national self-definition and progress within which majority and minority were born together, and the minority [was] born as disappearing" (McDonald 1993, p. 223). While this could produce profound and crippling internal dichotomies, in which peripheries become trapped in a paradoxical semiotic trap, held up as typical and simultaneously denigrated as backward (e.g., Herzfeld 1985), McDonald argues that the moral valence and polarity of these dichotomies could in some cases be reversed, turning to the peripheries' (semiotic, if not necessarily material) advantage. Thus, France in the 1960s saw a powerful revival of interest in the peripheral, the marginal; suddenly the primitive, the emotional, the intuitive came back to center stage as a positive and valued alternative to the perceived hegemony of stifling and soulless things such as modernity, rationality, and logic. The time was ripe for "the return of the native" (cf. Kuper 2005), and regionalist movements cast their differences from the rather shadowy entity of the French core in precisely the terms inherited from these earlier dichotomies: as more natural, more authentic, more soulful, more intuitive, and so on.

This chapter could in some senses be read as a Corsican version of this story, in which Corsica is discursively elaborated as a mysterious internal Other, a foil for the constitution of a rational and all-seeing French self. The discursive framework then flips over to accommodate an account of Corsica as an essential self: constantly misrepresented, unknowable to outsiders, immanently known to its natives. But insofar as it is primarily concerned with knowledge (the mysterious, the unknowable, the immanent), the account folds over onto itself to produce an extra layer of complexity. For one persistent issue which has dogged the anthropological literature on internal Others has precisely been that of the ontological status of these Others. In what Eduardo Viveiros de Castro has called "the constructivist nightmare," the Other, whether internal or external, is suddenly revealed as being no more than a figment of our imagination, no more than a version of the self (Viveiros de Castro 2003). Alternatively, if we take the Other's Otherness seriously, the entire account risks collapsing into yet another unveiling, when the false constructions of the center are revealed to misrepresent and distort an underlying reality. Read like this, the current chapter could just be added to the long list of works which claim to sweep clean previous prejudices in order to reveal what Corsica really is like. And, as Galibert perceptively notes, "the desire for originality is the very condition of [the] production of clichés" (Galibert 2004a, p. 3).

Some of the blame for this epistemological double bind should be laid at the door of Edward Said, who popularized the critical analysis of Othering through his famous work *Orientalism* (2003). As anthropologists such as James Clifford (1980) soon pointed out, there was more than a touch of philosophical inconsistency to Said's position, which at times suggested that Orientalism was a distorted and hence reprehensible account of the Orient and at other times that there is no reality behind Orientalism, no real Orient to which one might refer to redress the account. This wavering between the critical project of debunking misrepresentations and the more ambivalent project of describing discursive regularities has plagued much anthropological work on the construction of identity. Timothy Mitchell, in his work on the colonization of Egypt, addressed this problem head-on with admirable clarity:

> Am I saying simply that western representations created a distorted image of the real Orient; or am I saying that the "real Orient" does not exist, and that there are no realities, but only images or representations? My answer is that the question is a bad one, and that the question itself is what needs examining. We need to understand how the west had come to live as though the world were divided in this way into two: into a realm of mere representations and a realm of the "real." (Mitchell 1988, p. 32)

The history of the *mise en discours* of Corsica is a small sliver of this broader history of epistemology, in which objectivism and subjectivism (Daston and Galison 2007), rationalism and romanticism (McDonald 1993), are two sides of the same coin. What I have mapped, in other words, is not a false (French) interpretation of a radically different (Corsican) reality (since such binaries are internal to the discourses I have been describing), but a pervasive dualist modality of knowledge, which permeates the ways in which much of the time many people, be they Corsican or Continental, think and talk about Corsica. Quite predictably, mentions of *la Corse* in Crucetta brought up this kind of problematic: mystery, essence, unveiling, secrecy, a familiar economy of knowledge in which the world is split into mere representations and real essence and the game consists in trying—fruitlessly—to get these two shadowy entities to mate.

But there may be a way of evading this rather problematic alternative altogether, through a form of knowledge that is neither objective nor immanent, nor a combination of the two. The next chapter introduces a rather different way of thinking about knowledge, one which foregrounds connections and attachments, evading both the mirages of representation and the closures of essence. Rather than start from the Durkheimian opposition between thing and idea, in other words, the next chapter runs for a while with Gabriel Tarde's suggestion that a thing is no more than a society of which one is not (yet) a part (Candea 2010B).[7]

3

Place

This then, may be a way out of the dichotomy between the knowing subject and the objects-that-are-known: to spread the activity of knowing widely. To spread it out over tables, knives, records, microscopes, buildings, and other things or habits in which it is embedded. Instead of talking about subjects *knowing* objects we may then, as a next step, come to talk about *enacting* reality in practice.

—MOL 2002

[Fire is] an aerothermochemical phenomenon whose properties depend on the scale on which it deploys itself.

—PHYSICAL SCIENCES OF THE ENVIRONMENT
DEPARTMENT, UNIVERSITY OF CORTE, 2009

Metaphorical and Real Connections

I had been living in Crucetta for ten months when, on the afternoon of 29 June 2003, my upstairs neighbor Marie-Paule hailed me from her window as I wandered homeward. Marie-Paule is a tall, thin woman in her mid-forties, always impeccably dressed, with a keen sense of humor, and she was one of the first people to welcome me to the neighborhood in which I spent a year. She lived on the second floor of the tall stone house in the basement of which I was renting a flat, and she would often be seen sitting at her window, staring at the world outside, and often engaging in a running commentary in Corsican with her equally high-perched neighbor Mimi in the house opposite. What Marie-Paule had caught sight of this time, however, was not a neighborhood dispute nor a gang of schoolchildren throwing stones at the cats, but an ugly black column of smoke rising from the direction of the nearby village of Murettu. The fire had started in the past hour or so, Marie-Paule told me, but judging by the thickness of the smoke, it had swiftly grown into a serious blaze. The movement of the smoke suggested that the flames were progressing up the far side of the next large hill, toward us. Marie-Paule sounded alarmed at this prospect, but only mildly: this was far from being the first fire she had witnessed. Not so I. Pausing by my flat to pick up a notebook and pen, I ran down to the Place de la Mairie, the square outside the tiny town hall. As usual, the flat, tarmac-covered expanse was filled with parked cars, the Place de la Mairie being the deepest one could penetrate into the old village on four wheels. But I had not come here to pick up my battered Renault: I knew that, whereas Marie-Paule's window pointed southeastward, the Place de la Mairie surveyed a broad west-north-northeastern panorama, affording astounding views of the coastline and the surrounding hills—and today, an unbeatable vantage point on the approaching menace. As I had expected, a group of elderly male villagers sat on the stone wall, watching the progress of the fire. The usual jocularity had fallen out of their greetings as they quietly nodded to me to sit by them. Shoulders were tense, eyes fixed. I joined them, and together we watched the fire.

The link between people and land is central to the kinds of discourses about the unity of Corsica examined in the previous chapter. Over and over again, one comes across the intimation that Corsicans have a privileged and essential link with the island as a physical object. This claim can take many forms. As we saw in the previous chapter, eighteenth- and nineteenth-century French reports essentialized the link between the Corsican people and land in calls to cultivate both. Such tropes persist today in the somewhat related genre of tourist literature aimed at the continental French. These often portray the land and the people as an elemental unit, to be discovered together; as the main French guidebook *Le Guide du Routard* puts it:

> [Corsica is] a world filled with very uncommon places, a little rock, poised in a universe which is cut in two. Above, the past and its memories (vendetta, maquis, tragedy and mourning black), below, a sea for all seasons. The gods of the Mediterranean could have come here on holiday. If Corsica were a place of mythology,

it would be a kind of in-between world, empty and peaceful, inhabited by the gods and the smells of the maquis. But this island is no myth: see the staggering jumble of mountains and jagged coastlines, of clear bays and dreamlike beaches, of deep forests and lost valleys. It is also the cradle of a human community, the Corsicans, long-suffering victims of history. A Mediterranean people which has had to bear invaders, covetousness, isolation. That may be why Corsicans sometimes seem a little reserved when it comes to tourists. But don't listen to the most banal clichés. These sons of shepherds have heart and character. It is true. They have sharp minds. That is true also. And they have the pleasure of speech: eloquence. But down with generalisations! The first duty of the traveller in Corsica is to make friends amongst Corsicans. Like every island, . . . Corsica needs to be deserved. You will need time, real curiosity, and true love to discover its secrets. Know that she will need the same time to get used to you and allow you to step behind the postcard. . . . Hard and tragic, secret and wild, Corsica will never be just another *département* on the French map. Nothing here is rational: not the skyline, nor the climate, nor the passions nor the houses, nor, of course, the Corsicans themselves. (*Guide du Routard* 2003, p. 28)

Such depictions of an essential link between the Corsican people and the Corsican land are not merely external, French tropes: they are central to many Corsican discourses too. The starkest version is to be found in the underground nationalist paramilitary organizations which target the infrastructure of the French state and the holiday homes of continental French residents in the name of a fight against the "colonization" of the island. A more peaceful variant of this theme can be found in the official pronouncements of nationalist parties such as the coalition Corsica Nazione whose spokesman explained to representatives of the French state that "[Corsicans are] a people which has been *forged in the mountains,* which has its language, its culture, its history, which has *clearly defined frontiers*" (Cuq and De Roux 1997, p. 221; my emphases). Moving from the political to the anodyne, this link to the island is also reflected in the fairly widespread habit among Corsican men and women of wearing gold pendants in the shape of the island around their necks. In Corsican literature, as in proverbs and everyday speech, an enduring connection between Corsica and Corsicans is also often posited despite the evidence of important out-migration, with assurances that "a Corsican never leaves [the island], he is just absent for a while" (Jaffe 1999, pp. 53ff.). And indeed, among Corsicans who live on the French mainland or even farther afield, many regularly spend holidays and eventually retire on the island. There is certainly a widespread expectation that they will do so (ibid.).

As these various examples suggest, associations between Corsicans and Corsica are implicitly or explicitly understood against the background of the more superficial link to the land attributed to various non-Corsicans (primarily, the continental

French) living on or visiting the island. As in many other European contexts where tourism is an important feature of local life, these distinctions are centrally concerned with visuality. Relations to the land are often cast in terms of a distinction between locals who have an essential attachment to and deep knowledge of the land and visitors who merely come to look at the landscape, whose understanding is superficial and stereotyped, who may or may not be allowed to "step behind the postcard."

The notion of divergent relations to the land(scape) finds echoes within social scientific writing. From Raymond Williams (1975) to Pierre Bourdieu (1990), the idea of a disjunction between insiders who live their place and outsiders who objectify it has had a strong influence on anthropological theorizing. This is sometimes flanked by the notion of divergent cultural relations to space and place—a Western objectifying gaze versus various non-Western alternative experiences of place (Gell 1995; Blu 1996). In the case of Corsica, anthropologist Dominique Verdoni has suggested that a traditional, qualitative, differentiated rationality of space characteristic of island society can theoretically be counterposed to the indifferent technocratic space increasingly characteristic of Western modernity (Verdoni 1999). In a similar vein, the anthropology of tourism has often also drawn on a duality between outsiders and insiders, in the audience and backstage, official and local knowledge—although the reader is usually reminded that these form opposite ends of a continuum (Boissevain 1996).

Boissevain's reminder points to a slight wariness on the part of social scientists when it comes to describing a link between people and land. Eric Hirsch, for instance, has pointed out that stark oppositions between insiders who live their landscapes and outsiders who merely view it, such as that in Williams' account, smack of romanticism since they suggest that insiders are somehow more natural than outsiders (1995, p. 13)—which is precisely what is implied in the discourses we examined in the previous chapter. More radically, students of nationalism have long since highlighted the rhetorical and ideological use of land and territory in imaginations of community (Anderson 1991; Gellner 1983; Handler 1984). In the case of France, Anne-Marie Thiesse has argued that notions of a visceral link between landscape and people (*le paysage et les paysans,* in Thiesse's elegant formulation) was an extremely common trope in eighteenth- and nineteenth-century France, and it became intimately bound up with French nation-building. Thiesse calls this the "Montesquieu tautology" (Thiesse 1997, pp. 35ff.).

Montesquieu is famous for his thoughts on the way a people's character and constitutions (both physical and legislative) are shaped by climate and terrain (Montesquieu 1787, pp. 87–246). Thiesse, who studied the regionalist content of school manuals edited during the French Third Republic, notes that this causal relationship is often complemented by a metaphorical one, in which the land is given the (stereotyped) qualities of the people: the rivers are lazy, the mountains are haughty, the valleys are protective. Overall, she argues, "The land is like the people who live on it, the people are in the land's image: identity replaces the causal relation, proving conclusively that the physical or historical materialism which is regularly brought up to explain the intimate relations between a place and its inhabitants is no more than the vaguely scientific justification of an *a priori* tautology" (Thiesse 1997, p. 44).

For Thiesse, this metaphorical link, masquerading as a scientific or causal one, became a key component of the nation-building project of the French Third Republic. It enshrined the essential unity of the region as a "small fatherland" (*petite Patrie*) in which people were directly bound up with their land and history. This, in turn, formed a building block for the "great Fatherland" of the French nation (Thiesse 1997) in two ways. First, through representations of France as a patchwork of diverse yet harmoniously coordinated landscapes and "ethnotypes," a concentrate of north and south, sea and mountains, and so on. Second, through the application of pedagogical principles which, for some, were prefigured in Rousseau's *Emile:* learning was understood as the process of movement from the known and the concrete toward the unknown and the abstract (Thiesse 1997, pp. 17, 63). Thiesse shows how, in the Third Republic school manuals she examined, this principle was coupled with spatial representations to produce theories of the progressive emotional attachment of the child to family, region, and nation. According to the same logic, the child was to be taught, first of all, the history and geography of his region (an interesting use of the possessive), to which it was assumed he had a privileged, concrete, emotional attachment, in order to later have access to the more remote and abstract history and geography of France, and finally, to the history and geography of the world.

The notion of insiders' privileged link to the land was therefore one element of a broader metanarrative of national integration: progressively, locals were supposed to learn how to extend their visceral attachment from the region to the whole nation; while remaining grounded in their region, they would grow into fully rational, logical, political citizens capable of dealing with the abstractions of Frenchness and universal humanity, as well as with the concreteness of their local "heritage" (*patrimoine*). Thiesse sees the regionalist movements which rose up against the centralizing French state in the 1960s and 70s as unwittingly inheriting much of this originally state-sponsored rhetoric of regional heritage (Thiesse 1997, p. 120).

At the risk of simplifying, one might therefore detect an oscillation in anthropological writing between, on the one hand, accounts which implicitly shore up claims about the privileged link between a people and a place by pointing out the putatively deeper relationship to place of particular cultural modes of being and, on the other hand, accounts which debunk the rhetorical or metaphorical use of land for political purposes. Whereas the former approach assumes difference as its analytical starting point, the latter broadly deconstructive approach has been criticized for starting from an assumption of similarity. Karen Sykes, for instance, has noted that "[g]iving politics a kind of priority in cultural analysis gives the upper hand to Euro-American definitions of culture over those common in distant places" (Sykes 2007, p. 46). Even more radically, Eduardo Viveiros de Castro has argued, in an influential piece which has been taken as the marker of an "ontological turn" in anthropology, that "[t]he epistemological democracy usually professed by anthropology in propounding the cultural diversity of meanings reveals itself to be, like so many other democracies with which we are familiar, highly relative, since it is based 'in the final instance' on an absolute ontological monarchy, where the referential unity of nature is imposed" (Viveiros de Castro 2003, p. 18).

One might well adapt the argument to this particular case: to insist on the metaphorical nature of the link between the Corsican people and Corsican land would be to reduce such claims to a politicized trope overlaid onto a familiar reality in which land and people are, of course, separate. Furthermore, the trope itself is immediately recognizable and familiar: is it not another predictable offspring of nineteenth-century romantic nationalism (Kuper 2005)? Through the prism of this particular analytic, the supposed difference of Corsicans from non-Corsicans, which such claims attempt to establish, is explained away as little more than froth on the surface of an ocean of similarity.

This ontological critique of the social constructivist literature is timely and well met. However, it risks sending us back once again from the pillar of sameness to the post of difference. This is at least the case if the alternative to depicting Otherness as a mere political construct is a more or less strategic emphasis upon radical alterity, making of anthropology "the science of the ontological self-determination of the world's peoples" (Viveiros de Castro 2003, p. 18).

By contrast to the deconstructive tendency, this chapter does not treat the association between Corsicans and Corsica as ideology, as rhetoric, or even as metaphor. Rather more controversially, this chapter explores ethnographically (i.e., takes seriously) the surprising thickness and resilience of the link between people and place in the Corsican context, which points to a solidity far beyond the realm of the metaphorical. In this chapter, I will follow up Latour's (2005) suggestion that the resilience of society comes in part from the nonhuman components which are intricately woven into its fabric. Imagined in isolation, he notes, simple face-to-face social interaction between humans is a relatively weak and transient glue. Society is durable to a great extent because it is an assemblage of people and things, heterogeneous elements which extend and expand each other's grasp. Following this line of argument, we need to take seriously the manifold connections between people and things (including places) in the Corsican context in order to outline the very solid assemblages from which even the most obviously rhetorical or romantic claims about an inalienable link between people and land derive their resilience and power. Fires give us an unbeatable vantage point on this issue.

By contrast to the ontological tendency, however, this chapter also suggests that it takes some explicit and reductive work to transform this resilient link between people and place into some kind of radical alterity, something which straight-forwardly distinguishes insiders from outsiders, or Corsicans from the French.

Watching a Fire

The violent fires which often ravage the Corsican countryside and forests at the height of the tourist season are occasions in which such distinctions between locals and visitors, Corsicans and non-Corsicans, are strikingly mobilized. Pascal, the schoolmaster, often regaled me with tales of the very serious blazes which had erupted near the village in previous years. As an owner of one of the outlying villas, he described how villagers such as he had helped the firefighters to battle the flames which threatened their homes. In an indulgent but amused aside, he noted that the continental French families which rented flats in the area for the summer could be seen running out of their homes with their possessions on their heads while the Corsicans stood firm. Others in Crucetta told more acid-laced or outraged stories of tourists taking snapshots of the fires—stories which went to illustrate the general lack of sensitivity of visitors for whom the island is a mere backdrop.

Wildfires are a regular problem in Corsica, flaring up nearly every summer in the forests and underbrush of the island. The particularly dry and hot summer of 2003 was especially disastrous—16,000 hectares (almost 40,000 acres) of woodland burned down in Corsica during that year (against 14,000 hectares, or 34,600 acres, for the rest of France put together).[1] From the partial vantage point of Crucetta, one was able to spot a fire (near or far) almost every day throughout the month of August. In fact, 2003 was so severe that the French national research body, the Centre National de la Recherche Scientifique (CNRS), mandated its Physical Sciences of the Environment Department, based at the Corsican University of Corte, to create a new unit for the experimental study of fires. According to this unit's own definition, fire is "an aerothermochemical phenomenon whose properties depend on the scale on which it deploys itself,"[2] hence the need to study it in controlled conditions "on the scale of the field" (*à l'échelle du terrain*), by organizing experimental burnings in delimited areas of the island. These experimental fires are measured and in the near future will be modeled electronically and made available online through software developed by a researcher at the University of Corte.[3] In order to organize such experimental burnings, the University of Corte and its scientific partners, including the CNRS, established a five-year partnership convention (*une convention de partenariat*) with a number of other actors, including the Regional Natural Park of Corsica, the National Office of Forestry, and the Departmental Service of Fire and Rescue for Southern Corsica.[4] Wildfires, in this sense, can be seen as a prime example of what Bruno Latour has called a "matter of concern." These disputed matters of concern are to be understood by opposition to the notion of undisputed "matters of fact." Certainly not imaginary, nor yet stable objects, matters of concern are real and yet uncertain entities which are the focus of ongoing dispute, interest, and controversy: genetically modified organisms, the Gulf Stream, the social life of chimpanzees (cf. Latour 2004, 2005, pp. 125ff.). As the above suggests, wildfires are a key instance of a matter of concern in this sense.

The definition of a fire as a phenomenon whose properties depend upon the scale on which it deploys itself seems particularly apt, as the fires of 2003 deployed themselves as a matter of concern all the way from the Corsican forests and *maquis* (scrubland) to the national research institute and—through this effortlessly multi-scalar partnership among departmental, regional, and national entities (each with its own address in the town of Ajaccio)—back to the Corsican *maquis,* where they culminated in the propagation of a new set of fires, experimental, controlled fires this time, fires born to change the nature of firefighting.

Indeed, the aim of the research, as set out in the convention, is to enhance the practices of firefighting teams through the development of an accurate model to predict the spread of fire ahead of real time. But the research should also produce scientific evidence to inform firefighting practices, such as appropriate safety distances for firefighting personnel and the critical mass of scrubland beyond which preemptive "directed burning" is necessary to check the spread of potential fires.[5]

Back in the village square on the afternoon of 29 June 2003, the fire's presence was becoming more clearly defined. More defined visually, as the first flames appeared on the outline of the hill, a testimony to the fire's progress toward us. More defined, too, in a range of other ways. Besides the visible flames and smoke, the fire was taking shape in our discussion, acquiring an origin and a set of potential futures, opening up questions and performing, along the way, various operations of social engineering.

Let us begin with origins. A number of cross-cutting reports located the origin of the fire by the reservoir on the Murettu road—a thin strip of tarmac snaking along the hillside between Crucetta and the neighboring village. "Not an accident," one of the men said knowingly. He had been here when the fire started and had seen cars gathering suspiciously around the reservoir. His comment caused little stir, however, partly because the evidence was slight and partly because the human responsibility for fires in Corsica is as common an explanation as it is difficult to ascertain. Fires bring into stark relief a series of liminal and problematic figures who channel in various ways the search for causality. The "pyromaniac" (*pyromane*) is the generic designation used in common parlance for fire-starters. Sometimes, this word is used in the literal sense of a mentally unstable individual obsessed with fire. One of our little group told a presumably well-rehearsed story of meeting such a figure, a pyromaniac who had been responsible for devastating fires in the 1980s. "Ask him for a light," the nurse in charge of the pyromaniac had said. When the storyteller did, he saw the patient transfixed, fascinated by the flame. "Let me look after him," the storyteller had told the nurse. "I'll throw him off a bridge somewhere." In this case, the causal origin of the fire gets lost in the maze of an unhinged mind.

"Pyromaniac" is also used colloquially, however, to designate actors whose intentionality is more straightforward. One often hears accusations against unscrupulous developers, seeking to clear land on the cheap or exacting revenge after being denied planning permission; or against shepherds, for similar reasons. There is an enduring history to such intentional firings. Slash-and-burn techniques were once prominent and fairly regulated in Corsica, particularly among shepherds keen to clear land for grazing, before these techniques were outlawed by the French state in the nineteenth century (Wilson 1988, pp. 70ff.). As these practices faded into the realm of illegitimacy, they blurred into a broader category which included arson as part of ongoing feuds or as localized revenge by shepherds on landowners. When, from 1834 onward, the French state started laying claim to a number of forests previously considered communal property, fires were also started by locals in retaliation against these encroachments (ibid.). In one court case, a man was accused of starting a fire which devastated 1,000 hectares (2,500 acres) of the state-owned forest of Ota in August 1848 as an act of revenge against "the authorities, who had been trying to capture two of his cousins who were bandits" (ibid., p. 71).

Current uses of "pyromaniac" also point to unintentional fire-starters, such as those who throw cigarette ends or smoldering matches out of car windows. Signs discouraging such behavior have been put up along most Corsican roads, and it is often tourists who are believed to be the thoughtless actors in this usually unverifiable scenario.

In these various ways, fires are emplotted within a chain of human causality and acquire a whole range of different potential personalities, depending on whether they are the result of unscrupulous intentional calculation ("shame on you who burns the earth," exclaims in Corsican the leading Corsican nationalist website)[6] or bungling idiocy by uncaring outsiders, or whether their origin escapes back into the nonhuman through the incomprehensible mind of the true pyromaniac. But fires, of course, also outflank human agency in spectacular ways; they are, to use actor-network-theory terminology, "mediators" rather than mere "intermediaries" (Latour 2005, p. 58): their input does not determine their output. The aim of the newly created research unit at the University of Corte is precisely to reduce fires to intermediaries, fully modeled entities whose actions can be described ahead of real time. Until this is done, however, fires will continue to have, as it were, minds of their own. And the first thing a fire does is precisely cover its own tracks to destroy the clues and traces of its origin, giving rise in the same movement to the uncertainty and controversies outlined above. In doing this, the effect of the fire is to mobilize the common knowledge of locals in a search for origins, a search during the course of which this common knowledge is rehearsed, tested, and reconfigured.

Watching a fire in the present is no more straightforward than assessing its origin. From the first moment a fire is sighted, chains of mobile telephone calls are initiated, as people exchange their partial perspectives: from the four points of the compass, from the third floor of a mountain village house and the sea-level square of the nearby town, people relay their own tracking of the smoke and flames, putting together a composite image of the fire as a single entity—or, rather, as a single process, since the fire is never in stasis. With their own means, and in their own urgent real time, concerned locals are doing the same thing as the research unit at Corte: attempting to reduce the fire from a mediator to an intermediary. The fire as a visual entity combines multiple shifting perspectives, but it is always already more than this: potentiality and direction, vectoral projections and imaginative mappings. Which way will it turn? This depends on the wind, of course, but also on a range of other factors. As we sat on the Place de la Mairie, my companions discussed in detail which expanses of land in the adjoining valleys and hillsides were "clean"—that is, where had the thick undergrowth been cleared? Those areas would slow down the fire's progress. People also wondered which firefighting planes would be sent—the small white planes which drop a red chemical dust, or the huge *canadairs* which fill up with seawater? We discussed the fleet which was available locally, the size of the fleet at the large town of Bastia, the time it would take them to get here (which, of course, depended on what other closer fires they had to attend to). How many planes would the Continental firefighters lend to the island this summer?

And, of course, the fire's progress was not a phenomenon of uniform value. The fire brought urgency to people's knowledge of the land as property: whose fields was the fire creeping over? Whose house, hidden from view on the other side of the hill, would fall foul of the flames if the wind turned southerly? When another fire erupted a few days later even closer to the village, I was surprised to see the two brothers who owned the butcher shop jump in their small Peugeot and follow the huge four-wheel-drive fire truck as it trundled up the hill. "They have cattle up there," a bystander said laconically. But it is not just material interest which can turn bystanders into amateur firefighters. A mix of concern and sheer excitement drove youths from the village toward the flames. When I finally got up to leave my companions on the square, one of them held out a warning finger: "Don't go there, it's dangerous!"

·

Interconnaissance and Distributed Cognition

Slightly earlier, a continental French couple who had been renting a flat in the village for the past week had walked by us, laden with parasols, snorkels, and bathing towels. Some of my companions had switched their stare from the flames to the tourists, in the intense and somewhat intimidating form of public interaction to which I will return in the final chapter. The couple glided past us rather meekly, clicking a remote key at their gleaming rented car, which beeped in recognition, unfolded its mirrors, and flashed its lights with canine eagerness. Having packed their multicolored kit into the trunk, they slammed the doors and drove off with a pleasant and controlled hum. As the car snaked down the village streets and into the valley below, our conversation was briefly deflected in their direction. No one knew who they were or where they were staying, although one of my companions hazarded that they might be up at Madame Antonetti's flat. Be that as it may, their seeming lack of interest in the fire caused no end of muttering and adverse comment. At that moment, I recalled the equally disgusted reactions to stories of tourists' interest in fires: some actually took photos! On the face of it, it seems that, as a tourist, you're damned if you do look at a fire and damned if you don't.

The foregoing account of what is involved in watching a fire should give us some clues as to why this is the case. Watching a fire in the way described above is a process which is not exhausted by the usual definitions of the visual. First and most obviously, it calls upon a mass of accumulated and embodied knowledge—of the wind, the three-dimensional layout of the landscape, the human geography, the fire management infrastructures, the history of previous blazes, and the kinds of people (actual and imagined) whose actions feed into the blaze: those who start it, those who fight it, those who spectate. This is the kind of thing usually referred to as "local knowledge" (Frake 1996, p. 248), the sort of knowledge which cannot be subsumed in a map, which can be fed in tidbits to the eager anthropologist, but which often retains in anthropological accounts an almost mystical unity and thickness: "The power of local knowledge helps both to identify the outsider and to give the local the advantage" (ibid., p. 249). The phrase rings very true. But of what exactly is local knowledge made?

There is much to be retained from classic anthropological analyses of interpersonal knowledge, or *interconnaissance,* as the core of village sociality in France (Zonabend 1990) and in Corsica (Ravis-Giordani 1983; Meisterheim 1999, p. 9; Galibert 2004b, pp. 34, 150), which describe the daily (re)construction of a common knowledge which is "the semantic fabric without which no society can exist" (Galibert 2004b, p. 205). Village studies have often been stigmatized for reifying the local object or local culture (Boissevain 1975; Cole 1977; Grillo 1980; and, more recently, Gupta and Ferguson 1997). In fact, they often did precisely the opposite:

they grounded the seeming unity of a local object in actual traceable connections and relations, events and moments of a careful micro-sociology. On the question of "knowing," furthermore, these anthropological analyses already prefigured the idea that common knowledge is more than simply the sum of what everyone knows, and not just a store of information replicated within the minds of a select group of insiders. Neither of those perspectives captures the generative quality of such moments on the village square; one might say that it is not just information that is distributed and redistributed across different minds, but rather a cognitive process itself, a process which spreads to include different people, but also things and places (see Hutchins 1996; Gell 1998; Candea 2008). Knowing, in this sense, ceases to be a question of representation; it goes beyond even the common social production of a purely semantic fabric and becomes a question of belonging or mutual possession (cf. Candea 2009)—the interrelationship of people, places, stories into durable assemblages.

My aim, in other words, is to fuse anthropological discussions of local or common knowledge with the notion of distributed cognition, in the sense in which this expression is used by Edwin Hutchins (1996). Like navigating an amphibious helicopter transport in Hutchins' account, watching a fire is a process which draws on knowledge which is distributed in uneven and redundant patterns across a number of different minds. That much is easy: not everyone knows everything, and watching fires together is partly about sharing information and learning—local knowledge and local people co-constructing each other. But Hutchins argues further that some cognitive properties cannot be crammed into individual minds and can only be understood as properties of groups of minds in interaction with each other and with artifacts in the world (ibid., p. 62). The broader philosophical implications of this point have been spelled out in an influential article on the "extended mind" by Andy Clark and David Chalmers (1998), but an anthropological genealogy for this approach can also be traced through Alfred Gell, who famously claimed in *Art and Agency*, "The Kula system as a whole is a *form of cognition,* which takes place outside the body, which is diffused in space and time, and which is carried on through the medium of physical indexes and transactions involving them" (Gell 1998, p. 232).[7] Keeping a minute-by-minute record of the position of a ship, in Hutchins' account, requires such distributed cognitive processes, and so does keeping tabs on something as monstrously large and processual as a wildfire. Unless and until researchers at Corte manage to pack into a stable single entity—a computer program—the many simultaneous measures, processes, and predictions which can reduce a fire from a fickle mediator to a predictable intermediary, fire will remain an open-ended matter of concern, and locals and firefighters will have to watch it and act upon it as a composite of many points of view, surmises, and predictions—often incommensurable and assembled ad hoc.

In this distributed process, people are helped by a range of nonhuman entities: mobile phones, planes, helicopters, but also fields, hills, houses. The terrain can slow down the progress of the fire, but in a more basic sense, the terrain also helps one to see. Whether in an emergency or in the everyday, knowing a place is itself a distributed process, relying on connections between landmarks which are only marks to the knowing eye and on eyes which are only knowing in the right place.

The fire is watched, fought, and coerced by such assemblages of people and things, and it is against them that it fights back. The fire was a matter of concern for my companions on the square because it could hurt them, to varying degrees, in their flesh and in their fields, in their friends and in their homes, in their cattle and in their landscape. The fire brings home in a frighteningly immediate way the extent to which persons are themselves distributed across and invested in a range of human and nonhuman entities; the fire makes it obvious that they belong to such entities as much as the reverse (Edwards 1998; Edwards and Strathern 2000).

Neither Dichotomies nor Continua

What does the above account describe if not a powerful, collective, deep, complex, and enduring link between people and land? People who configure places and places which configure people, thrown into stark relief by the blaze of a wildfire. If we had to choose between metaphorical and essential connections, the above account would go toward substantiating and filling in claims to an essential link between people and place. Almost, but not quite. Because neither timeless essence nor rhetorical ploys are needed here: this is an account of how essence is put together, of how it emerges from connections which themselves are contingent and shifting.

Along with the notion of timeless essence, the specter of radical alterity is also shooed away. For the tourists, too, are connected. No radical disjunction operates de facto between their experience of watching fires and that of the locals. As recent studies of tourist engagements with place have convincingly argued, the tourist gaze is nothing like the two-dimensional objectification which it was often reductively imagined to be (Crang 1999; Franklin 2003; Larsen and Haldrup 2006; Sheller and Urry 2004). Even at their most stereotypical, when hidden behind a camera, tourists are also mobilizing complex assemblages of human and nonhuman entities; they, too, participate when they spectate.

The difference between their way of watching fires and that of my companions on the square is not therefore one of kind; as an early approximation, one might think of it as one of degree (although I leave this for now as a placeholder for the more complex description which appears below). However concerned tourists might be at the sight of the fire, their concern enlists a far more limited number of entities, a far smaller range of connections. The fire is a part of their world, too, but it belongs to it by far fewer connections; they have less of a handle on it—and it has far less of a handle on them. They may deplore the ecological disaster, feel sorry for the locals, fear for their possessions; they will also try to assess the progress of the flames and to figure out where the fire is going, but they are more thinly distributed, lack associates—in the people as in the landscape—who could multiply, enhance, and distribute their vision of the fire.

What the fire brings into view, in other words, are the tangibly divergent ways in which people and places are assembled and entangled. If we now return to issues of rhetoric, ideology, or metaphor, these appear rather less flimsy, flat, and obvious than they might have seemed to begin with. *Le Guide du Routard*'s depiction of Corsicans and Corsica as an elemental unit suddenly sounds rather less naïve. And when Jean-François Bernardini, the singer of the Corsican world-music band I Muvrini, says that "to be Corsican is to cry when the *maquis* burns," the statement suddenly has a different ring. Indeed, one might want to temper some of the more functionalist undertones of the notion of distributed cognition, with its talk of mechanisms and operations, by exploring the affective aspects of human/nonhuman relations. What is distributed across the participants, the places, the stories, the winds, and the flames are not merely cognitive processes, but also affects (see Thrift 2004; Navaro-Yashin 2007). And yet, while we can appreciate the extent to which such associations of people and land transcend the metaphorical, we do not have to fall into a reiteration of the romantic opposition between locals who live their land and tourists who merely gaze at it.

Were we to stop here, however, we would have simply redescribed, in a needlessly sophisticated form, the fairly simple idea that insiders and outsiders are at opposite ends of a continuum. But the case of the researchers at Corte throws a wrench in the works of this neat, unilineal progression. For the researchers' own relation to the fire and to the land is different again, mobilizes a different set of entities in a different set of connections. And while we may be tempted to fit the locals and the tourists into neat regionalizations (a Corsican way of seeing against a French or Western one, perhaps?), the researchers do not lend themselves to that kind of analytical manipulation. Like the fire itself, they explicitly deploy themselves on different scales (cf. Latour 2005, p. 269). They associate themselves to regional and national bodies (including similar organizations in the United States and Scotland) which allow them to create delimited local experiments in the Corsican *maquis* based on which they produce knowledge for a global audience, to be distributed over the internet.

The position of the researchers breaks the temptation to resolve the situation into a dualism (outsider versus insider perspectives) or into a continuum (more connections for insiders, fewer connections for outsiders), which is little more, after all, than a wary dualism. It is not merely a question of the quantity of connections, as if reality were a series of uniform dots to join, as if identity could be resolved into a numerical comparison. No, the relationship to land varies substantively according to which connections are made, and to what. In a context in which spectatorship is always already participation, insiderness and outsiderness are not stable states which can be found sitting quietly at opposite ends of a continuum. Each person will find something slightly (or wildly) different as the connections accumulate. As the French sociologist Gabriel Tarde put it, "each one of us, however orthodox he [may] be, has his own religion, and each, however precise, his own language and ethics; the most commonplace of scientists has his own science, and the most bureaucratic of officials his own system of administration" (Tarde 2000, p. 87). Each, too, has her own way of being local: her own personally acquired set of landmarks, associates, numbers stored in her mobile phone; her stakes, fears, and blind spots—which go into making her a (particular) local person.

Difference Out of Similarity, Similarity Out of Difference

This leaves us with a problem. How does this generative, shifting multiplicity solidify into the kind of binaries with which this chapter began? This is particularly hard to explain when watching fires is described as a distributed process. For, as Jean Lave has pointed out, notions of distributed knowledge and cognition also suggest that "learning is ubiquitous in ongoing activity, although often unrecognised as such. . . . It is not the case that the world consists of newcomers who drop unaccompanied into unpeopled problem spaces. People in activity are skilful at, and are more often than not engaged in, helping each other to participate in changing ways in a changing world" (Lave 1996, p. 5).

If watching a fire is one of the many activities through which one can slowly and progressively become local (albeit in a myriad of different ways), one of the ways one can acquire and become acquired by the manifold connections which are being mobilized, whence then the instances of disjunction, opposition, boundary making which one can observe in the square, as in the stories with which I opened this chapter? The answer is that researchers at Corte are not alone in manipulating scale and context: so does everyone else. And when my companions on the square manipulate scale to make themselves local, they grab the passing tourists as their non-local Other. They incorporate and appropriate them, in other words, but only by one tiny facet of their person: as a disconnected, oculocentric tourist. And one is unlikely to feel like helping such a figure "to participate in changing ways in a changing world." One is much more likely to grumble about them and use them later as a framing device to substantiate one's own insiderness. In a sense, what my companions did to the passing tourists in this instance was what they were attempting to do to the fire: they reduced them from complex, unpredictable mediators to mechanical intermediaries, fully modeled entities which hold no surprises. And at the precise moment when the tourists were turned into such a thinly defined presence in my companions' world, I would wager that the converse was equally true: the tourists were quite probably dealing with another instance of "those unfriendly Corsicans who mutter about you as you walk through the village square" (see chapter 7). If they had read *Le Guide du Routard,* they might well have concluded that they were in the presence of that "thing," Corsica, which declined to let them see behind the postcard. In the meantime, my companions were faced with "typically rude and insensitive tourists." Here, difference, even radical difference, emerges out of everyone doing the same kind of thing—but doing it to each other, rather than doing it together.

The paradoxical ways in which such radical and clear-cut differences can emerge from an ambiguous field of shifting connections and disconnections are the subject of the next three chapters.

4

Things

The difference between ambiguity (continual and contingent indeterminacy) and clarity (ontological knowledge) is not as enormous as the literature implied, at least in terms of what generates the sense of there being authoritative accounts.

—GREEN 2005

The Phone Book

Mimi, a woman in her late seventies, is sitting on a white plastic chair outside her house, in the shade of an overgrown vine. This spot of shade outside Mimi's house is just off the main expanse of my local square in the center of the old village, Piazza à O,[1] a convenient place for the elderly and not so elderly women of the neighborhood to sit and chat of an afternoon—comfortably within eyesight and out of earshot of the men sitting on Piazza à O proper. Today, the necessities of the anthropological interview intrude upon this gendered pattern, but Mimi is bearing my intrusion with good grace. Mimi is a widow who has spent her whole life in Crucetta, and I am asking her to tell me about her experiences as a pupil in the village school. Her son Pierre, a tall, balding baby-boomer with square shoulders and a strong jaw, has been doing most of the talking. His fluent French, upon which a Corsican accent draws swirling patterns, intertwines with Mimi's mostly Corsican speech. He, too, went to school in Crucetta, although he now works as a postman on the French mainland. He returns every summer and most holidays to visit his mother and the many friends and relatives he still has around Piazza à O. His most salient memory of school was the daily lighting of the stove, for which each child had to bring his own portion of wood. That, and the blinding blow Mr. Fiorelli once landed him, which sent him flying and knocked his temple into the corner of the wooden desk. The flimsy plastic chair trembles under him as he mimics the savage swipe. He grins broadly and recalls how later, during a break, the teacher asked him if he was all right, and he answered yes, he was. This turns out to be a story about a fond moment of rapport, then, rather than a grudge.

Mimi recites, in French and in a slightly incantatory voice, the list of obligatory school items (*le matériel d'école*) which she claims parents had to buy their children—although it is not clear whether she is thinking of her school days or her son's. Then, mother and son compete to recall the names of successive schoolmasters and -mistresses and the various places in which classes were held: the one down by the church, the other one up at L'Olmu, you know, by the monument . . . no, by Savini's house . . . This inexperienced interviewer, however, is getting a little restless. I take profuse notes to hide my discomfort, but I just can't escape the niggling feeling that this is somehow beside the point, not great data, in a word, banal. I haven't been an ethnographer for very long by this point and have not yet learned to be ethnographic about that feeling itself. As it happens, I am missing the most important: the real, crucial stuff, the fabric of locality and "interknowledge" which forms the focus of a large part of this book. But that realization will only come much, much later. For now, I attempt to prod the discussion in another direction.

Regionalist historiographies in Corsica, as in other parts of France, are filled with the specter of the systematic eradication of the local language by militantly French-speaking schoolmasters (Jaffe 1999; McDonald 1989). The absolute ban on speaking anything but French in school, the pernicious punishment of the *symbole*, a visible marker of shame which a child caught speaking a dialect or patois would have to wear until he could pass it on by discovering another culprit—these had become the stuff of regionalist legend. Perhaps I could elicit some examples, some counterexamples? So I ask if, in their experience, children were ever punished for speaking Corsican in school. No, they weren't: "in fact we spoke Corsican more than French," Mimi's son notes, his mother repeating the statement in Corsican: "Parliamu piu Corsu chi Francese." Well, she corrects after a while, in the playground, that is. But sometimes in the classroom, too. And the teachers were all Corsican,

Pierre adds, and sometimes spoke it themselves. But not much—it wasn't their job, after all, was it?

This settled, Mimi's son returns to the litany of names and places which I have attempted to deflect, leaving me unsure as to what exactly my line of questioning has achieved. But Mimi has another idea. Wiping her hands purposefully on her pristine apron, she springs up and strides into the house. A few moments later, she emerges from the cool, dark corridor, carrying an armful of large, yellow objects, which, on closer inspection, turn out to be telephone books. "Here you go," she says, squinting slightly at the sunlight through her tiny spectacles, "this is what you need: this has got the Corsican things, the sayings and so on." The phone books she has brought out are not the standard France Telecom kind, but a parallel phone book called "The Corsican" (*U Corsu*), edited by a small company on the island. In the introductory section usually reserved for important general information, these phone books contain a somewhat random selection of information on traditional Corsican food, proverbs, and customs.

"This is what you need: this has got the Corsican things"—there is no hint of irony in Mimi's voice; she is being absolutely straight and helpful. I wanted to know about Corsican things, and well, here are the Corsican things. The irony is unintentional and on a completely different level: receiving preformatted information is a fitting punishment for an anthropologist who asks questions to which he thinks he knows the answers. I have learned my lesson and drop the pen. We spend the next hour or so revisiting the meaning of reflexivity: I read aloud traditional Corsican proverbs from the phone book, and Mimi and her son tell me whether they have ever heard them. When they have not, the three of us together try to guess the meaning, with mixed results.

Much of the anthropological literature on identity or ethnicity has been centrally concerned with the ways in which persons are fitted into groups and categories, often with a particular interest in the ways such identities or ethnicities are discursively elaborated, constructed, or contested. In Crucetta, too, people were constantly categorizing each other in inclusive and exclusive ways, and the issue of whether a person was Corsican, French, Continental, Arab, or possibly two or three of those things at once was an extremely important part of everyday reality (I will examine this in the next chapter). And yet, I have purposefully chosen to preface the more in-depth discussion of Corsican and non-Corsican persons with a brief chapter on Corsican and non-Corsican things, because approaching identity through things brings out the paradoxical ways in which identity is both set apart and banal, both profound and contrived. Mimi's phone books, as "Corsican things," were set apart from the complex, everyday reality of her own and her son's recollections: they were distinctive and instantly recognizable, they were "the things I needed." And yet, in a sense, they too were intensely banal, things one happened to have somewhere in one's house, to which one does not usually give much thought, but which might be of interest to a researcher.

The question of persons being or not being Corsican in Crucetta shared this air of thingness, in the double sense of irrevocable factuality and sheer banality. Thus, Petru frowned in genuine incomprehension when I asked him one afternoon whether a person could ever become Corsican. He had me repeat this question, in the tone he often used to correct my early, stumbling attempts to speak Corsican. When he realized that I had actually meant this nonsensical question, he replied firmly, as to a small child: "No, no, you are Corsican or you are not. You are Corsican if you are, well, from here, you know." This reply perfectly summarizes the paradox of identity in Crucetta: categories of identity packed the punch of an unambiguous answer (you are Corsican or you are not), and yet they also had this uncertain, trailing-off quality when it came to actually defining what it was that made a person (or, indeed, a thing, a foodstuff, a kind of behavior) Corsican. The unexpected thing was that this did not in any sense lessen the power of these categorical distinctions, just as, in a fractal view, "one's grip on a tool is no less secure because on an infinitesimal scale, skin and wood do not touch" (Strathern 2004, p. xxiv).

A Roba Corsa

Rather like Jane Cowan (1990) in the Greek town of Sohos, I found that the people with whom I worked often had a very clear sense of what should be the relevant object of my research. Like Mimi when she lapsed from the mode of personal recollection to that of being an interviewee, when people treated me as a researcher, they would direct me toward what was known as "the Corsican things" or "the Corsican stuff" (a roba Corsa), which cultural activists, nationalists, and local intellectuals sometimes referred to, in a more lyrical idiom, as "our things" (a roba nustrale).

These "things," "goods," or "stuff" (roba) included physical objects, foodstuffs, tools, items of clothing; more immaterial things such as proverbs, sayings, songs, rhymes; and, more broadly, behaviors and events which were considered traditional or cultural. Brought together under the designation of Corsican things, these various items were united in a solidity and an out-there-ness that defied easy distinctions between real objects and mere ideas. Corsican things were thus an unavoidable and extremely pervasive part of reality: even though cultural activists would sometimes balk at this usage, the adjective Corsican was commonly applied in Crucetta to a class of things far wider than the usual paraphernalia of authenticity, tradition, or heritage: there were not just Corsican proverbs and Corsican cheeses, Corsican polyphonic singing and Corsican houses; there were also Corsican pizzas, Corsican pop music, Corsican stand-up comedy, Corsican soft drinks (*Corsica Cola*), Corsican jewelry, Corsican license plates, and Corsican ways of driving; there were Corsican jokes, Corsican pigs, Corsican dogs (a race called *u cursinu*), Corsican roads, Corsican knives, Corsican classes in school, Corsican political issues, and Corsican legal particularities; there were Corsican history books, Corsican poetry, and a Corsican university; there were Corsican radio stations, Corsican sections in bookshops and supermarkets, Corsican TV shows, Corsican websites.

The sheer pervasiveness of the adjective Corsican in everyday life in Crucetta left one reeling with the impression that every thing might have its Corsican variant, counterpart, or subsection—that, in other words, the world was made up of things and Corsican things. Corsican things, as the above list suggests, proliferated across the realms of culture, politics, entertainment, tourism, consumption, education, etc. It is this connectedness of Corsican things above and beyond the many distinctions of domain or relevance that explains why a question about speaking Corsican in school in the mid-twentieth century would prompt Mimi to bring out a phone book containing Corsican proverbs.

Within this mass of Corsican things, of course, people were constantly making distinctions between the authentic and the spurious, the trivial and the crucial, the old and the new. A subset of these Corsican things were often set apart as "really Corsican" or "very Corsican" (*vraiment Corse, très Corse*), rather than "merely Corsican" in an unmarked, everyday kind of way. Thus, Crucetta was, of course, Corsican in the sense that it was located on the island, but people had serious doubts as to whether it was "really Corsican." My neighbors in Crucetta often objected, for instance, that I had come to the wrong place. Crucetta wasn't deemed Corsican enough: I should go farther inland, up the mountains, in those small villages "up there" (*quàssú*), where, I was told, everyone spoke Corsican. "I mean, look at this place," people would exclaim: it's got a block of council flats and it's full of newly built villas; Continentals are buying up all the old houses in the center of the village—surely, this isn't the place you should be studying! A more theorized, diffusionist version of the same argument was put forward by some who claimed that the central mountainous regions of the island had preserved much more of their cultural authenticity, being less exposed to the waves of sea-borne invasions which form the pivot of most accounts of the island's history.

Such comments were fired by a sense of a lack of distinctiveness, of being ordinary, uninteresting (Green 2005, p. 13). This in turn pointed to a very strong sense that real Corsicanness was elsewhere: in a village farther up a hill, in the front pages of the Corsican phone book, in the Corsican section of the bookstore in Ile Rousse. This form of Corsicanness at times appeared to be a standard by reference to which

Crucetta was found lacking. Rosemary McKechnie, in an extremely sophisticated article on the intricacies of Corsican identity, has described this standard of real Corsicanness:

> Temporally, Cursichezza [Corsicanness] was spoken about as characterizing life on the island before the First World War. It was located spatially on the island in the mountains. Particularly in the Niolu, which was generally represented as the most "remote," untouched region of Corsica. Unlike other French regions, the shepherd rather than the peasant was perceived to be the last living embodiment of traditional Corsican life. (McKechnie 1993, p. 129)

As in my experience, she found that, while people were keen to point her in the direction of this real Corsicanness, they "assumed that their own life today would be uninteresting to me, banal. It was much the same as life elsewhere" (ibid., p. 132).

However, this was not quite the whole picture, for there was a fractal quality (cf. Strathern 2004; Green 2005) to such ascriptions of authenticity. The same logic which made some people reject Crucetta as not "really Corsican" allowed them to make finer distinctions within the village itself: some parts of the village, some people, some behaviors were more Corsican than others. For instance, the old village, with its intricate maze of crooked streets overhung by bridges between tall terracotta-hued houses, was generally considered to be far more Corsican, in the sense delineated by McKechnie, than the villas. The village itself, in this sense, repeated the pattern of the island as a whole: authentic interior, compromised periphery. But these distinctions proliferated within each of these parts of the village, too: in the old village, there were houses inhabited by Corsicans and others bought by incomers, whereas, as we saw in the first chapter, local people considered those living in the newer villas as, in the main, the really autochthonous population of Crucetta. The fractal pattern continued on a more minute scale: among Corsicans living in the old village, there were, as McKechnie suggests, some occupations which were seen as more Corsican than others. Thus, I was repeatedly directed toward Petru the shepherd as a valuable "informant" and someone I absolutely had to meet, rather than, for instance, his next-door neighbor Stephane, a Corsican man in his early forties who worked at the local supermarket. But, on even closer inspection, only some parts of the activities of shepherds such as Petru qualified as really Corsican.

This was brought home to me one day when I accompanied two schoolmistresses on a local ramble with their class of four- to six-year-olds. The central purpose of the ramble was to put the children in touch with their local surroundings, to counteract the presumed nefarious influence of video games and TV with a slice of Corsican rurality. On the way back, we wandered past a field whose gate was cleverly improvised from an old ironing board and a rusty segment of an old bed frame. One of the schoolteachers took this occasion to lecture the children on the dangers of littering, showing them this recycled contraption as an example of the way nature is destroyed by people who just throw their garbage outdoors. In the meantime, the other teacher complained to me about the bad habits of such local farmers and shepherds. This kind of unaesthetic improvisation clearly did not qualify, in their book, as part of what makes shepherds "really Corsican." Rather, this is part of what makes them "rustics" (*rustiques*), a word which, when applied to people, loses the connotation of healthy trustworthiness (as, for instance, when it is applied to furniture or bread) and becomes straightforwardly derogatory. I thought of Petru—to whom both teachers often referred in the most positive terms as the paradigm of the authentic Corsican shepherd—and of his sheepfold, where the water troughs were an old bathtub and a sink propped up with rocks, and the headboard of an old bed formed part of the fence. Although he would probably have resented the suggestion that these constituted garbage or litter, Petru was no more likely than were the two schoolmistresses to point to these particular items as particularly Corsican. As I suggested in the first chapter, he had as keen a sense as anyone of the tools of his trade that would qualify as authentic (such as his donkey and its wooden saddle) and those that would not.

Explicitly elaborated forms of cultural distinctiveness have been a focus of anthropological theorizing for some time. David Schneider, for instance, noted in his classic *American Kinship* (Schneider 1968) that there is often a structural format to diversity. As Simon Harrison puts it:

> [Schneider's] respondents all viewed their ethnicities as distinctive, and ascribed this distinctiveness to the peculiar role of their mothers. Yet in sharing this notion they were indistinguishable. . . . It was as though American culture possessed a generic schema of "The Ethnic Minority Family," a single model for conceptualizing any ethnic group and the "distinctive" attributes it ought typically to have. (Harrison 2003, p. 344)

There is now a well-developed literature in anthropology on such "structures of common difference" (Wilk 1995, quoted in Green 2005, p. 38) or "symbolic complexes" (Chapman 1978; McDonald 1989, 1993), which make everyone seem different, and different in the same way (cf. Strathern 1995). These studies attest to the power of "taxonomic form" (Herzfeld 1989, p. 4) in organizing people's experiences of difference and similarity.

An important effect of such taxonomic, recognized ways of being different is that they render certain things visible or salient at the expense of others. For instance, Sarah Green showed in Epirus how the kinds of cultural distinctiveness which are valued within the broader framework of national and European development programs come to assume a standard, recognizable form: "for people, there would be costume, food, music, myths and legends, language or argot, festivals and traditions, and so on; for the places with which the people are now indigenously associated, there would be the traditional settlements as well as the untouched natural beauty of the flora and fauna" (Green 2005, p. 39). As Green shows for Epirus, these packaged forms of distinctiveness make some things visible and others invisible, they draw lines between what is deemed representative and typical—those bits of reality which can be made to stand for a region or a group of people—and the everyday, uninteresting, humdrum stuff that could, presumably, be found anywhere else. This was the fate of the main area in which she worked: "Pogoni as a place and Pogoni peoples remained somehow nondistinct, unclear—unrecognized, to use the language of recognition politics" (ibid., p. 8).

Anthropologists have often pointed to the disjunctures between such "structures of common difference," such packaged ways of being distinctive, and people's everyday experiences. In *We Are Not French,* for instance, Maryon McDonald describes the monumental quid pro quo at the heart of Breton nationalism: while educated militants in the Breton movement strove toward the authenticity of rural Breton-speakers, these rural populations saw the activities of the militants as alien, as "that Breton thing." And whereas the militants proposed to liberate the peasants from the alienation which made them desire Frenchness, the peasants, paradoxically, only came to appreciate—and partially emulate—the model of traditional Bretonness proposed by the militants when they came to see it as the latest trend from Paris (McDonald 1989). Similarly, in McKechnie's account of Corsican identity, the standard of real Corsicanness erased, rendered invisible, or undervalued many aspects of people's everyday lives; for some young nationalists and cultural activists, she argued, real Corsicanness could come to constitute a painfully unattainable ideal, against which their own behaviors, their cultural competencies, their habits, desires, or sexualities stood out as imperfect, incongruous, unsatisfactory. "The over-definition of identity," she found, "could result in real anxiety" (McKechnie 1993, p. 139).

The image of a packaged, distinctive, objectified Corsicanness standing out against and contributing to the muting of an everyday life, which it renders as unmarked, undistinctive, and humdrum, goes some way toward describing the use of the category Corsican in Crucetta. People were indeed, as we have seen, constantly making distinctions between really Corsican things and the rest of reality, and the former were often cast in the recognizable terms of costume, food, music, myth, and legend. And yet the more one tried to pin this distinction down, the more it tended to slip away. The humdrum could suddenly become typically Corsican, and the typical humdrum—not, as in McDonald's case, in the slow interpenetration of mismatching world views, but rather from one moment, one sentence, one interpretation to the next. There was no distinct line in Crucetta between fixed, stereotypical, or essentialist versions of Corsicanness and fluid, contextual, ironic, or playful categorizations. The "really Corsican" constantly spilled over into the "merely Corsican," as in the following story about knives.

Three Knives

In the spring of 2003, I lost a knife. This was a pretty, thin penknife with a rosewood handle, made by the French company Laguiole, whose distinctively shaped productions can be purchased in every hardware store and most tourist shops across the country. The knife had been given to me years previously by a school friend while on a hiking trip in the Pyrenées and, after living a mostly ornamental life, had suddenly come into its own during my Corsican fieldwork as a practical implement for whittling, cutting strings, and dislodging bits of things from other things in which they should not have been lodged.

The practical need for a knife, together with the approaching end of my time in Corsica and the associated idea that I might bring back a keepsake from the island, put me in mind of the beautiful Corsican knives displayed by local artisans at various fairs around the island. When I mentioned my general interest in Corsican knives to the schoolteacher, Pascal, he told me of his uncle, a shepherd who lived in a small village in the inland valley of Asco and made what Pascal described as traditional Corsican knives. The very next day, Pascal brought to school a beautiful glossy book on the history and present variety of Corsican knives (Bianchi 2002), which the author had signed and gifted to Pascal's uncle, who featured in it, in a section on amateur cutlers. Perusing the book, I learned that some of the contemporary Corsican knives which I had seen at fairs and in shops were produced by a small elite of professional artisans who had come together under the guidance of a retired schoolteacher, Mr. Santoni, who had set about to salvage traditional Corsican knife making, reproducing as far as possible under similar technical conditions every known form of Corsican small blade tool and rustic weapon. He, in turn, inspired and taught his techniques to others who now combine historical recreation with the invention of new models made from carbon or Swedish steel—all extremely expensive, reaching, in some cases, the equivalent of $1,000 or more. Alongside this refined and circumscribed art cutlery, a flood of industrially produced "Corsican knives" of uncertain international origin have flooded the Corsican market and become as ubiquitous in Corsican gift shops and tobacconists as the Laguiole knife is in the rest of France. These are often stamped with the outline of the island, the "Moor's head" of the Corsican flag, and/or a Corsican-sounding (and sometimes inaccurately spelled) name, and they draw the scorn of advocates of Corsican culture such as Pascal.

Pascal's uncle's knives were different again: he made them himself, in a makeshift workshop behind his house, from the salvaged metal blades of sheep shears or hedge trimmers. Eschewing the generic curved shape of what has come to be recognized as the typical Corsican shepherd's knife, he made his knives' handles long and rectangular, with a toothed pattern at one end which was known as the "dog's head" and which had once been specific to the valley in which he lived. Most important from Pascal's point of view, he made them for his own use and amusement, or for close family, and although he could occasionally be persuaded (and, in my own case, eventually was) to sell one here and there, that was emphatically not their purpose. Interestingly, in the aforementioned glossy book, pictures of Pascal's uncle's knives appeared not just in the section on amateur knife makers, but also earlier in the historical section, to illustrate descriptions of traditional knives.

When Petru the shepherd heard, some time later, that I had bought a knife for the equivalent of $200, he gave me one of his looks. Taking a glance at my purchase, he stood up unceremoniously from the plastic-tableclothed table at which we were drinking our afternoon coffee and beckoned me toward a darkened, concrete-floored room at the back of the house. This was Petru's storeroom and workshop, and, opening an ill-fitting drawer in the rough-hewn workbench, he exclaimed: "You want a Corsican knife? You should have asked me. I have knives, here you go." In the bottom of the drawer jostled a number of standard, factory-produced hunting knives and penknives of different ages and in different states of disrepair. Picking through these carefully, Petru selected a big hunting knife, and then changed his mind and told me to choose my own. After some reflection, I picked up an aged Laguiole, identical to the one I had lost but for a plain black handle and a blade worn down by long use and repeated sharpening.

The boundary between the authentic and the inauthentic in this story of knives is as elusive as the boundary between Crucetta and Ile Rousse proved to be in the first chapter. In each case, really Corsican objects are opposed to merely Corsican or to frankly inauthentic, banal, or unimportant ones, according to different regimes of value which partially clash and partially overlap (see Appadurai 1986). When, at the end of a hunting trip some weeks later, I participated in skinning a boar with Petru's Laguiole and told my fellow hunters who had given me the knife, one of them remarked on the blade's sharpness: "Jean's father's knives—they really cut, don't they?" In the context of this discussion, Petru's Laguiole was a real Corsican knife, enmeshed in the webs of kinship and value of an unself-consciously Corsican—and thus truly authentic—rurality, by contrast to which Pascal's uncle's knife became an expensive, nostalgic implement. And yet, the latter had its own superlative authenticity, which allowed it anachronistically to illustrate a bygone age of Corsican knife making. Its "real Corsicanness" stemmed from different sources again from the even more expensive art objects produced by professional neo-traditional Corsican cutlers, which in turn put to shame the fabricated productions

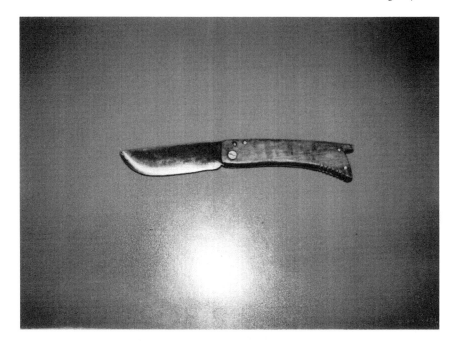

FIGURE 4.1. Pascal's uncle's knife

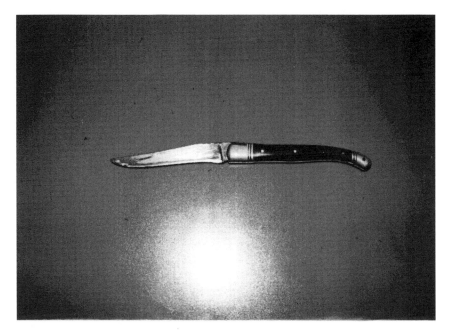

FIGURE 4.2. Petru's knife

of the tourist industry sold in hardware stores around the island alongside . . . the kind of Laguiole which Petru had just given me.

In Crucetta, distinctions between really Corsican things and banal, normal, mere ones constantly shifted, disappeared, and reemerged. While this made room for much debate, discussion, and disagreement over issues of authenticity, what emerged as patently obvious to everyone was the existence of such a distinction, its evident and unquestionable nature unaffected by the difficulty of pinning it down. There was enough there to drive to distraction any anthropologist bent on the deconstruction of claims to authenticity (Linnekin 1991). The evident, unquestionable existence of things which were Corsican and things which were not emerged unscathed from an observable mass of indeterminacy and contradiction as to which exactly these might be. This interplay of ambiguity and clarity extended to the question of people's Corsicanness, and the distinction between Corsicans and non-Corsicans in Crucetta had a similarly disconcerting tendency to fade in and out of view.

5

People

[Cultural difference] is experienced in contradictory ways
by Corsicans. Are they different from the French? A majority will respond[,] we are French! So, you are the same as the
French? Oh no, not at all, we're Corsican and proud of it!

—CULIOLI 1990, TRANSLATED IN JAFFE 1999

You are Corsican or you are not. You are Corsican if you are, well, from here, you know.

—PETRU, PERSONAL COMMUNICATION

Seeing Like a (French) State

In 1991, the highest French legal authority, the *conseil constitutionnel,* ruled that
the expression "the Corsican people" was contrary to the French Constitution.
This decision was a response to a drafted bill which, in its first article, referred
to "the living historical and cultural community which constitutes the Corsican
people, a component of the French people" (quoted in Hossay 2004, p. 420). The
conseil constitutionnel ruling canceled this first article, thereby reconfirming that
Corsicans were not to be officially distinguished or set apart as a group within "the

French People," which "must be considered a unitary category, unsusceptible of any subdivision by virtue of the law" (Conseil Constitutionnel 1991).

Unsurprisingly, there were some immediate reactions on the island. Corsican nationalists who had been calling since the 1970s for official recognition of the Corsican people were outraged. By contrast, the influential Corsican center-left leader Paul Giacobbi endorsed the decision in the strongest terms, claiming that "[w]hen you recognise the Corsican People within the French people, you are making a racist distinction!" (Giacobbi, quoted in Hossay 2004, p. 420).

It is thus not an overstatement to say that the question of Corsican identity and difference from the French is one of the key ongoing matters of concern and public debate on the island. There is a broad consensus about the existence of "Corsican" and "French" as categories. Debate mostly occurs over their proper definition, de jure and de facto. Do claims to Corsicanness imply cultural, sociological discontinuities with Frenchness or even, as some nineteenth-century Corsican regionalists once tried to claim, racial ones (see Pellegrinetti 2005)? Should such differences be recognized and regulated by (French) law? Is Corsicanness the same kind of category as Frenchness? Are the two compatible, hierarchically ordered, mutually exclusive? Can/should Corsican culture change, and in what way? Can one become Corsican, and how? These debates are inflected by a set of existing legal and material provisions and constraints which make the category French, on the institutional level at least, seem far more solid than Corsican: however complex, shifting, and elusive such oft-invoked objects as French identity, culture, or national consciousness might be, French nationality at least is a straightforwardly verifiable fact (Stolcke 1997). Thus, the majority of people in Crucetta are French in this sense: they have in their possession passports and identity cards which state this fact and are counted in the national census as French. This Frenchness derives from and is defined by a set of simple criteria: French people in Crucetta were either born in France, or of French parents, or have been naturalized.

The category Corsican, by contrast, benefits from no such de jure reality. For instance, the INSEE national census of 1999 (the most recent at the time of my fieldwork) reported that the population of Crucetta was at that time 838 people, 743 of whom held French citizenship. There were 537 residents of Crucetta, the document noted, who were born in Corsica, 190 in continental France, and 111 abroad. It went so far as to tell us that 98 people who were living in Crucetta in 1999 lived in mainland France ten years previously, and thirteen lived abroad. This is precise, detailed, and interesting information to be sure, and it tells the reader much about the migration patterns of the population of Crucetta, but one cannot discern from it the kind of distinctions which were ethnographically highly salient in Crucetta among Corsicans, Continentals, and Arabs, for instance. The invisibility of such categories in state statistics is, of course, not an omission. It is consistent with the constitutional council's decision, noted above, against the recognition of the Corsican people, which in turn is motivated by the explicit principles of what has been termed French republicanism and, principally, the French state's refusal to recognize sub-national minorities as collective political entities or as bearers of group rights (Lloyd 2000; Silverstein 2004; Bowen 2006)—although the French government has, since the time of my fieldwork, initiated a broad strategic discussion of the desirability of ethnic statistics (see *Actes du Colloque Statistiques "Ethniques"* 2006).

One of the clearest statements of the republicanist position can be found in a response to a report by the European Commission against Racism and Intolerance (2000) in which France was admonished to recognize what the ECRI described as its "multicultural" and "multiracial" nature. The response was penned, in an appendix to the report itself, by the French authorities.[1] It quotes the first article of the French Constitution, according to which "France shall be an indivisible, secular, democratic and social Republic. It shall ensure the equality of all citizens before the law, *without distinction of origin, race or religion*. It shall respect all beliefs" (European Commission against Racism and Intolerance 2000; my emphasis). The writers invoked not only ideals, but "sociological reality" itself: "Although ECRI feels it must consider that 'de facto, [minority groups] exist' . . . it must be pointed out that there is no consensus of opinion on this assessment of French sociological reality in the country itself" (ibid.). Indeed, the notion of a society subdivided into ethnic or religious communities, they argued,

> cannot be applied to the situation in France. For example, how does one identify persons "of North-African origin," the expression used in the report, among the French population? Should one distinguish between those who, while living in France, have Algerian, Tunisian or Moroccan nationality and those who were born in these countries but now hold French nationality? But if this is the case, how far back should one go to establish the criterion of "origin"? Should religious beliefs also be taken into account? And is it wise to put Tunisians, Algerians and Moroccans all in the same group? Finally, and above all, do the interested parties want or claim to be identified in this way or to belong to this group? . . . The legal concept of "minority" does not exist in French law, which does not mean that the specific characteristics of people's identities are not recognized. But they lie within the realm of individual, private choice governed by freedom of thought and conscience and are not based on objective criteria. (Ibid.)

This republicanist approach has been widely debated (and, in the main, critiqued) by anthropologists and sociologists, and I do not propose to rehearse these debates here but rather to examine the effects of this approach in Crucetta.

Corsican Citizenship

Some people in Crucetta were directly involved in trying to alter what they perceived as a legal imbalance between Frenchness and Corsicanness. I was thus rather surprised one day when one of my nationalist friends proudly told me that he had applied for a Corsican identity card. What he was referring to was the recently set up nationalist project of a Temporary National Assembly: the Assemblée Nationale Provisoire, or ANP (Chemin 2002b; Associu per a Cunsulta Naziunale 2002). The current regional government of Corsica has limited powers granted to it by the French state. Furthermore, it is voted for by all French citizens residing on the island, including, for instance, Continental civil servants who, many nationalists feel, are not committed to the island's welfare; for hardliners, these civil servants are part of the French state's "population colonization" (*colonisation de peuplement*) policy. By contrast, the projected ANP would consist of representatives elected exclusively by members of the Corsican people. Since it would operate entirely outside of the official structures of the French state and was heavily criticized by the then French minister of the interior, Nicolas Sarkozy, such an assembly would have no legal power. The hope of those who set it up, however, is to use it to register and reveal a truly *Corsican* opinion which, they feel, is masked by the residency-based voting principles of local government. Such a revelation would call into question the democratic nature of the French voting process, by proving the existence of a Corsican minority with a distinctive and muted voice: it would effectively challenge the state's claims about French sociological reality as described above. There is also the wider aim of creating a representative parallel institution "to make ourselves heard, particularly at the international level" (Jean-Pierre Santini, quoted in Chartier and Larvor 2004, p. 33). This points to the increasing importance in Corsican nationalist policy, alongside direct antagonism toward and appeals to the French state, of appeals to the European Union's stated interest in supporting regional cultures and identities (Shore 1993).

As my friends in Crucetta pointed out to me, a website was set up which offers an online voting system for members of this newly constructed Corsican electoral body. The first step is to apply for membership in this body, a service also available through the site. This attempt to give formal life to the Corsican people, despite the French state's opposition, involves a translation of the rather elusive notion of a "living historical and cultural community which constitutes the Corsican people" into actual applicable rules of nationality—a problem with which France itself has struggled repeatedly since the revolution, each new citizenship regime an accommodation between "voluntarist" and "organicist" concepts of the nation (Stolcke 1997, pp. 62–63). The rules of eligibility for Corsican nationality are as follows: a person is eligible for Corsican nationality either by descent (at least one parent is eligible for Corsican nationality), or by marriage to an eligible person, or after ten years of residence in Corsica. As one of the proponents of the scheme, Jean-Pierre Angelini, explained, ten years of residence is the same period as the one imposed by French nationality rules—with the difference that the French state reserves decision after that period, whereas for Corsican nationality, eligibility after ten years is automatic.[2] The applicant by residence, however, must be "committed to furthering the political, economic, social and cultural interests of the Corsican nation." Successful applicants are issued a Corsican national identity card—complete with barcode and photo—printed on a machine which the organizers have purchased for 4800€ (Chemin 2003).

Underlying this Corsican citizenship policy is a broadly held definition among Corsican nationalist parties of the Corsican people as a "community of destiny" (*communauté de destin*), a concept which mirrors the often ambivalent ways in which French nationhood has been defined. The notion of the Corsican people as a community of destiny was explicitly formulated, for instance, during hearings for an official government inquiry by the spokespersons of two nationalist groups (Cuq and De Roux 1997). In answer to the question of whether the Corsican people is defined as an "ethnic, territorial or cultural" entity, the spokesperson for the Movement for Self-Determination (MPA) answered that the community of destiny is a population living on a given territory who share a history and a culture, and that the main characteristic of this culture is its openness to new people and a capacity to integrate new influences. She then expanded on what she described as the recent integration of many North Africans into the Corsican people (pointing to a fluency in Corsican as an indication of this integration). On the question of the Corsican diaspora, she noted forcefully that there were many people of Corsican origin who, as far as her party was concerned, belonged to the community of destiny of other French regions. Belonging to a community of destiny, she reiterated, is not about origin, but about the contingencies of life. The spokesperson for the more radical coalition Corsica Nazione took a slightly different line. In reply to a question about the precise definition of the Corsican people, he stated:

> M. PAUL QUASTANA: [The Corsican people] exists, this is an obvious fact. Corsica is a nation. It has suffered invasion after invasion. It is a people which has been forged in the mountains, which has its language, its culture, its history, which has clearly defined frontiers. To deny it is to deny the obvious.

> M. RENAUD DUTREIL [INTERVIEWER]: I am not denying it, I am simply asking you to be more specific.
> [The nationalist spokesperson runs through specific examples of who would and wouldn't qualify, with a number of asides on French policy in Corsica. He concludes with the following definition:]

M. PAUL QUASTANA: . . . By "Corsican people," we are referring to any person living on this land, potentially whatever their nationality [*éventuellement quelque soit leur nationalité*], who is involved in an economic development which does not go against our interests. (Mission d'Information Commune sur la Corse 1997)

Although in the final instance this definition eschews any explicitly ethnic element, the tone throughout suggests a distinction between an original us (forged in the mountains, against a long history of invasions, etc.) and a potential them (who are invited to join us insofar as they do not go against our interests). In more recent definitions of the Corsican people, this is sometimes explicitly articulated in terms of a distinction between the wide "community of destiny" and the original "historic community" (Chartier and Larvor 2004); another definition of the Corsican people is "a community of destiny bringing together Corsicans by origin and Corsicans by adoption" (Culioli 2003). The notion of origin, here, is carried over from broader French ways of talking about nationality, where it plays an interesting and semi-submerged role. French nationality (be it given at birth or acquired later in life) in principle erases, as we have seen, other possibilities for official categorization on the basis of ethnicity, for instance; however, a French national who was born as a national of a different country will commonly refer to himself as "French of X origin" (so, in my case, "French of Romanian origin": *Français d'origine Roumaine*). Similarly, children or grandchildren of Algerian immigrants, say, may choose to refer to themselves as "French of Algerian origin," in what comes close (but significantly does not equate) to the type of hyphenated identity categories deployed in Britain and the United States. The difference between these two ways of signifying complex identities is a concentrated key to the differences between multiculturalist and republicanist modes of citizenship. The notion of origin also lends itself to subtle deployment in the everyday marking of differences: so, for instance, it is often acceptable to ask people of what origin they are (*vous êtes de quelle origine?*) in contexts in which it would be considered rude or outright racist to explicitly query their Frenchness. Origin thus reintroduces into acceptable conversation an ethnic categorization which is officially under erasure. In Corsican as well as in French identity talk, an implicit concern with ethnicity therefore persists within official discourses of abstract or color-blind nationality.

More broadly, anthropologists, sociologists, and historians of France have become increasingly suspicious of the supposed binary distinction between a French, abstract model of citizenship and a German, cultural model of nationalism, as can be seen in the recension of this distinction in recent debates about French republicanism versus Anglo-Saxon multiculturalism. Rather than being two opposed national traditions, these emerge from late twentieth- and early twenty-first-century analyses as two poles internal to nationalisms across Europe, "a tension with the fabric of western nations" (Silverman 1992, p. 5; see also Balibar and Wallerstein 1991). Authors have shown the historical (Stolcke 1997) and continuing (Silverstein 2004) intertwining of integralist claims to cultural rootedness and universalist notions of citizenship within France. Unsurprisingly, as the preceding shows, Corsican nationalists are facing the same ambiguities in their attempts to define a Corsican nation, people, and citizenship.

Telling

An involvement in conceptually refined debates about and operations upon the status and nature of Corsicanness was, however, the exception rather than the rule in Crucetta. There were those who had applied online for a Corsican identity card and were awaiting its arrival through the mail; in this irreducibly local way, they were participating in the constitution of the Corsican people as a particular kind of entity, attempting to reveal a truly Corsican electorate within the undifferentiated mass of French citizens counted by the INSEE. For many others, however, the legal imbalance between Corsicanness and Frenchness was a mere fact, denoting differences between the kinds of category that French and Corsican are: the former a legalistic, formal, and in some ways more remote one; the latter deeper, ineffable, and no less incontrovertible albeit less straightforwardly verifiable. This articulation of two categories was expressed succinctly in the language of another time—which clashes strangely with the proprieties of the current discussion—by the English writer Dorothy Carrington, who wrote: "the Corsicans are Corsican by race and French by Nationality" (Carrington 1962, p. 48). Of course, the idea of a Corsican "race" (to which a few people in Crucetta did make occasional implicit or explicit reference) was overwhelmingly recognized as an illicit and inaccurate categorization, and yet Carrington's formulation reflects the way many Corsicans in Crucetta treated the two categories as complementary. For many, being French and being Corsican simply pointed to different levels of the same reality.

My landlord, Xavier, an affable giant of a man, was a living embodiment of this intertwining of Corsicanness and Frenchness: having worked in Paris for nearly all of his adult life, Xavier never tired of telling new tenants of his joy at finally reaching retirement age. Beaming over a plate of delicious fish and potatoes on my first evening in Crucetta, Xavier tells me of his last day at work. His colleagues offered to have a celebratory drink: "Allons arroser ça," they had said, a common French idiom which literally translates as "let's water it." "You know what I said to them?" Xavier delays the punchline with a barely suppressed giggle, his huge forefinger waving like a police officer's baton. "You know what I said?—I said go outside and you'll be 'watered' by the rain." Characteristically, Xavier has packed into this succinct joke both his denigration of the many years spent on the French mainland (what is there to celebrate?) and the main reason for this denigration, rooted in the kind of place the Continent is: a rainy place, the weather a metaphor for everything Xavier—like the many other Crucettacci who had been driven to the Continent by the tough postwar years—had left behind in Corsica. The story underscored the strong sense, throughout Xavier's account of his life history, of exile and homecoming: "Back then, you had to leave. There was no money, no work." And then, slightly defiantly: "I don't regret going!" With the money he made on the Continent, Xavier built this large home on the outskirts of the old village, where he now settles in contented retirement, the end point of a continental odyssey of many years. But his unconditional attachment to Corsica, which constantly emerges in Xavier's narrative as the pivot and framework of his own self-description, doesn't entail much sympathy for Corsican nationalism. He says, sweeping aside my question about the island's potential for autonomy: "Alone, what could we do? If there's three days' strike of the maritime transports, we have a famine here. We can't sustain ourselves." The project of a "Europe of regions" does not appeal to him either: "Every region has to give something. What can we give?" No, for Xavier, "Corsica's never had it as good as since it's been in France." Corsica and France, in other words, bring up distinct voices in Xavier, the former singing of direct experience and visceral attachment, while the latter intones economic and political logics, a dual harmony of compatible categories.

This play on categories was highlighted by a set of proprieties around the proper terminology for talking about non-Corsican French people in Corsica. Somewhat confusingly for the uninitiated reader, Anglophone authors writing about Corsica often refer to the non-Corsican French simply as the French, or use the labels French, Continentals, and continental French interchangeably (cf. Jaffe 1999; Jensen 1999; McKechnie 1993), whereas these categories can be deployed with subtly different, but often far-reaching implications. People in Crucetta (however they self-categorized) occasionally referred to those they wished to mark as non-Corsican French simply as "the French," just as they might refer to continental France as just "France." However, such usage was not unmarked or banal. In one sense or another, it suggested a framing in which Corsica and France were mutually exclusive entities. Hence, Corsicans of a nationalist persuasion might consistently speak of "the French," but this is definitely seen as a marked thing to do. Similarly, Continentals with particularly strong views on the Corsican question might follow this usage, restricting (in their disapproval of the island) true Frenchness to the mainland. Other Corsicans and Continentals also occasionally used "French" and "France" in this way, but this was usually treated as a slip of the tongue, quickly corrected to "Continental" (*Continental*) and the "Continent" (*continent*), often with an embarrassed laugh or comment. The markedness of this usage and the uneasiness around it was strongest when addressing strangers, and especially in situations where a Corsican/Continental distinction could be understood to cut across the company. Continental thus tiptoes around the political implications of French, aiming for the (supposed) impartiality of geography. The problem disappears in the Corsican language, given the existence of a specific word, *pinzutu,* to denote the non-Corsican French. *Pinzutu* literally translates as "pointy" and is sometimes said to be a reference to the pointy *tricorne* hats worn by French soldiers at the time of Corsica's annexation.[3] The flexibility of *pinzutu* obviates the problem: in theory, Corsican and *pinzutu* could be used as two subcategories of "French" (whereas Corsican and French obviously cannot), but crucially, *pinzutu* doesn't necessarily imply this categorical subordination of Corsican to French. Its (supposed) roots in the history of France's military invasion of Corsica hark back to a time when Corsican and *pinzutu* were in no sense part of an overarching whole. Its flexibility matches the complexity of the situation. This is why I suggest that the closest French translation of *pinzutu* in its current Corsican usage is "Continental" (and not "French"; cf. Ravis-Giordani 1983, p. 231).

But this asymmetrical approach to the categories French and Corsican had more than terminological implications. If Frenchness was—in one sense at least—verifiable from one's passport, Corsicanness was in practice a matter of fine contextuality and what Baumann has termed "telling" (the near-immediate categorization of people based on tiny details of appearance and deportment, a social game of which Crucettacci were extremely fond; see Baumann 1996, p. 4). Telling was an acquired skill. As a newcomer to Crucetta, informed by a literature which seemed to suggest that the question of relational identity and boundary maintenance in the Barthian sense was the single most important issue an observer might encounter on the island (McKechnie 1993; Desanti 1997; Desideri 1997; Jaffe 1999; see also Ravis-Giordani 1983, p. 231), I was surprised to find that the distinction between Corsicans and non-Corsicans was rarely articulated explicitly. In time, however, I came to recognize the subtle and often silent ways in which people sounded each other out on this issue or wove it implicitly into discussions of a third party. It took an experienced eye, in many cases, to note this telling, the ways in which people would seek clues to unknown interlocutors' Corsicanness in certain physical features, items of clothing and jewelry, hairstyles, accents, attitudes, occupations, and so on: this person's mainland French accent, this other's way of standing, the car this couple drove, which although it had local plates was too shiny not to be rented. Language, however, was the prime marker, although not in the sense one might first expect. As I will elaborate in the next chapter, linguistic distinctions in Crucetta were far more complex than a simple binary: "Corsican for Corsicans," "French for Continentals." While it was indeed usually assumed that only Corsicans spoke Corsican well, it did not follow that all Corsicans spoke it; furthermore, everyone (also) spoke French, and French was almost invariably the language of first address. Distinctions resided rather in accents and smaller particularities of speech, such as the use of *corsismes* (words or grammatical turns drawn from Corsican) in French speech, typical Corsican interjections, or the pronunciation of Corsican proper names. Little by little, a number of initially strange silences or reticences, or slightly forced or edgy comments, or, on the contrary, unexplained bursts of hilarity came to make sense in view of the ways people's interactions and expectations of each other were implicitly informed by the question of whether or not the various people present were Corsican.

It would not be an overstatement to say that first meetings between people invariably involved an implicit resolution of this question. If one could not tell on sight, a few politely indirect questions as to one's interlocutor's village and relations would soon settle the matter. Direct questions as to one's Corsicanness, however, were fairly rare, and this was not because people always guessed right. Indeed, Corsicans, particularly those who had spent time on the Continent, were constantly telling amused or outraged stories of being mistaken for Continentals while traveling in other parts of the island. Stéphanie, for instance, a very elegant fifty-something schoolteacher who had spent most of her life near Paris, used to return to the island every summer, before she finally moved back for good—not, however, to her own village in the center of the island, but to Ile Rousse, from where she commuted to a job at the Crucetta primary school. Stéphanie and her Continental husband were both extremely keen motorcyclists and had motored quite widely around the island. On one occasion, as she stood in a queue for groceries in a tiny village along the way, Stéphanie inadvertently hit the woman in front of her with the motorcycle helmet she was carrying in her hand. As she apologized, she heard the woman mutter in Corsican, under her breath, *pinzuttaccia*—a term of abuse for Continentals. Stéphanie retorted indignantly in the same language, "no more *pinzuttaccia* than you!" (*pinzuttaccia cum'è voi!*). Similarly, Pascal told me, as he was giving me advice on how to negotiate the often narrow and dangerous local roads, of a Corsican friend who was often mistaken for a Continental not just because he drove a large car with continental plates, but because he drove it rather too gingerly around difficult bends, slowing down traffic. Irate Corsican motorists would be surprised to hear the *pinzuttacciu* reply in Corsican to their abuse. This, in turn, suggests why directly asking someone whether they are or are not Corsican might be impolite and inappropriate: if one needs to ask, one runs a serious risk of offending one's interlocutor (since they might turn out to be Corsican).

The Elusiveness of Boundaries

To put matters in this way, however, suggests an incontrovertible and clear (albeit politely muted) boundary between Corsicans and non-Corsicans. But I will be making a rather stronger and more counterintuitive argument here: the implicit and undefined way in which people sought out each other's Corsicanness or otherwise was not a polite fudging of a clear-cut phenomenon. What this way of "doing" identity meant in practice was that establishing one's Corsicanness was not an isolated question, but was inseparable from a number of other assumptions concerning one's class, life history, educational background, etc., which were similarly deduced from infinitesimal clues rather than expressly discussed. These various distinctions and connections faded into and out of one another. The indeterminacy and fine contextuality were intrinsic to the kinds of distinctions these were: seemingly obvious, binary, either/or, and yet in practice very hard to pin down.

Take, for instance, the inhabitants of my neighborhood in the old village, a cluster of houses and streets generally referred to by the name of the local square, Piazza à O. Some cases were fairly unambiguous, such as the Viltanés and Cécile, a schoolteacher in Paris who had bought a house in the village one year before I got there and came back every school holiday. At the other end of the scale were Mimi and Petru, Crucetta born and bred; he lived with his wife, Marie-Josée, who was a native of the neighboring *commune* of Murettu, and their son Jean. But what of Suzanne, the daughter of villager Patrick, who had spent her early childhood in the village but had long since moved to the Continent and came back for one month every summer with her Parisian husband and their two children? What of Jeanne, who worked as a nurse, ministering mostly to elderly and bedridden patients in remote villages in the hinterland of Crucetta? She had moved into the house next to mine two years previously from the French mainland and now lived there full time with her two daughters, her mother, and her Corsican stepfather. And what of the Cousins couple who had discovered Crucetta many years ago, bought a house on the square, and even celebrated their wedding on Piazza à O? A decade later, the party was still vividly recollected and took up many pages in Petru's collection of photos of memorable Piazza à O occasions. Mr. Cousin traced his ancestry to the south of the island, but he and his family were usually referred to on Piazza à O as "the Parisians" (*les Parisiens*).

It was not that people—apart from the occasional naïve incomer such as myself—were habitually confused about who was or was not Corsican. It is rather that the polite indeterminacy around liminal cases was constitutive of the way in which the Corsican/non-Corsican distinction operated in general (even in the most obvious cases, such as those of Petru or Cécile): being or not being Corsican was not a matter of bounded (albeit overlapping) categories with a set of clear and commonly acknowledged selection principles, but rather a situational and often unelaborated matter. Unlike French citizenship, or Corsican citizenship as imagined by Corsican nationalists, there was no theoretical counterpart to the situated practice of telling, no explicit principles of selection which could exhaustively and definitely determine whether a certain person was or was not Corsican. While obvious cases of Corsicanness or Continentalness went without comment (no rules needed to be invoked), ambiguous cases remained indeterminate (no rules could clarify them into a binary). The fractal image of a hand gripping a hammer while infinitesimally not touching it is apposite here. Ambiguity would prompt not a clear resolution, but a deeper delving into detail: one's parent or grandparent may have been Corsican, or may have lived on the island, etc. What these seeming boundaries resolved into, therefore, was a set of potentially infinitely traceable connections (Edwards 1998; Edwards and Strathern 2000). Of course, commonsense expectations occasionally came to interrupt the often tenuous craving of some for Corsican credentials. As the Corsican funny paper *A Macagna* put it, in an article on tourists: "It's not because your great-uncle was from my village that you're Corsican and that you're my cousin!" As I will argue in more detail in chapter 7, Edwards and Strathern's claim about the self-limiting nature of English notions of kinship rang true of claims to Corsicanness: "social and biological claims . . . , each endlessly ramifying in themselves, serve equally to link and to truncate *one another*" (2000, p. 159).

But no explicit and agreed-upon cut-off point operated in terms of depth of generational attachment or length of time spent on the island. The question of Corsicanness in such cases became, as I argued of insiderness in chapter 3, neither a binary, nor a range, but a specific and ultimately individual configuration of attachments to people, places, and histories.

Les Arabes

For people as for things, then, there were many different ways of being Corsican, merely Corsican, or really Corsican (McKechnie 1993), subtle distinctions woven into life histories, between, say, Pascal and Petru, or between either of them and Mr. Cousin, the Parisian. In practice, these distinctions could easily trump the commonalities, and Corsicanness would fade out of view when Mr. Cousin and Mr. Viltané discussed French politics or when Pascal and I discussed Petru. Certain differences, however, were not so easily disposed of.

In Corsica, as in the rest of France, one often hears the label *Arabe* or *Maghrébin*[4] used to refer, interchangeably and en masse, to the now elderly first-generation migrants from the former French colonies in North Africa; their children and grandchildren, many of whom were born and grew up in France and are French citizens; and recent labor migrants from North Africa. People in the latter category,

McKechnie wrote in the early '90s, "are to a great extent invisible on the island. They work in the countryside and many live there, often in barrack accommodation. They are seldom seen in shops, virtually never in the bars or nightclubs of smaller towns. They appeared to be outside the social life of the community" (McKechnie 1993, p. 134). Even though in Crucetta a number of North African families lived in the center of the old village, their patterns of socialization were similarly very far removed from those of the other inhabitants. Their invisibility to other inhabitants was matched only by their discretion and reticence when it came to the presence of a strange and inquisitive anthropologist. While, as I argued in the first chapter, the very idea of studying any place from the inside as part of a community is problematic in view of the multiplicity of partial intimacies which brush past each other, the case of North Africans is an especially accentuated version of this phenomenon.

For all their misunderstandings and the often tenuous and partial nature of their interactions, my other neighbors in the old village did at least engage with one another on a day-to-day basis. This was rarely the case, in my experience at least, with the North African families: not only were Franco-Maghrebians never seen in the cafés and bars, and only rarely and fleetingly at the grocery store, but in the squares, which formed the focus of most casual social interaction in the old village, where old men would sit together of an afternoon and passersby might stop and chat a while, North Africans would never stop. In one very rare case in which a North African woman was outside, letting her young son play in the square near her house, a group of Corsican men who usually patronized that square was sitting observing her suspiciously from the opposite corner of the square. At the beginning and end of the school day, mothers would stand and chat outside the gates. But even then, the three Moroccan mothers usually formed a separate group and, outside of the teacher, did not greet anyone, nor were they greeted, and they politely ignored me when I tried to engage in conversation. During religious festivals and processions which left the village and concentrated around the village church, or when parties were organized at the events hall near the council flats, Franco-Maghrebi children and youths might occasionally be seen observing the excitement from the sidelines with expressions ranging from skepticism to defiance to unconcern. This separation was far less stark in the nearby town of Ile Rousse: at the supermarket at which I worked during the summer, Franco-Maghrebians, Corsicans, and Continentals worked together in an atmosphere of only occasionally tense banter and jocularity, and there were many cases of friendships and socializing across these boundaries—which, for all I know, may very well have existed in Crucetta too. In public in Crucetta, however, the isolation of North Africans was more marked, and like McKechnie, I never managed to get more than fleeting conversations, in passing, in an alleyway, or for the duration of a hitchhiker's ride to the nearby town. As a result, like previous ethnographers, such as McKechnie, I was reduced to principally studying Franco-Maghrebians' absent presence in the discourses of the Corsicans and Continentals who lived alongside them.

McKechnie has argued that Franco-Maghrebian "workers . . . played a central role in Corsican self-image by occupying the lowest rung of social and economic status, and by providing a 'pariah' group, defined in opposition to Corsican values of family, cleanliness, pride and intelligence" (McKechnie 1993, p. 135). In my experience, however, the discursive emplotment of Franco-Maghrebians into accounts of Corsicanness was rather more complex and ambivalent, as *les Arabes* were occasionally held up in Corsican discourses as instances of "how we used to be." If everyday depictions of *les Arabes* were rife with the kinds of Orientalist stereotypes one might encounter throughout the rest of France, this took on an added layer of complexity given the salience of a form of "internal Orientalism" in French (and, indeed, in Corsican) discourses about Corsica (for a similar phenomenon in Italy, see Schneider 1998). Stereotypical depictions of Franco-Maghrebians as "traditionalist," "very religious," "authoritarian and inegalitarian in terms of age and gender," "having high birthrates," "touchy on the subject of honor," and so on, which are rife throughout French discourses on Franco-Maghrebians, could in many ways also apply to Corsicans' accounts of their own past, and many in Crucetta made these comparisons explicitly. I overheard an argument between two Corsican women about an investigative journalism program aired on French TV, which focused on the much-discussed topic of "the oppression of Muslim women." One of them alleged, on the basis of the program, that *les Arabes* were "barbarians," to which the other responded that, in many ways, Corsicans used to be very much the same not so long ago. "Well, I'll like them when they've evolved then" was the angry retort. In a more positive vein, schoolteachers often complained that Corsican and Continental children were far too sedentary, staying in all day and playing computer games. By contrast, they pointed approvingly to *Arabe* children who, they said, spent all day outside, "playing in the dust, like we used to do when we were children." As a result, some teachers argued that, whereas the Corsican and Continental children were good at "fine motor skills" (*motricité fine*), Franco-Maghrebian children were far better at outdoor games and sports, enjoying the kind of rude health which the teachers associated with their own childhoods. In a similar vein, older Corsicans would sometimes compare Corsican youths unfavorably with *les Arabes* in terms of the latter's willingness to work. As one pensioner noted, in an aside from his discussion of the old days, "Young people [*les jeunes*], they don't want to work." "That's right," chimed in his friend, sipping a pastis with one elbow on the counter. "If you want a manual worker, now, there's no young people to do it. All you find is Arabs." The first man nodded sadly and, spreading out his palms, completed his friend's thought: "The young people, the Corsicans, they're too ashamed to do it."

Rather than a straightforward case of Barthian boundary maintenance and *a contrario* definition, then, discourses about *les Arabes* in Corsica betray a complex mix of ambivalently recognized similarities and differences, a partial "denial of co-evalness" (Fabian 1983) which places "them" in the past—rendered more complex by the fact that this past is itself a valued and romantic horizon. These discourses are reminiscent then, on the one hand, of common ambivalent representations of "the British Asian family" which have been described for the United Kingdom, in which nostalgia for a golden age of "traditional family values" is fused with the "anxiety of being 'taken over' as well as overtaken by a population not granted the status of really belonging" (Rattansi 1995, pp. 68–69). On the other hand, these similarities between marginalized North African workers in Corsica today and the marginalization of Corsican workers on the French mainland could provide, at least in theory, grounds for empathy with the plight of North Africans, another economically dominated people, poor workers who have had to leave their home and face a hostile land. Anti-racist Corsican writers such as Culioli make such comparisons explicit: "Employed illegally, exploited when not actually mistreated, the guest workers of the 1960s have accepted to live as pariahs so that their children may have a better life. The same was true for many Corsicans in the early 20th century" (Culioli 2003a, p. 46; see also Cole 1997 for a similar argument about Sicily).

However, despite the best efforts of Culioli and others, despite the plausibility of such framings, and despite the accumulated weight of similarities which Corsicans, however ambivalently, recognize between themselves and *les Arabes,* the fact remains that such examples of solidarity remained thin on the ground in Crucetta. This suggests that an understanding of what kept *les Arabes* marginalized cannot be sought entirely in the realms of discourse and Othering—although these are certainly partial explanations. The weight which meant that, as we have seen, *les Arabes* consistently appeared in discourses as effective gaps in the social fabric of Crucetta ("there's no young people to do it. All you find is Arabs"; "before the houses were full, now's there's the Arabs in them") is also partly to be sought in the multiple minute and powerful ways in which they were actually disconnected, more so than many Continentals, from the webs of interknowledge (*interconnaissance*) which tied together, however partially and revocably, many other inhabitants of Crucetta.

Anthropologists' broadly speaking Barthian approach to identity, in terms of the discursive construction of differences and boundary maintenance, has often tended to suggest that, as Galibert puts it, "when a group cohabits with another group, it is truer to say that it cohabits with the image it has of it" (Galibert 2004b, p. 29). The truth of this insight is probably stable (familiarity does not necessarily dispel prejudice), but its importance is inversely proportional to the thickness of the connection between people of the respective groups. In other words, the thought that interaction in and of itself dissolves boundaries is naïve and belied by a profusion of cases of schismogenesis. However, the thickness of connections across boundaries, while it may well reinforce the perceived salience of these boundaries, also brings in a wealth of other relevant frameworks for contextualization. Thus, in the case of Corsicans and, to a lesser extent, Continentals, the practice of "telling" brought along with it a wealth of contextual details about class, wealth, education, and personal trajectories, which might provide actual traceable commonalities at the very moment at which they highlight distinctions in terms of "who is what." By contrast, in the case of Franco-Maghrebians, the sheer lack of contextual knowledge and actual social interaction left the categorical distinctions bare of discursive elaboration; the gaps that North Africans' absence left in many Corsicans' accounts of Crucetta are in this sense partly homologous to the gaps left in this ethnography by the absence of a detailed account of the North Africans' intimacies and experiences.

Categories and Connections

Many anthropologists have pointed to a double face of identity, its propensity to assume by turns essential and fluid forms (Turner 1993; Werbner 1997; Baumann 1999; Grillo 2003). Often, this distinction between fixity and fluidity is mapped onto a distinction between state-imposed categories and local ones, between explicit categorization definitions and the myriad implicit ways in which people "do" identity in practice. Thus, Michael Herzfeld has suggested that anthropologists should look for identity in the interplay between, on the one hand, the fluid, relative terminologies of identity in people's everyday usage and, on the other, the fixed, essentialist identity categories of nationalist or statist definitions (Herzfeld 1997, p. 42). The kind of fixed and bounded ways of categorizing people which are enforced— sometimes violently—by states and bureaucracies interrupt the contextuality and revocability of people's everyday categorizations of each other. Herzfeld's description of a rigid state imposing its essentialist categories onto the fluidity of the everyday is particularly convincing for anthropologists, because it echoes a critique internal to the discipline itself: the notion that classical anthropological attempts to map categories and kinds of people fall short of the complexity and fluidity out there. This argument has been leveled at the anthropological concepts of culture (Clifford and Marcus 1986) and ethnicity (Edwards 1998) and at anthropology's engagement with objectified Others more generally (Fabian 1983). In this vein, Gerd Baumann has mapped in his extremely perceptive ethnography of multiethnic Southall the interplay between a "dominant discourse" of state multiculturalism, in which people are divided into cultures mapped onto communities, and the many "demotic" discursive moves through which Southallians challenge this equation between culture and community and reinterpret the meanings of the terms themselves: "Southall culture thus entails a dual discursive competence, embracing the dominant as well as the demotic, and it is the dominant that enables the conservation of existing *communities* and the demotic that allows Southallians to re-conceive *community* boundaries and contest the meaning of *culture*" (Baumann 1996, p. 195).

In one sense, the situation in Crucetta could be seen as the inverse of Baumann's account of Southall. If anything, the dominant discourse is one which, through the refusal to recognize groups as political actors and to make minorities statistically visible, attempts to render invisible the differences between people, claiming that they are a matter of individual choice and not based upon objective criteria. By contrast, if there are demotic voices to be found in Crucetta, they reside precisely in attempts to highlight the power and irrevocability of these differences, to ascertain and locate people, for better or for worse (and against the grain of official representations of an undifferentiated French citizenry), as Corsican, Continental, or Arab.

The respective values of fluidity and fixity, too, seem to some extent reversed, or at least blurred. On the one hand, it is true that French state categories (and their Corsican nationalist counterparts) attempt to fix into abstract principle who might and might not be considered French (or Corsican), whereas the everyday, situated practices of telling in Crucetta paint much more contextual pictures. But, on the other hand, there is no doubting which of these ways of thinking about identity was locally perceived as the more solid and irrevocable. This was powerfully evidenced in the sense of remoteness which attached in practice to discussions of nationality and citizenship.

As an avatar of this detachment, I will cite a comment on the institutional debate over the Corsican people drawn from the Corsican comedy website www .atechja.com,[5] whose humor was not lost on inhabitants of Crucetta to whom I showed it. The comment is in the form of an article within a section of the website entitled "Amusing Ethnology of Corsica." A large photograph features a man's empty clothes laid out on the floor alongside a lighter, a pair of glasses, and some car keys. In the place where the head would be is an issue of the national daily *Libération,* whose headline reads: "The Corsican People Is Dissolved." The text accompanying the picture reads:

> Remember: In 1991 the interior minister . . . presented his project concerning the status of Corsica to the National Assembly. The very first article of this draft astounds the islanders who wonder whether their favorite daily newspaper hasn't gone mad: without anyone bothering to warn them, it seems that there now exists *a living historical and cultural community which constitutes the Corsican people, a component of the French people.* Sadly, at the same moment, other higher and more powerful personages make the same discovery, and the axe soon falls: the 9th of May 1991, the constitutional council cancels the first article . . . concerning the existence of the Corsican people, judging it anticonstitutional! The media however failed to document the strange events which subsequently hit

Corsicans everywhere. A TECHJA, in its relentless search for truth, presents you this exclusive document. . . . On the day following the decision, every Corsican, on the island, on the mainland, and worldwide, whether or not he approved of the projected status, whether or not he had over-indulged the *apéritif,* suddenly found himself transformed into a sort of invisible man. This lasted for about ten minutes during which only his clothes and accessories remained un-dissolved. Don't worry, things are fine now and *Homo Corsus* has reconstituted himself. . . . On the other hand, *Populu Corsu* [the Corsican people] is still struggling to be accepted [*se faire admettre*].

The atechja.com piece is a wry comment on the distance between categorical debates over Corsicanness and Frenchness, and the experiential reality of being Corsican which these debates attempt to regulate. The implication, not to put too fine a point on it, is that these grandiose debates are epiphenomenal to the real fact of being Corsican. The Corsican reader, the heavy irony of the piece suggests, does not need his daily newspaper to inform him of the existence of a Corsican community any more than a legal decision by powerful, high-up politicians can make real Corsican people melt away.

We have thus a reversal of the usual anthropological wisdom[it is the state's definition of citizenship and nationality which appears fluid and amenable to negotiation, quite literally, through political protests, voting, and public debate.]By contrast, the "local," "demotic" ways of thinking about identity emerge as essentialist and fixed, since they hark to the unequivocal obviousness of being Corsican (or Continental, or Arab). After all, when Petru claimed that one cannot become Corsican, that one either is, or is not, he was being far more essentialist than the Corsican nationalists who laid down rules for Corsican citizenship, which involved at least the possibility of naturalization. Petru's essentialism, however, has one interesting characteristic, which one does not usually associate with essentialism, namely, that it is ultimately unbounded: "You are Corsican if you are, well, from here, you know." No clear criteria, no explicit bottom line underscores this seemingly straightforward, unambiguous fact of being Corsican.

Similarly, in the atechja.com piece, the obviousness of the existence of the Corsican people is grounded in the same fine contextuality which is involved in telling: the remains in the picture may look fairly generic to the untrained eye, but the collection of objects adds up fairly unambiguously to the stereotypical costume of a young Corsican man: jeans and black T-shirt—the latter printed with various symbols of the island—gold chain with an island-shaped pendant, gold bracelet, ring, with lighter in one hand, car keys in the other. Trite and circumstantial as these may seem, it is such small clues and cues, and the feeling of insiderness produced by the capacity to identify them, which help to make obvious the reality, the tangibility, of being Corsican. It was this obviousness, in turn, which informed and grounded people's reactions to discussions such as those about the existence or not of a Corsican people, without the article providing at any point a definition of what this might mean or a guideline as to whom in practice might be included or excluded. The explicit debates around the proper categories—is there or is there not a Corsican people?—albeit carried out in the shadow of the state, are amenable to reversal, discussion, resolution, whereas this implicit web of connections seems to delineate much stronger attachments and more impassable divides.

This is almost the story, but not quite. For to leave it at that would be merely to rediscover the old nineteenth-century sociological opposition between the implacable rootedness of traditional ways of belonging against the abstract associations of modernity; the distinction, in other words, between Tönnies' *Gemeinschaft* and *Gesellschaft* or between Durkheim's mechanical and organic solidarity. This kind of distinction between concrete, rooted, local belonging, inarticulate yet profound, and the abstract heights of citizenship which free the individual and enable rational debate was, of course, internal not just to sociology, but to the French nation-building project itself. As we saw in chapter 3, it was by virtue of such an opposition that regions were engulfed and subordinated within a broader national whole (Thiesse 1997). Today, these two strands are still in continuing tension within French state and Corsican nationalist definitions of identity: a French passport does not exhaust the meaning of Frenchness, as shrill debates about whether naturalized immigrants "really belong" and about the "cultural unity" of France constantly demonstrate (Silverstein 2004; Bowen 2006); nor do definitions of the Corsican people as a "community of destiny" quite manage to erase the constitutive distinction within Corsican nationalist discourse between an original us and a naturalized them.

The authoritative ambiguities around identity in Crucetta which I have described are therefore not the local, essentialist counterpart of national abstract definitions. They partake of the same interplay between organicism and voluntarism, between the abstract categories of citizenship and the stuff (historical consciousness, cultural commonality, community of interests, and, among a self-defined racist fringe, claims to biological relatedness) which fills identity up and gives it form and conviction. Crucetta is, in this sense, a location in which the "ambivalence of modernity" (Bauman 1999) plays out; it is one of the numerous places in Europe where, as Silverstein notes, following Holmes (Holmes 2000, p. 30):

[T]he romantic foundations of European nationalism expressed in integralist notions of rooted cultural belonging—present from Herder's cultural philosophy through contemporary neo-fascist cant—run headlong into parallel republican and scientific modernist discourses of a social body united in organic solidarity that underlie Durkheimian sociology as appropriated by the architects of European federalism. (Silverstein 2004, p. 30)

Observing this phenomenon in Crucetta adds something to the analysis, however. It adds the realization that, in practice, this confrontation is not so much the clash of two discourses (essentialist/fluid or dominant/demotic) as the intertwining of *two heterogeneous forms:* on the one hand, *categories* of identity (Corsican, Continental, French, Arab) and, on the other, the myriad *connections* from which these categories draw their experiential power. The former (categories) are explicit, debatable, they allow one to say identity, to label it ("you are Corsican or you are not"), and by that very token, to contest it, to formalize it, to define and redefine its boundaries and its rules of selection (from the most essentialist to the most inclusive). The latter (connections) are often implicit, they are deduced from the myriad tiny details of dress, speech, or deportment which allow people to "tell," they inhere in the multiple relations of value and use which make things more or less Corsican. Connections weave actual networks of relations within and across the supposed boundaries between people, imagined in the language of categories, as they do between really and merely Corsican things. These connections thus simultaneously fill the categories with a sense of obviousness, make them appear essential and irrevocable, and blur their edges, making them hard to pin down and define.

This distinction between categories and connections is thus not a return to the distinction between fixed statist essentialism and fluid local ways of doing identity: both categories and connections can be fluid, open to agentive manipulation, and both can be essentialist, limiting, or fixed. Their power, for good or ill, is in their combination as, for instance, when the category of the village is mapped onto the myriad often translocal connections which give it form, content, and persuasion. The implicitness of connections, the ways in which they blur the edges of clear categorical distinctions is not necessarily a guarantee of freedom, a challenge to authority—in fact, quite the opposite. As Sarah Green has noted, the ambiguous, the "shifty," the marginal, have often been associated with resistance and counter-hegemony, with the hope that multiple, decentered, fluid identities will somehow destabilize the often oppressive ways in which things "are made to seem clear, bounded and fixed" (Green 2005, pp. 4–8). And yet, as she also points out, "[t]he difference between ambiguity (continual and contingent indeterminacy) and clarity (ontological knowledge) is not as enormous as the literature implie[s], at least in terms of what generates the sense of there being authoritative accounts" (ibid., p. 12). The two parts of Petru's statement, in other words, are not inconsistent, as it might at first seem, but rather mutually constitutive: what makes being Corsican seem such an unavoidable fact, what makes it in practice such a difficult category to shift, to acquire, or to rebel against, is precisely the difficulty of pinning the boundary down; it is the paradoxical interplay of a clear categorization and a potentially open-ended set of connections. Just like the conviction that the world is divided into things and Corsican things is in no way undermined by the difficulty of pinning down a fixed inventory of these two categories, or a set of agreed-upon rules of selection, it is precisely at their most ambiguous that assertions of identity are the most authoritative.

6

Languages

The information passed in Breton conversation is not . . . of a different and more intimate kind than that passed in French. . . . the linguistic resource is one that is used to map people and events in a very sophisti- cated way; you need to be bilingual in order to appreciate how this is done. [However, y]ou are not, as a French monolingual, excluded from secrets.

—CHAPMAN 1992

The men of Gilead said unto him, "Art thou an Ephraimite?" If he said, "Nay"; then they said unto him, "Say now Shibboleth": and he said Sibboleth: for he could not frame to pronounce it right. Then they took him, and slew him at the passages of Jordan.

—JUDGES 12:6

The Corsican Language

Crucetta primary school, on a Wednesday morning. Pascal is standing in front of a class of eight- to ten-year-old pupils whose ears are still ringing. Over the grumbles and protests, he reminds them playfully that that is what they get for not being quiet when he asked them politely, and he puts his feared referee's whistle back down on the desk. Tucking his glasses onto his forehead, he announces that it is time for the

Corsican language lesson. As the students scramble, automatically, for their blue exercise books, putting away the red ones (math), Pascal starts to tell them, as an introduction, about his two grandfathers, born in the nineteenth century. Despite the sun outside and the stifling heat inside, he manages to grab and keep the students' attention through his characteristic mix of good storytelling and interactivity. He soon gets to the point of the story: linguistic competence. His grandfathers were fluent Corsican-speakers, Pascal notes, and he continues, with frequent interjections from the class (the entire exchange is in French):

> PASCAL: You [all] speak Corsican less well than I do. That's normal. But I speak less well than them! But they couldn't read or write it. Why?
> JULIA [FROM THE BACK OF THE CLASS]: Because no one taught them!
> PASCAL: That's right, and where did they learn French?
> MARIE: In France!
> PATRICK [SIMULTANEOUSLY]: On the Continent.
> PASCAL: No, in school. It was a foreign language, like English for you.
> PATRICK [SLIGHTLY PUZZLED]: But then, they were illiterate!
> PASCAL: Yes. [pause] But it wasn't their fault. On the other hand, they *spoke* Corsican really well.
> ALEXANDRA: As well as French?
> PASCAL [HESITATING]: Yes . . . at least . . . Now, when I was at school, we were punished for speaking Corsican. . . . That's why we forgot and why today children don't speak Corsican any more.
> ROGER: Where was this school?
> PASCAL: Everywhere.
> PATRICK: Even here?
> PASCAL: Yes. . . . So, we weren't allowed to speak Corsican.
> ROGER [IN A SING-SONG VOICE, BEING SILLY]: And now, we're not allowed to speak French.
> PASCAL [WITH ONLY THE MILDEST STRAIN OF CONTAINED IRRITATION]: No, we're allowed, but we can also speak Corsican.

A little later on the same day, I am sitting in the shade in the Piazza à O with Petru, Jean, and their friend Dumé, engaging in sparse conversation. A couple of tourists from continental France walk by, both in their fifties, dressed in white: he wearing shorts, sandals, and a polo shirt, she with bronze curled hair and brown sunglasses. They have been here for a couple of days, renting the large house on the corner of the square. Their opening conversational gambit, in the amiable way one hears throughout southern France, is to note that we are sitting in the shade, and isn't that nice? My thoughts whizz to a document I recently perused, in which "greetings referring to the other person's activity" were singled out as a part of the curriculum of Corsican language and culture.

While the anthropologist is figuring that one out, Jean asks the tourists if he remembers rightly that they are from Toulon, and the husband confirms that before launching into an enthusiastic panegyric to Crucetta: "It's a beautiful village, and not touristy like . . . like others. Here, you hear Corsican being spoken everywhere!" And, clinching his hand with the appreciative gesture of a man weighing a satisfactory amount of produce: *Ça parle Corse!*—literally, "it speaks Corsican," a passive grammatical form, as one might say "it rains." Petru nods amiably. "Ah yes, you should learn!" he says, in his heavily accented, gravelly French. The man, who accurately interprets Petru's comment as a pleasantry rather than a serious suggestion, smiles slightly vacantly, his eyes focusing in the distance. "Yes, it speaks Corsican," he repeats with emphatic admiration, before saluting us and beginning to walk away, arm in arm with his wife. As the couple wander off, Jean comments to us, in Corsican: "They're a pain in the ass, they are!" and proceeds to detail the way they bargained with their landlady over the price, after they had moved in, and a multitude of other such breadcrumb sins.

In 1864, a survey indicated that over 90 percent of the population of Corsica did not speak French (Marchetti 1989, p. 119); in 1996, a report published by the European Commission estimated that fewer than 10 percent of the population of Corsica spoke Corsican as their first language. What these statistics point to is, first, a shift, and, second, a continuity.

The nature of the shift is obvious: Corsica's entry into France in the late eighteenth century entangled the island's population in a long-standing French project of linguistic unification, which is often traced as far back as the Edict of Villers-Cotterêts in 1539, the first official act in which French was enshrined as a state language (Noer 1988, pp. 20–21)—although the political concerns, motives, and meanings which accompanied the signing of the edict, not to mention the language described as French, have undergone numerous shifts and permutations in the intervening period (McDonald 1989). This project of linguistic unification was famously given a huge boost by the institution of free, compulsory schooling across France in 1882 (Weber 1976; Reed-Danahay 1996). Although historians have highlighted the complexities and ambivalence of schoolteachers' actual attitudes to regional languages and have helped to destabilize the stereotypical image of teachers as fanatical Francophone indoctrinators (Di Meglio 2003; Thiesse 1997; Ozouf and Ozouf 2001), the fact remains that a huge language shift took place in Corsica during the twentieth century.

While the shift is obvious, the nature of the continuity is perhaps slightly more elusive, but no less important. It concerns a certain way of thinking about and problematizing language. Both surveys, in the very form of the questions they asked, assumed languages to be more or less discrete entities which individuals speak or do not speak. Furthermore, they were both driven by a set of problems concerning the way languages map onto named groups of people. The nineteenth-century survey makes sense within the above-mentioned problematic of linguistic unification, whose end point is to produce a fit between French citizens and French-speakers. The statistical inquiry works to identify problem areas where this fit is not perfect. Similarly, the 1996 report, entitled "Euromosaic," fits within a broader project of building a "people's Europe," which would also be a Europe of peoples (Shore 1993), a mosaic of cultural units, each with its "costume, food, music, myths and legends, language or argot, festivals and traditions, and so on" (Green 2005, p. 39). It seeks to interrupt the overcentralization of national entities by encouraging the "flowering" of regional cultures (Shore 1993). While the two projects clearly point in different directions (unification versus diversity), they share, on a more profound level, a set of assumptions about the way languages should map onto named human populations (cf. Green 2005, p. 81) and, by extension, an evaluative framework in which disturbances to this order of things (as when French citizens do not speak French, or when a people has lost its language) are unhealthy or problematic.

This logic undergirds the extremely strong feeling of Corsican nationalists, such as François Alfonsi of the Corsican People's Union (UPC), here speaking in response to an official investigation led by the French National Assembly into *le problème Corse:*

> I consider the question of the Corsican language a humiliation. It is a status discrimination. When my son entered secondary school [*sixième*], we received a piece of paper asking whether we wanted our son to receive Corsican language lessons. It took me three days to answer, and I finally filled in the piece of paper, but I am humiliated. What? In my country, I must ask for my son to be allowed to learn Corsican? . . . We have always refused violence and have never practiced it. We have been hit with unjustified smoke grenades. We have been held in unjustified custody. All of this I can forget. But if tomorrow, my son doesn't speak Corsican, that I will not forget. (Cuq and De Roux 1997, p. 237)

This assumption of a one-to-one correspondence between a language and a people is a comparatively recent phenomenon. During the brief period of Corsican independence in the eighteenth century, the language used by the leaders of the Corsican nation was mostly Tuscan, and while Pascal Paoli's concern with knowledge and education was manifested in his famous institution of a university at Corte, no effort was made to officialize, bring to the fore, or teach a language specific to the island or corresponding to the nation (Di Meglio 2003). While the fact that people in Corsica spoke differently from people in other, nearby places was sometimes noted, the nature and extent of this difference was not a subject of much debate or concern. At the beginning of the twenty-first century, "the Corsican language," or simply "Corsican," has become an incontrovertible fact, albeit one whose value and characteristics, like those of other languages, remains a matter for dispute and controversy.

One could tell this as a story about the imposition of a fixed grid of territorialized difference onto a teeming multiplicity of ways of speaking (Irvine and Gal 2000; cf. Green 2005, p. 81). But we also need to recognize that in the field of language, more straightforwardly than in most, such impositions are to a great extent self-realizing. Insofar as they are understood as misreadings of an underlying reality, it is hard to fathom the extent to which they actually are on a par with and a crucial and formative part of the reality they describe. It might be more productive to think of the notion of discrete linguistic entities as a representation with teeth, one capable of changing the reality it describes (Green 2005, p. 33 and passim). But while this in itself takes care of the general principle, it begs a more specific description of how this process might work in this particular case. This is what this chapter will explore.

Counting as One: An Entity Comes into Being

In the Corsican case, the emergence of the entity which is now the Corsican language is well described by one of the contributors to this process, the sociolinguist Jean-Baptiste Marcellesi, through his coinage of the term "recognition-birth" (*reconnaissance-naissance*), which he defines as: "the symbolic glottopolitical decisions which apply to a linguistic system hitherto classified as dependent [on] another, their linguistic differences being minimized, and which erect these differences into significant distances, thus proceeding to a recognition of that which already existed on the terrain and giving birth by solemn declaration to a new language" (Marcellesi 1986, quoted in Marcellesi 1989, p. 170).

A link between a distinctly Corsican language or dialect (patois) and a Corsican national consciousness was made explicitly from the late nineteenth century onward in Corsican journals such as *A Tramuntana* and, later, *A Cispra,* and authors such as Ghjacumu Thiers have suggested that isolated attempts to establish a Corsican linguistic consciousness can be traced back to the eighteenth century (Thiers 1989, pp. 34–37). It is generally acknowledged, however, that the height of this process in Corsica as in other French regions was during the final three decades of the twentieth century, when Corsican academics explicitly and purposefully set apart the entity that would become known as the Corsican language from what had previously been generally thought of as an Italianate dialect. A foundational moment of this process was the following statement, in the orthography manual *Intricciate è Cambiarine,* by linguists Marchetti and Geronimi: "We name [the] Corsican language, the sum, of all the idioms [*parlers*], distinguished by meagre variations, which are used on the territory of the island of Corsica" (Marchetti and Geronimi 1971, quoted in Di Meglio 2003, p. 520). This heralded, on the one hand, a process of isolating a multiplicity and "counting it as one" (see Badiou 1988, pp. 104ff.) and, on the other, a shift in value terms, from treating the way Corsicans spoke as a (mere) patois to treating it as a (proper) language.

This involved producing an account of a specific set of grammatical regularities for the Corsican language (see Chiorboli 1991). It involved devising a specific orthography which reflected and erected into significance the language's specificities of pronunciation, particularly through the new "trigraphs" *chj* and *ghj,* as alternatives to the Italianate conventions *ci* and *gi* (Marchetti and Geronimi 1971; see Jaffe 1999, p. 218). Perhaps most strikingly, it involved a monumental work of vocabulary reassessment, with five dictionaries appearing since 1997 (Di Meglio 2003). For some, this meant distinguishing and in some cases excluding words which had been borrowed from French and producing neologisms to describe objects which had entered into Corsican reality together with their French designation. One such successful neologism, for instance, is the now fairly widespread use of *scagninu* (from *scagnu,* desk/drawer) to refer to cassette tapes (metaphorically, "little drawers"). An unsuccessful one was the attempt to rename television *spichjafonu* ("mirror-phone," from *spechju,* mirror). This process closely mirrors the ongoing effort by French linguists to keep up with technological advances and thus avoid, more or less felicitously, the inroads of English terminology into French speech (Walkman becomes *baladeur,* email becomes *courriel,* etc.).

As Alexandra Jaffe has shown in her excellent monograph of Corsican language politics (1999), this process of recognition-birth was fraught with a number of internal debates, polarizing the proponents of the Corsican language into various camps: organic versus strategic essentialists disagreed about the ultimate philosophical status of the language; purists who attempted to exclude French (or, in some cases, Italian) influences and unify local divergences clashed with sociolinguists who presented the language as a living "polynomic" entity, where polynomic languages are defined as "languages whose unity is abstract and results from a dialectic, not from the ossification of a single norm, and whose existence is founded on the mass decision of its speakers to give it a specific name and to declare its autonomy from other recognised languages" (Marcellesi 1984, quoted in Chiorboli 1991, p. 8; cf. Thiers 1989). This latter approach, focused on the abstract unity of complex multiplicities, was an extremely interesting deviation from the classic model of discrete, mutually exclusive linguistic entities (Jaffe 1999), but its rather complex theoretical underpinnings made it difficult to put across to a lay audience and, indeed, to translate into teaching practice (Di Meglio 2003; Jaffe 2005).

These somewhat arcane debates notwithstanding, a general sense of Corsican's existence as a language, and not as a mere dialectal subset of another language, had, by 2002, become an element of public consensus in Corsica and in France more generally. This is perhaps not so aptly described as a "mass decision of its speakers" as much as a set of effective and ongoing language planning moves (see Urla 1988). As Chiorboli noted, "the man in the street wants to be spared the explanation, the numbers and the nuances: he wants the 'specialists' to tell him, for instance, whether yes or no, Corsican is a language" (1991, p. 5). The specialists have overwhelmingly said that it is, and the public sense of Corsican as a legitimate language has increasingly been strengthened as differently situated social actors have been enlisted into taking the Corsican language seriously. This has involved a number of media developments, including Corsican-language radio stations (for an excellent account, see Jaffe 1996), Corsican-language sections in newspapers, regional TV programs in Corsican, and some admittedly cautious institutional changes (bilingual signs for town and village names, regional government funding for Corsican-language projects, and most of all, increasingly liberal provisions for teaching the Corsican language in state schools). This is not to say, of course, that ambivalence about the status of the language does not persist, nor that use of Corsican in the media necessarily or uniformly has acted as a real legitimating force, since some people have reacted negatively to what they perceive as an inauthentic form of Corsican (Jaffe 1999; Jensen 1999).

More broadly however, there has been an increasing shift in France and in Europe toward a vocabulary (if not yet in all cases an effective politics) of recognition (Taylor 1994). As the Corsican nationalist leader Jean-Guy Talamoni noted as early as 1996: "All the political organisations now recognise the need to teach the Corsican language. That wasn't the case twenty years ago. Twenty years ago many said it was useless, that one should learn to speak French and English. . . . Today no-one says this any longer; indeed it wouldn't be politically correct to say that the Corsican language is useless; on the contrary everyone is for the Corsican language" (quoted in Cuq and De Roux 1997, p. 214). This general consensus partly explains why, by the end of the millennium, as linguistic anthropologist Janne Jensen noted, the Corsican language had "ceased to be a hot potato politically" (Jensen 1999, p. 85).

And indeed, there was very little trace in my experience in Crucetta of the kind of social stigma attached to speaking patois (as opposed to "proper French") which McDonald (1989), for instance, describes for rural Brittany in the 1970s. On the contrary, Corsican was almost universally held up, by speakers and nonspeakers alike, as an unambiguously good thing in itself—although, as we shall see in the next section, with some reservations concerning its appropriate context. Certainly, the notion that there was a proper linguistic entity which belonged to the category of people known as Corsicans was a matter of no dispute whatsoever. So much so, in fact, that a number of Corsicans to whom I spoke in Crucetta told me rather cautiously that they didn't speak proper Corsican, just "a dialect of Corsican."[1] In other words, whatever we might think of the model of bounded linguistic entities, ethnographically speaking, the Corsican language has been successfully brought into existence as a distinct entity since the 1970s. It is now one of the realities which stalk broadly unquestioned through places such as Crucetta, to the same extent as more banal realities, such as the French language, Corsica, or society. It has fairly successfully made the leap, in other words, from being a "matter of concern" to being a "matter of fact" (Latour 2005; cf. chapter 3).

Counting as Two: Bilingual Schooling

Alexandra Jaffe rightly notes that the elaboration/reconstruction of the Corsican language has to be understood in the context of a broader history of French language politics, and one could characterize the various approaches to the Corsican language in terms of differing responses to a set of French practices and theories about language. In particular, her work shows the extent to which Corsican debates about language since the 1970s operated within and against a broader linguistic ideology, put forward most explicitly by French revolutionary thinkers such as the Abbé Grégoire,[2] author in May 1794 of a report on the necessity of eradicating the dialects and patois spoken on French territory (DeCerteau et al. 1974). The so-called Grégoire Report established a number of linked dichotomies: patois was to French as languages of the past to the language of the future; as the means of a feudal tactic of divide and rule was to the single language of a free and equal people; most important, as languages of the heart were to the language of the mind. Grégoire asks:

> If in our language [French] the political part has barely now been created, what can it be in dialects [*des idiomes*] some of which are full, in truth, of sentimental expressions to depict the sweet effusions of the heart, but are absolutely void of terms relating to politics; while the others are rude and heavy jargons, without any determinate syntax. (Grégoire, in DeCerteau et al. 1974, pp. 300ff.)

The rhetorical choices are illuminating: on the side of dialects, he uses expressions, sentimental, sweet, heart, rude, heavy; on the side of French, he uses terms, politics, syntax. A few months earlier, Barrère, author of a similar report, had put the distinction even more violently. He described French as "the most beautiful language of Europe, the first to have frankly consecrated the rights of man and citizen, the one entrusted with transmitting to the world the most sublime thoughts of freedom and the grandest speculations of politics" (Barrère, in DeCerteau et al. 1974, pp. 291ff.). On the other hand, "Federalism and superstition speak lower-Breton; emigration and hatred of the republic speak German; counter-revolution speaks Italian, and fanaticism speaks Basque. Let us break these instruments of damage and error" (ibid.). Grégoire and Barrère's framings of the difference between the local and the national idioms contributed to establishing an enduring discourse around language, structured around a set of linked dichotomies, structural oppositions forming a "symbolic complex" (Ardener 1989; McDonald 1989; Chapman 1978) within which the opposition between core and periphery came to make sense and was accompanied by its own enduring structures of value—region:France:: patois:French:: nature:culture:: heart:mind:: feeling:reason:: superstition:knowledge:: entrapment:freedom:: old:new:: particular:universal, etc.

Alexandra Jaffe has argued that post-1960s Corsican language politics in Corsica can be categorized in terms of differing kinds of resistance to the hegemony of French (Jaffe 1999, pp. 23–32). "Resistance of reversal" consisted in resisting French language domination but not its structures of value, attempting to show that Corsican, like French, was a proper language with grammar, rules, etc. "Resistance of separation" involved internalizing the diglossic model of Corsican and French as different kinds of language, but reversing or at least equalizing their value—wanting to retain that which made Corsican different from French (warm, private, family-centered, not official). The final form of resistance, which Jaffe terms "radical," attempts to challenge the entire diglossic framework through notions such as that of a polynomic language.

The fragmentation of these different forms of resistance could be seen as responding to some constitutive ambiguities within the process of French linguistic unification itself. The power of the "symbolic complexes" described above, as twentieth-century historians of French nation-building have shown, was precisely that they lent themselves not just to violent denigration (as in the revolutionary rhetoric of Grégoire and Barrère) but also to a more subtle play of hierarchical and pedagogical intertwining, within a broader logic in which the large fatherland engulfs and subsumes the small fatherland (Thiesse 1997). In this vein, the Corsican schoolmaster Jean-Pierre Lucciardi wrote in 1923:

> There have been presidents of the council [the highest political office in Third Republic France], ministers, members of parliament who have spoken out in favor of regionalism, and particularly in favor of an attachment to the language of the small fatherland, and their claims can be summed up in this familiar phrase . . . : a man is allowed to speak the language of his region [*patelin*], indeed, it

is very good for his intellectual development. . . . Not only is Corsican not a
hindrance to the teaching of French, or only a very slight one, but we will further claim that—paradoxical as this may seem—it can even help in learning the
national language. (Quoted in Di Meglio 2003, p. 514)

So, while the current teaching of Corsican in schools such as that in Crucetta
is often portrayed by its proponents as the culmination of a long struggle against
the centralist vision of French schooling, a vision which was often imagined to
come straight from the principles of the French Revolution, a more detailed history
of Third Republic schooling policies shows rather more ambivalence toward and,
in some cases, actual support for all things regional. Anne-Marie Thiesse (1997)
shows the importance given to regional history, geography, and ethnography in early
twentieth-century French schooling. As in Lucciardi's comment above, this regional
content was included following two interlinked principles. First, there was the pedagogical principle according to which learning should proceed from the immediate,
the near, the concrete, toward the more distant and abstract: thus, geography lessons
would start with a description of the *commune,* before moving on to the region,
France, the Continent, and the globe, while history lessons would begin with a roll
call of the region's great citizens, before moving on to the more distant facts of French
and world history. To start near home was thus deemed good for one's intellectual
development. The second principle was a progressive metanarrative of national integration: by starting with regional content and then moving outward in concentric
circles of increasing distance and abstraction, national schooling would help those
people imagined as locals to extend their visceral attachment from the region to the
whole nation. As they learned that their local heritage was part of the greater national
heritage, children's local pride and patriotism would thus grow and be channeled
into national patriotism, a higher sentiment which would combine the virtues of
intellectual abstraction and primordial attachment (Candea forthcoming A).

Some aspects of a similar logic permeated French governmental support for
regional languages at the end of the twentieth century. The official justification for
the teaching of regional languages in public school was expressed in the following
way by the French Ministry of Education: "The Éducation Nationale's duty is to
make this cultural heritage live, to encourage the development of regional languages
and to contribute to their transmission. To forget this responsibility would not be
a mark of modernity. It would lead, on the contrary, to a loss of substance of the
national cultural heritage" (Éducation Nationale 2001, n.p.).

Returning also to the pedagogical principle of concentric circles of belonging
and the move from the concrete to the abstract, the ministry grounded its support
for the teaching of "regional languages and cultures" in the programmatic slogan:
"anchoring oneself so as to be more open."[3] The idea, as Pascal explained every

year in his initial parents-teacher meeting, was not to learn Corsican language and culture in isolation, "for the sake of it," to "stay closed upon oneself," but as the basis for a wider opening onto the world. A pragmatic opening, first of all, since a Corsican-speaker could communicate with Italians and, therefore, Pascal argued, would have an important advantage in this nearby job market. But it would allow also a more general opening up of intellectual and ethical vistas: Pascal, like other proponents of Corsican/French bilingualism, explained that linguists, psychologists, and pedagogues had shown that early bilingualism is good for a child's intellectual development. Without going into technicalities, he explained to parents that it helped children to learn more languages later, but also the early realization that there could be two words meaning the same thing opened up their minds to a kind of multivocality which was not accessible to the monolingual. With bilingualism, Pascal explained, the child realizes that "chalk [French: *craie*] is also *chalk* [Corsican: *calchinella*]. In Dijon, chalk is just chalk." In accordance with the official slogan, the argument was that to be anchored in a double reality is to be more open to the universal (cf. Jaffe 2007).

Deborah Reed-Danahay argues that "local schools, even in the centralised system of France, may work to reinforce local identity, as parents and children resist aspects of national culture and state power" (Reed-Danahay 1996, p. 4). But what happens when the local school, in accordance with state directives, takes it upon itself to reinforce local identity? In a striking inversion of Reed-Danahay's case, some parents and pupils in Crucetta resisted this move, standing up in defense of French remaining the official school language; this position did not usually imply a denigration of Corsican, but a belief that it belonged in the private sphere—a mix of Jaffe's resistance of reversal and of utilitarian approaches to language use. Pascal's attempts to portray the teaching of Corsican as the grounding for the universal, for instance, were often countered by parents arguing that English, rather than Corsican, would be a more appropriate, useful choice—a theme introduced by Pascal himself when he made the link to Italian. To these arguments, Pascal usually replied with an argument about the intrinsic value of Corsican-as-heritage, noting ironically that Corsican in Crucetta was "not exactly a foreign language." In this, the French Ministry of Education and Pascal were in a contingent and somewhat unstable agreement with the Corsican nationalist François Alfonsi who, when asked whether Corsican would be of any use, replied: "Is it interesting to maintain the Corsican language? This is not a question I even ask myself. From an ethical point of view, is it interesting to make a culture disappear in Europe?" (quoted in Cuq and De Roux 1997, p. 239).

But maintenance is not the only aim, and Pascal often repeated that the Corsican language should not be taught only in association with Corsican "cultural content" (*contenus culturels*) or "Corsican things" (*roba Corsa*), "otherwise," Pascal commented, "we're just going in circles." One critical aim of bilingualism is to change the status of the Corsican language and to put it on a par with French— Jaffe's resistance of reversal. This new status cannot be achieved if one limits the use of Corsican to Corsican things, even though these have remained a part of the curriculum.

Thus, in a region-wide training course for bilingual teachers, which I attended, one afternoon was given to writing songs in Corsican and dancing the traditional square dance–like quadrille. For the latter event, tables were pushed to the sides of the room, and four couples took the floor, while everyone else sat around, laughing and clapping. The first eight dancers were Pascal, three other experienced Corsican teachers, and myself—ever the enthusiastic anthropologist—along with three young and embarrassed teachers who had been jeered, tugged, and coaxed into joining us. Lively violin-led music started pouring out of the karaoke machine, and I was surprised at the participants' precise memory of the moves—performed with varying degrees of grace—of which we had been given only a brief reminder before the dance. I flailed somewhat, but the whole exercise was done in a general atmosphere of slightly embarrassed fun, amid claps and shouts from all sides. After the first dance, I asked where they all got their dancing fluency from. One of the more experienced teachers, as it happens, was a member of a regular quadrille group. The young teachers, on the other hand, had learned the quadrille at teacher training college (Institut Universitaire de Formation des Maîtres; IUFM). I quite candidly asked why that was. Pascal laughingly took up my question: "that's a good question. Why *do* they teach quadrille at the IUFM?" He was partly acknowledging everyone's slight embarrassment at the situation and partly making a dig at the new academic teacher training colleges—a common target for the older teachers trained at the *écoles normales* (the previous, more practice-oriented teacher training schools). A young teacher replied rather stiffly: "well, it's the culture" (*ben, c'est la culture*). The uncomfortable proximity of some of this *contenu culturel* and older definitions of Corsican folklore did not, as this example shows, go unnoticed, and there was some uneasiness among the teachers when it was felt that a concern with the paraphernalia of authentic Corsicanness was taking up too much space in the curriculum or being taught for its own sake.

This was the logical justification for one of Pascal's practices which was most often criticized and misunderstood, not only by parents who were openly opposed to bilingualism but even by those who were generally sympathetic, namely, the teaching of subjects such as math and biology in Corsican. Pascal went to great effort to teach such subjects in Corsican. Since the scientific vocabulary of Corsican was until the 1970s non-existent, teaching math or biology in the language meant learning to use unfamiliar terms created by Corsican linguists in recent decades. In fact, the capacity to teach scientific subjects in Corsican was one of Pascal's claims to fame in the world of bilingual teachers, many of whom found it very difficult to go beyond the more well-trodden paths of subjects such as history and the arts. Therefore, the children who, in Pascal's class, learned to speak in Corsican about spatial geometry and the workings of the human body possessed a competency which few native Corsican-speaking adults had—unless they happened to be linguists or very experienced Corsican bilingual teachers. This is why the practice of teaching sciences in Corsican was often difficult to get across even to fairly responsive parents. Its logic appears, however, in the context of the enduring metaphorical complexes examined earlier. This often misunderstood teaching practice highlighted one of the main breaks between twenty-first-century bilingual teaching and previous region-oriented French schooling practices: the attempt to break with any remaining hint of hierarchical relation between Corsican (for culture) and French (for everything else). Teaching math and biology in Corsican was thus a bold attempt to operate directly upon the nature of the Corsican language.

Naturalizing Competence: 1. Continentals

In the previous chapter, I described the interplay between categories of identity and the multiplicity of connections which simultaneously gave them substance and blurred their edges. Similarly, French and Corsican as clear-cut linguistic entities were present in Crucetta not just in the classroom, but in many village spaces, with people constantly making distinctions in terms of whether or not (or how well) they and others spoke these languages. And yet they were present alongside and in interaction with a multiplicity of ways of speaking which fell in between clear-cut linguistic boundaries.

Whereas Pascal, in his classroom, was attempting to turn a group of mostly Francophone children, many of whom were Continental, into a bilingual population, at the level of general categorizations, essence was often assumed to trump process. I was thus often told, by Corsicans as well as Continentals in Crucetta, that Continentals couldn't ever *really* learn to speak Corsican. Alexandra Jaffe notes (personal communication) that, in her own fieldwork, she encountered Continentals who were held by Corsicans to be very competent speakers, which suggests (as do Pascal's efforts) that such essentialized attributions of (in)competence, while common, were not universal.

Where such essentialized binaries were invoked, however, they drew much of their persuasive power from fine-grained distinctions in pronunciation, which provided a seemingly empirical anchor. Both Corsicans and Continentals in Crucetta often claimed that Continentals can't pronounce in the Corsican fashion, with the proper stresses and sounds. Often singled out by Corsican-speakers were Continentals' failure to emulate the distinction between open and closed vowels (both are used in Corsican, but in patterns which differ markedly from French patterns) and, most important, stress patterns. French stress patterns almost invariably fall on the final syllable, whereas in Corsican the tendency is toward the penultimate syllable. Continentals who had mastered this (to a Francophone ear) counterintuitive stress pattern were then thoroughly stumped when they encountered the fairly wide range of words which were stressed on the antepenultimate syllable. A short example of the range of pronunciation differences for one name may be clearer than a long description (see figure 6.1).

Ponte Leccia is a small town in the north of Corsica. I have purposefully picked the example of a proper name here because of their saliency even within French speech: Corsicans tend to pronounce Corsican proper names in a distinctly Corsican way while speaking French, whereas many non-Corsicans do not. This is also true of other Corsican words and even many Italian ones. Thus, for instance, many Corsicans pronounce *pizza* as a Corsican word in French speech and give it the Corsican/Italian plural *pizze,* rather than the French *pizzas.* Pronouncing a Corsican name (or word) correctly within French speech is thus one of the more salient clues to Corsicanness which people pick up on during "telling," as discussed in the previous chapter.

In turn, and as a result, this habit of mixing Corsican pronunciation with French speech was often identified and emulated by Continentals who were keen to demonstrate a more long-term experience of Corsica. Continentals in Crucetta often noted in vernacular discussions of the way Corsicans spoke that the latter "swallow the last syllable"; that is to say, they read the unfamiliar penultimate syllable stress pattern as an actual elision of the final syllable—probably encouraged in this belief by the fact that certain final vowels of Corsican words are weakened, or truncated, although they are rarely completely eliminated. Continentals in Crucetta were clearly not alone in this misreading of Corsican pronunciation. For instance, the popular and authoritative French guidebook *Le Guide du Routard* gives the following advice to Continental tourists: "In Corsica, you will soon notice that the inhabitants usually 'swallow' the endings of names. Thus Bonifacio is pronounced 'Bounifatch'; Porto-Vecchio, 'Porto-Vèk' and Sartène, 'Sarté'" (*Guide du Routard* 2003, p. 60). This text is particularly revealing in that the writers fail to distinguish between the Corsican pronunciation of the town of "Buni*faziu*" (four syllables, accented on the penultimate) and the fact that the Corsican name of Sartène is actually "Sar*tè*" (two syllables, accented on the last). Missing this subtle distinction, they represent both of these as truncated versions of the French names.

These mistakes become, for Continentals, privileged insider knowledge into Corsican ways of speaking. So, to continue the example above, the Corsican pronunciation of Ponte Leccia is reproduced by many Continentals as Ponte Letch.

"Ponte Leccia" is a small town in the centre of Northern Corsica

---

1)"Corsican" pronunciations of this name (with tonic accents marked by ˈ , and sub-tonic marked by ˌ) is: [ˌpɔn.ntɛ.ˈlɛ.tʃia] or sometimes [ˌpɔn.nta.ˈlɛ.tʃia].

The marking characteristics of this pronunciation being:

➔   tonic accent on the penultimate syllable

➔   open [ɔ] and [ɛ] sounds and stressed [n]

➔   regional variation over pronunciation. A now extinct name for the town (which I came across in 19th century documents) was "Ponte alla Leccia", hence the vestigial /a/ in certain pronunciations

2)"French" pronunciation of the same is: [pɔ̃.ˌte.le.ˈtʃia], sometimes [pɔ̃.ˌte.le.ˈʃia] or [pɔ̃.ˌte.le.ˈkia]

the marking characteristics of these pronunciations are

➔   tonic accent on the final syllable

➔   nasalised [ɔ̃] ("on") sound and open [e]

➔   uncertainty over pronunciation of final "ccia" sound

FIGURE 6.1. Pronunciation of Ponte Leccia

Ironically, this way of pronouncing, which many Continentals consider to be pronouncing *à la Corse,* is recognized by many Corsicans as just another Continental mispronunciation.

Another set of issues which crystallize around the pronunciation of Corsican names are those of actual comprehension. Jaffe notes that, in dealings with certain Continentals (in her example, a Parisian travel agent), Corsicans will often pronounce their own names in what I have described above as the French fashion. This reflects their acknowledgment of the fact that, pronounced in the Corsican manner, their names would most probably be misunderstood.[4] Similarly, many Corsicans, especially those working in tourism-related jobs, pronounced place and people names in the French manner when they feel they are speaking to a Continental who might be disoriented by the Corsican pronunciation—or, simply and more generally, out of habit, even with other Corsican-speakers.[5]

I remarked on this to my Continental neighbor Cécile and gave her the example of a Corsican employee in a tourist-oriented bar who, in conversation with me, had pronounced the name of the village Pigna [pi'ɲa] (with French stress) instead of ['pi ɲa] (with Corsican stress). Cécile answered, "It's normal; they put themselves on [the tourists'] level. Me too, at first, when I arrived, I appreciated it when people said [pi'ɲa]. [piɲ] isn't on the map." Cécile's response deserves some unpacking. First, she is distancing herself from the basic Continental tourist, both through her life history ("Me too, at first . . .") and linguistically, by her use of the "Continental approximant" [piɲ]. While arguing that Corsican-speakers should show deference to Continental tourists, she marks the fact that she herself can play on both codes (even though her [piɲ] is not the same as my ['pi ɲa]—but this is a difference she does not recognize, while a Corsican-speaker would). This example shows the intricate process through which distinctions between languages and ways of speaking constantly emerge, fade, and reemerge, while assumptions that there is a boundary remain stable.

My own slightly special case highlights the saliency of pronunciation in people's definitions of each other's language competence. As it happens, Romanian pronunciation has a partially overlapping set of differences with French in terms of stress patterns and vowel sounds, and being a French/Romanian bilingual helped me to get attuned to the specificities of Corsican pronunciation (where they mapped onto Romanian) faster than would have been possible for a French monolingual. As a result, from my first few weeks in Crucetta, even when my spoken Corsican still consisted merely of a few words and stock phrases, I was repeatedly shown off by Corsicans to their friends for my pronunciation. "Wait, listen to this," my upstairs neighbor would say to a dubious and unimpressed cousin who had come to visit from another hamlet, and to me: "say 'babbu' [father]." And I would obligingly switch from my markedly Parisian French into an emulation of her pronunciation, which in the International Phonetic Alphabet, one might transcribe as ['βaβu]—a slightly attenuated *b*, a closed *a*, and a stress on the first syllable. My neighbor would rest her case: "There! Even ours [i.e., her children], they can't say it. They say [ba'bu]"—hard *b*, open *a*, stress on the final syllable—"He speaks Corsican like us!"

This was so excessive an overstatement, given my lack of even basic vocabulary, that it highlights the importance given to pronunciation in people's definitions of language competence. More generally on this issue, I refer the reader to Jaffe's excellent discussion of the complex reactions to a foreign learner of Corsican, which involve contextually overestimating or underestimating the personal ability of the learner (Jaffe 1999, pp. 191–200). Jaffe, who was also repeatedly told that she spoke Corsican "like us," notes in particular that very low expectations of foreign learners mean that their fluency tends to be widely overestimated. Although this certainly rings true, I would add that, as my own case suggests, this overestimation of competency was not just a result of my making fewer mistakes than expected, but rather to my making, as it were, the wrong mistakes. Both in terms of pronunciation and later even more obviously in terms of grammar and vocabulary, I made a number of mistakes based on my mapping Corsican onto Romanian, or in some cases onto Spanish. Such mistakes, however, were often inaudible to ears attuned to French-based errors. This gives an interesting insight into the ways in which clear distinctions are built out of a myriad of tiny connections and disconnections.

This general consensus on Continentals' linguistic incompetence found further confirmation in the fact that many Continental holiday makers and part-time residents expressed their keenness to learn the Corsican language—as part of a more general *engouement* for an authentic experience of Corsica—but rarely ever got around to doing so. In most cases, Jaffe has argued, this is partly because their own commitment was often rather superficial, as was the actual encouragement among their Corsican-speaking neighbors and acquaintances (Jaffe 1999, pp. 192–193). Continentals who had lived for a while in Crucetta often claimed that they could speak some Corsican, but didn't dare, or that they could understand but not speak, at least not beyond a short greeting or phrase. Petru, in the context of a broader discussion of Continentals' affection for traditional Corsican farm implements and the like, thus noted, in Corsican (French text in italics): "Everyone who comes here, all the Parisians and such, they all want to learn Corsican. But it's difficult for a Parisian—a real Parisian, not like you—it's very difficult. Maybe they can say 'va be' ['how are you,' which Petru mispronounced as a French-speaker might: babé], but no more than that. Maybe '*The donkey is* the donkey [*l'ane, c'est* u sumere].'"

The consensus on Continentals' incapacity to learn Corsican was such that real Corsican fluency was automatically taken to imply that one was Corsican, in the fine contextuality of telling which I described in the previous chapter. This was brought home to me one day near the end of my stay, when I had been conducting a fairly lengthy discussion with a Corsican colleague at the supermarket at which I worked during the summer. This was our first meeting, and after we had implicitly ascertained that we both spoke Corsican, we switched to that language. I saw my colleague becoming increasingly puzzled as my account of myself wore on and I mentioned studying in England, growing up in Paris, being born in Romania. At this point, she interrupted me and asked, with a sharpness which bordered on anger: "But *are* you Corsican then or not?" Clearly, she had taken my—relative—fluency not just as a sign of Corsicanness, but as tantamount to a clear statement to that effect, and she felt cheated to discover that I was not, as if I had been engaging with her under false pretenses. This episode made me rethink retrospectively the tenor of another such first meeting in which I had spoken to a stranger in Corsican. A few sentences in, this man, a fluent Corsican-speaker who was the caretaker at a chapel I had been visiting, told me point-blank and without to my mind any kind of *à propos,* that he was a *pinzutu* (a Continental). I remembered my puzzlement at the time, particularly given the slightly derogatory nature of this term. In retrospect, he was probably trying to avoid precisely the kind of uncomfortable situation in which I had found myself with my colleague. He was, incidentally, the only self-proclaimed Continental I met during all of my time in Crucetta who had—or was willing to exhibit—any level of fluency in Corsican.

Naturalizing Competence: 2. Franco-Maghrebians

This naturalization of Continental incompetence was particularly interesting by contrast to the ways in which the linguistic abilities of other populations were evaluated. I was surprised a few months into my fieldwork when a new acquaintance, to whom I had said a few phrases in Corsican, exclaimed for the benefit of the whole bar that I "spoke Corsican like an Arab." The statement implied that I spoke it well, although given the marginal position of Franco-Maghrebians in Crucetta, it was a rather ambivalent way of giving praise. Following this incident, I started to clock Corsican-speakers' attitudes to the linguistic abilities of those they designated as *les Arabes.* Just as widespread as the belief that Continentals couldn't speak Corsican properly was the belief that many Franco-Maghrebians had fully mastered the language. From my own limited experience of working at the supermarket, it did not seem to be the case that the Franco-Maghrebians who were held to or claimed to speak Corsican had a much higher level of fluency than their Continental colleagues—although to test the impression would have required a more intensive ethnography of Franco-Maghrebian ways of speaking, particularly in more private contexts.

Certainly, both Continentals and Franco-Maghrebians working at the supermarket tended to be aware of a set of stock Corsican salutations or simple phrases. What set Franco-Maghrebians apart from Continentals in practice, however, was their willingness to use said phrases. Younger Franco-Maghrebians would often hail Corsicans loudly in Corsican: *chi faci?* (what are you doing?), *ti campi?* (are you enjoying yourself?), or answer their French requests with *va bè* (that's fine). These expressions were usually delivered in a joking tone, as part of the generalized banter which formed the fabric of relations among Corsicans, Continentals, and Franco-Maghrebians in the supermarket. On one occasion, while I was discussing my return to Cambridge, one of the Franco-Maghrebi employees who was on very good terms with my (Corsican) boss suggested, in front of him and a large audience, that I take my boss back with me to Cambridge as a specimen of the "primitive Corsican man." He proceeded to imitate the boss's Corsican accent, caricaturing it into an idiotic gurgle. My boss, in the same joking tone, told him to enjoy playing the funny man while he could, because one of these days he was going to get "bumped off."

Although in this case perfectly amiable, there was an obvious underlying tenseness to this kind of banter in the broader context in which stories frequently circulated about actual acts of mob violence in which Franco-Maghrebians had been beaten or even killed, and Franco-Maghrebian families driven from villages by groups of armed and masked men. It is perhaps unsurprising, therefore, that the linguistic competence of Franco-Maghrebians was not always straightforwardly a ticket to integration. Edwin Ardener wrote of Pakistanis in Lewis that they "may not all speak the fluent Gaelic that legend says, but the legend marks their assimilation to the averageness of strangeness that characterizes incomers. No amount of Gaelic would turn them into Gaels, but their existence is used to contrast with those incomers who have learned no Gaelic at all" (Ardener 1989, p. 220). Many Corsicans, such as Pascal the bilingual teacher, were similarly convinced of the integrative virtues of Franco-Maghrebians learning to speak Corsican, and examples of Franco-Maghrebians who had learned Corsican were often held up as marks of success by proponents of bilingual schooling and, in a different sense, by nationalists promoting an open definition of the Corsican people as a community of destiny (see chapter 5). This belief in the integrative value of the Corsican language reflected broader French discourses about the integrative potential of French, as described, for instance, by Ralph Grillo in his study of institutional attitudes toward immigrants in 1980s France (Grillo 1985).

And yet, linguistic interactions in the supermarket pointed to the limits of this model in the case of Corsican. Not only was it the case that (perceived) linguistic fluency did not straightforwardly negate deeply held assumptions about Franco-Maghrebians' difference, but this fluency in itself could occasionally become an object of resentment. It was not uncommon, for instance, for a Corsican worker who was addressed in Corsican in this bantering tone by a Franco-Maghrebian to answer quite seriously in Corsican *va a cacà* (piss off), or mutter darkly along the lines of "oh, so you speak Corsican now, do you?" One Corsican man went so far as to tell me explicitly that he simply hated to hear an *Arabe* speak Corsican. Outright racism, although clearly present in his case, is not by itself sufficient to explain this rather strange sentiment, which also harks to enduring models about the respective value of French and Corsican.

On the one hand, the rather ambiguous place of working-class Corsican-speakers within broader French regimes of value may form part of the backdrop for these virulent reactions. The positive valorization of Corsican through cultural regionalism and tourism is not so hegemonic as to have completely eradicated other stigmatizing discourses of Corsican as patois, as a marker of rurality, peripherality, and lack of distinction. In this context, the bantering use of Corsican by non-Corsicans was often interpreted as a form of outright mockery. This was not always a misreading on the Corsicans' part: in some contexts, the Franco-Maghrebians (and, I might add, some Continentals) *were* explicitly mocking the Corsicans, as in the preceding anecdote of the "primitive Corsican man." Down this road lie some of the most virulent and unpleasant forms of integralism born of parallel experiences of disenfranchisement and competing discourses of victimhood (Holmes 2000; Hewitt 2005; Candea 2006).

On the other hand, common conceptualizations of Corsican as a language of closeness, familiarity, and intimacy (Jaffe 1999, pp. 92–103) make it available for such reactions of possessiveness and rejection, marking out a space of cultural intimacy (Herzfeld 1997) into which Franco-Maghrebians might be perceived as intruding. The dynamic is very different in the case of French, as the following episode illustrates. At lunchtime, many supermarket employees would retire singly or in twos and threes to a small air-conditioned common room in the back of the building. A few feet from the milling throng of eager shoppers and confused tourists, we relaxed for a while, and while some stuck to their pre-prepared sandwiches or lunch boxes, others took their chances with the yucky/exciting lottery of the large fridge, which was full of damaged or unsalable items brought in by various employees over the course of the morning. Strange how a windowless, neon-lit yet reliably cool room can at times seem a preferable alternative to the sensory whirlwind of sea, mountain, and sky; smells, sun, and wind, which hit you even in the supermarket parking lot. A strange space of intimacy this was, and on that particular day, it revealed itself as a highly revocable one, too. Two Franco-Maghrebian young men, who were chatting in Moroccan over their sandwiches, were rudely interrupted by a French colleague, a teammate of one of them. "Hey you bloody *bics,* speak French, you're not in your country [*chez vous*] here." *Bics* is a racist term, derived from the word *biquot,* or billy goat, and the phrase *chez vous* is an untranslatably situational way of saying "at home," in your country, on your own turf—a mix of all of which was implied in this particular context. The sentence was so outrageous that the four or five onlookers, myself included, were convinced that this had to be a particularly tasteless and unsubtle bit of banter; some, including one of the two young men, the teammate of the man who had spoken, giggled. His friend, however, looked the slightly older man straight in the eye and replied steadfastly, "I am *chez moi* here." To which the first man, far from backing down, replied: "Yeah, you think so, but really you're not!" The argument escalated until the first man shouted: "Here, you speak French!" and standing up with a final look of menace, stormed out of the room. A heavy silence followed, emphasizing the slight yet maddeningly persistent hum of the neon lights.

While French, as I have argued above, following Grillo, could easily come to stand both for an avenue of integration and for a coercive marker of incorporation, it would have been unthinkable for this exchange to center on an injunction to speak Corsican. In this complex maelstrom of linguistic essentialisms, mapping languages onto people and policing "who spoke what" were enduring concerns which clashed powerfully with the valorization of multilingual fluencies in Pascal's classroom.

Interlanguages

This concern with mapping languages onto groups of people also clashed, at least at first sight, with the multiplicity of ways in which people spoke, the interlanguages which formed the shifting ground against which the vision of bounded languages was made to stand out, just as the myriad connections and disconnections of identity were resolved into categorical oppositions. Indeed, like the Corsican things discussed in chapter 4, Corsican ways of speaking broke down into very different genres: alongside the academic Corsican spoken by linguists at the University of Corsica and schoolteachers such as Pascal, there were the various "dialects of Corsican" as many people in Crucetta described their own ways of speaking. But there were also a number of often minute language practices which marked out as Corsican the French speech of some people. Between the two poles of speaking French with a "Corsican accent" (*l'accent Corse*—with its specific rhythmic and tonal patterns) and speaking Corsican, the majority of people's actual speech was made up of what Jaffe has described as "mixed language varieties in which there is an interpenetration of both lexical and syntactic features from Corsican and French" (Jaffe 1999, p. 112). These have been classified by the Corsican linguist Filippi into two categories: "regional French of Corsica" (Français régional de Corse, or FRC), and Franco-Corsican (Francorse), which I will use here rather loosely, because it maps onto a distinction which people in Crucetta themselves drew (albeit not in those terms). As defined by Filippi, FRC is French with a range of pronunciation features, grammatical constructions, and lexical shifts taken to be derived from Corsican, while Francorse refers to the introduction into French speech of neologisms based on Corsican words (Filippi 1992, quoted with examples in Jaffe 1999).

Common features of FRC which I encountered in Crucetta include:

- the repetition of a phrase at the end of a sentence for emphasis—a usual feature in Corsican, but absent from standard French: *"Je roule comme il faut, je roule"* ("I'm driving at the right speed, *I'm driving*")
- the use of the hypothetical future: "Il roulait trop vite, il *sera tombé* dans le ravin" ("He was driving too fast, he *will have fallen* in the ravine")

- certain pronunciation features, which are further inflected and localized by micro-region and even occasionally by village

On the other hand, examples of Francorse used by people in Crucetta included words such as:

- *goff,* to mean "ugly," "nasty," "bad" (French: *moche*), from Corsican *goffu*
- *apitchigué,* to mean "hanging on" (French: *accroché*), from Corsican *apichjicatu*
- *chtoumagué,* to mean "disgusted" (French: *dégouté*), from Corsican *stumacatu*
- *briague,* to mean "drunk" (French: *saoul*), from Corsican *briacu*
- *s'affaquer,* meaning "to arrive, to come over" (French: *s'amener*), from Corsican *affaccà.* The reflexive form is taken from the French construction.

In Crucetta, the distinction between FRC and Francorse mapped onto a generational and evaluative difference. The more marked linguistic forms covered by what Filippi calls FRC were usually associated with elderly and/or rural and/or working-class people and commonly depicted (rightly or wrongly) as resulting from an imperfect grasp of French, while Francorse tended to be seen as the province of the young: an amusing, inventive, and *new* way of speaking, even though many people, first and foremost the schoolteachers, rejected it as a corrupt slang. This is reflected in Filippi's own terminology, which if treated ethnographically, has strong evaluative correlations: the official, scientific-sounding FRC covers most of what is usually referred to as (merely) a Corsican accent and, to some extent, consecrates the lexical shifts which, as Jaffe notes, are often perceived and mocked (by Corsicans themselves) "as funny/shameful bilingual malapropisms made by Corsicans for whom French was a second language" (Jaffe 1999, p. 211). It was FRC, for instance, which in the previous section, formed the basis of my Franco-Maghrebian colleague's parody of my Corsican boss's way of speaking. On the other hand, Francorse is modeled on the more common Franglais ("Frenglish") which was so heavily ridiculed, lampooned, and feared in certain intellectual French circles in the 1980s and '90s (cf. Ager 1999). Like Franglais and unlike Français régional de Corse, Francorse carries a negative connotation of linguistic impurity. This type of negative evaluation of Francorse was common among bilingual schoolteachers who, by their position, considered themselves experts on both French and Corsican. They often commented, between amusement and consternation, on their pupils' (and their children's) use of Francorse expressions, which they found highly unaesthetic when they were not undecipherable. This complex double evaluation reflected in part the fact that the schoolteachers perceived Francorse as a challenge to the integrity of

Corsican, which was conceived as a language-in-making whose integrity had to be preserved, whereas FRC (while it reflected badly on its speakers) could hardly be seen as a challenge to the French language as a whole.[6]

Another salient interstitial feature of Corsican language practices was the common use of interjections. Some were actual Corsican words, such as *mi* (look) or *aetta* (to express surprise and disbelief, from the Corsican word for lightning, *saetta*); others were merely expressive sounds, such as *po po po* (to indicate surprise or concern),[7] *umboh* (to indicate one doesn't know something), or *aiò* (meaning "come on"). Greetings between rural and working-class Corsicans in Crucetta, for instance, were often reduced to the interjection *euh!* A sketch performed by the young Corsican comedy duo Tzek and Pido on an open-air stage in Ile Rousse illustrates both the importance of such interjections and the ambivalence of Corsicans' attitudes to their own linguistic practices: the sketch begins with a voice-over announcing that Corsican regional television is about to broadcast a scene entirely in Corsican for the education of its viewers. The two comedians then enter and play out the meeting of two old friends. The first few minutes, during which the friends spot and greet each other, sit down at a café, order, express their surprise at their sudden meeting and their general feelings about the situation, are conducted entirely through these interjections, without a single actual word being uttered. This is, of course, an exaggeration, but while part of the comedy resided in Tzek and Pido's mime work, most of the humor lay in how close this scene was to the type of real-life situations the audience had encountered and taken part in. The sketch was also a wry comment on the different regimes of value within Corsican language practices, resting on the obvious mismatch between the official educational announcement (associated with academic Corsican) and the interjectional speech (associated with Corsican rurality).

It was interesting in this context (and obviously unknown to the various parties involved) that the official curriculum for Corsican language and culture in primary schools includes a section on "onomatopoeia expressing sentiments or reactions: aiò, anh anh, à eh, auh." On one occasion, Pascal, upon hearing a pupil preface a French sentence to a friend with *mi!* interrupted the lesson to comment on this, telling the class they could always tell Corsicans by the fact that they say *mi*. If they went to Paris and heard someone saying *mi!* he explained, they could be certain that person was Corsican. On another occasion, while I was tape-recording a Corsican session in Crucetta's pre-primary classroom, among the mostly French speech of the pupils, four-year-old Jacques, who was being pushed by his friend Mohammed, shouted, "*Aiò,* Mohammed!" The teacher laughed and told me: "There, you'll have a beautiful *aiò*." As with Corsican things in chapter 4, then, distinctions between merely Corsican and really Corsican language practices were constantly shifting in and out of view.

In practice, however, what is described as accent, FRC, Francorse, interjections, and even actual code-switching (Jaffe 1999, pp. 108–112) were combined seamlessly to create forms of language practice which were crucial to the practice of telling described in the previous chapter. While being able to speak fluent Corsican was almost infallibly taken as a sign that one was Corsican, there were many people on the island who self-defined as Corsican and who couldn't speak the language. Gradations of accent, interjections, and use of stock phrases formed a complex and variegated field within which a person's Corsicanness or otherwise could be quite finely mapped—albeit not always correctly.

Here is a detailed example of one such instance, after I had nearly backed into someone's car in the Ile Rousse supermarket's parking lot. The driver honked, I braked in time, and we both continued parking. I got out of the car and said apologetically (Corsican text in italics):

"Ah, je suis vraiment désolé. *Po po po!* Je conduis vraiment mal, hein?" ["Ah, I'm really sorry. *Po po po!* I'm such a bad driver, eh?"]

To which he replied:

"Oh, vous inquiètez pas, ça va, *m'hè dijà accadutu!*" ["Oh don't worry, it's OK. *It's happened to me before.*"]

I took the code-switching hint and answered:

"*Scusatemi,* hein, *ùn faccia micca attenzione,* enfin je suis desolé." ["*I apologize,* right, *I wasn't paying attention,* anyway, I'm sorry."][8]

My interjection (together with other factors, such as my physical appearance, the fact I was driving a car with Corsican license plates, and my accent in French, which by that point had begun to sound quite distinctly Corsican) signaled a Corsicanness to which my interlocutor responded with a brief code-switch by which he signaled his. I followed up with a sentence spoken mostly in Corsican, with brief switches to French. It is difficult to mark out, even in my own case, how much of this kind of "linguistic flirtation" or my attempt at "phatic communion" (Malinowski 1972) was intentional—to a great extent, the assumption of recognizably local forms of speech became an ingrained habit in situations of stress or unfamiliarity. Experientially at least, this was not an attempt at mimicry or disguise, but a form of familiarity and politeness, a way of establishing connection, and putting the other person (and myself) at ease. The fact that this habit was more than utilitarian was brought home to me when I realized that I had carried it over to situations of stress or unfamiliarity in Paris—where a Corsican accent was no longer a social asset in any meaningful sense.

Descent and Alliance

The interlanguages I described in the last section blurred distinctions between French and Corsican not just in the direct linguistic sense of borrowing between two languages, but also in another, more pervasive sense. After my fieldwork, I spent some time with a friend who, though a long-time resident of Paris, is originally from the south of France. When we discussed these interlinguistic practices, I was surprised to find how many phrases, words, and expressions—and also forms of accentuation and intonation—she recognized as characteristic of southern France. Some of this may be explained by a strong Corsican presence in the south of France. Primarily, however, this is an instance of the "denied resemblance" (Harrison 2003) which is involved in the delineation of geo-linguistic boundaries. In other words, some (although by no means all) of what in Crucetta was identified as a specifically Corsican way of speaking French would have been identified in Marseilles as a southern French way of speaking French.

This realization involves a shift in the way we think about relationality, somewhat analogous to the classic opposition in anthropology between descent and alliance theories of kinship (Dumont 2006): the interlinguistic practices described above are often seen by speakers, and sometimes by linguists, as arising from the mixing of two distinct languages (rather like the way, in descent theory, alliance is a problem for kinship groups). By contrast, what I have been tracking in this chapter is the way in which distinct languages are produced out of the indeterminacy of a contingent and shifting field of ways of speaking (rather like the way kinship groups are an effect of patterns of alliance)—a field of ways of speaking whose characteristics are not exhausted by the designations Corsican, French, or romance. This production is the effect of various framing devices, such as the recognition-birth implemented by Corsican linguists or the bilingual teaching of Pascal, and also of people's everyday ascriptions of essentialized competencies to each other, or attempts to police who speaks what in the supermarket.

These framing devices operate upon the multiple ways in which people actually use language in Crucetta and their different ranges of competencies: not simply linguistic fluency in French and/or Corsican, but fluency with the complex language practices described above, which are inseparable from their equally complex valuations—as mixed, incorrect, old, young, funny, inventive, shameful, etc. What Malcolm Chapman argues for Brittany resonates to some extent with the Corsican case: "The information passed in Breton conversation is not . . . of a different and more intimate kind than that passed in French. . . . the linguistic resource is one that is used to map people and events in a very sophisticated way; you need to be bilingual in order to appreciate how this is done. [However, y]ou are not, as a French monolingual, excluded from secrets" (Chapman 1992, p. 45). Of course, two Corsican-speakers may choose to exclude non-Corsican-speakers (be they Corsican or Continental) from their conversation—and bilingual teachers often shake their heads sadly at the fact that parents often switch to Corsican when they want to keep secrets from their children. But many people on the island (Corsican and Continental), while unable to engage in a conversation in Corsican, or even to follow one, are still aware of and fluent in the linguistic subtleties of accent, pronunciation, Francorse, and FRC. Their occasional exclusion from a conversation between Corsican-speakers was little compared to the wider disconnection of the more recent incomers who are not able to play on and appreciate the subtle and complex language practices which I have touched on so briefly above. In other words, what Chapman describes as an opposition between monolingualism and bilingualism shades here into a multiplicity of degrees and kinds of fluency, each bringing with it its own degrees and kinds of (always partial) intimacy.

7

Knowing

The tree imposes the verb "to be," but the rhizome is
woven of the conjunction "and . . . and . . . and . . ."

—DELEUZE AND GUATTARI 1980

Collisions and Connections

This story starts with a crash. On a rainy Thursday morning in February 2003, as
I was heading toward the regional archives in Bastia, I lost control of the car in
a particularly treacherous bend and collided rather spectacularly with an oncom-
ing van. Luckily and rather incomprehensibly, no one was hurt, although the
small bottle-green Peugeot which I had bought soon after arriving in Crucetta was
crumpled beyond (affordable) repair. In the following weeks, I realized quite how
much I had come to rely upon the fragile lump of metal which was now deposited
on the tarmac of a garage in Ponte Leccia. But the now immobile vehicle was fast
turning into a millstone around my neck. I could not afford to fix the car and on my
relatively meager research budget could barely face the expense of having it towed
to a dump, and the garage owner was threatening to charge for my use of his space.

Fortunately, I knew someone. A colleague of my mother in Paris was close friends with a young Continental woman who was living with her Corsican fiancé in Bastia. Stéphanie was an energetic woman in her late twenties who had recently finished a master's thesis on Proust, and when I met her she was a secondary school teacher and an aspiring novelist. Her fiancé, Antoine, was a short and muscular man some years her junior—calm, kind, and collected. Antoine, who worked as a part-time firefighter, sported short dark hair and a close-cropped beard, and never parted from his knife. "It's a Corsican thing," he once explained, acknowledging with a wry smile that it produced no end of teasing from his colleagues at the Bastia fire station, who called him Conan the Barbarian or "the little shepherd." Be that as it may, Antoine made no secret of his attachment to Corsican things: his knife, his band which sang polyphonic songs, his village, and the little chapel in which he and Stéphanie would be married in the summer. Antoine was also into online role-playing games, a passion Stéphanie found hard to fathom. All in all, there was more than enough warmth and happiness in Antoine and Stéphanie's flat in the suburbs of Bastia to spare for a stray, disoriented anthropologist—and I sought their haven more than once.

Antoine, it turns out, had a brother, Phillippe, who knew about cars and many other things. So, when I called Stéphanie in desperation after my accident, she suggested Phillippe might be able to fix things. I arranged to meet Phillippe at the garage in Ponte Leccia, some fifty kilometers away from Crucetta, to hand over my car keys. He agreed to tow my car using his pickup truck and to give me some money for the remains of the wreck. He had his own uses for it. But first, I had to get to Ponte Leccia, and thus see Corsica through the eyes of the carless. The journey which I had so far only experienced as a straightforward half-hour drive suddenly looked very different. It now involved walking the five kilometers to the nearest train station in order to catch the one eastbound train of the day, which left at 6:45 AM. I then had the option of either hitching a ride back or waiting for the westbound train from Ponte Leccia at 5 PM. Having hitched countless rides between Crucetta and the nearby town of Ile Rousse, in the early days before I had a car and since the crash, I carelessly assumed that hitching a ride back from Ponte Leccia would be equally unproblematic, particularly since Ponte Leccia, although a tiny town, is the central node of the entire road system of northern Corsica.

My crucial mistake was that Ponte Leccia was not a place in which I was known. As I stood by the road for three hours, watching cars whizz past, I meditated on the fact that nearly every single ride I had ever hitched had been with someone who was either an acquaintance or who at the very least had seen me around in Crucetta and was keen to satisfy their curiosity. Finally, a car stopped—or rather, it returned after a ballet of indecision. The young woman driver apologized for this hesitation as I stepped in: "I know this is Corsica," she said, "but you never know." The car was a Peugeot 306, shiny pretty things hung from the mirror, and the young woman drove it fast, with her sunglasses on her forehead and a cigarette in one hand. As we snaked through the bends and careened down the straights to the Latin American reggae tunes of Manu Chao, she spoke about her boyfriend, about drugs, about her family. "I can tell you this," she said with a sidelong glance, "because you don't know anybody I know." When she has children, she said proudly, they will speak Corsican and will have Corsican first names. And a Corsican last name, too; she paused to see if I got it. I did. When she marries, it will be a Corsican, she insisted. "Not that I'm racist, you know, I'm all for mixing and all that. But I do get the feeling that we're becoming a minority in our own island. We'll soon have disappeared completely if things go on this way."

And now for a very different anthropological voice:

> We must enquire as to the future of the rural community and the functions of the family group and the web of kinship as we have described them here. Are these forms of social organisation part of a superseded mode of production? Do they still have a function today in the construction of this bipolar society (Corsica/Continent)? . . . [O]n the Continent, the salience of ethnicity maintained and continues to maintain the memory, the nostalgia and the desire of a village sociability which has not altogether broken down. It is thus to the village that one turns. . . . But a social structure is needed to ensure the maintenance of this link: this structure is not the rural community, which, in the absence of its territorial framework and its agro-pastoral economic system, can no longer sustain itself; it is not the *partitu* [clan], whose functioning is intermittent; it is the family and the web of kinship. Of course, the structure of the family group has itself changed; it no longer much resembles the domestic group we have been describing. . . . Due to emigration it is a multipolar group, almost a network; but a network whose mesh is still very tight . . . a network which is able to hold together the elements of a society which emigration has stretched but not yet dismembered. . . . We could thus put forward the idea that it is the family group, and to a lesser extent, the web of kinship which support, one might say at arm's length, a rural community which as we have seen is now resting on a multi-polar economic activity. . . . But the family group, by virtue of its small size, is highly dependent [on] the impulsions of the individuals which compose it: each with his personal adventure, his life-choices, his social experience, brings to the group his own style, imparts to it his own movement. . . . [T]he sociological "mass" of various family groups is too small, their economic basis too complex, their history too diverse, to allow them, either individually or together, to impart to the process of social reproduction the same continuity and the same regularity imparted by the rural community of the older type. (Ravis-Giordani 1983, pp. 380–381)

The correspondences and differences between the two accounts above map the pervasive ways in which the notion of society in Corsica brings with it a host of worries. In the press, as in everyday conversations in Crucetta, the phrase "Corsican society" is more often than not associated with the notion of what is wrong with the island, and this in turn is usually something to do with connections. There are those for whom the problem is too little connection, a progressively thinning web of social relations, a social fabric which is growing threadbare, an equilibrium being thrown off, a social body growing weak. Georges Ravis-Giordani's monumental structural-functionalist account of Corsican society is interesting here both because it very accurately reflects the scholarly background to these popular concerns and as a body of scholarship which continues to provide a wealth of insight into the minutiae of Corsican relationality, long after the demise of the Fortesian theoretical armature which undergirds its description of stable systems.

For others, the problem is not too few connections, but rather too many: patronage, insider dealing, occult and hidden webs of influence which pervert the proper civic functioning of the island. Such discourses about society are clearly informed by pervasive tropes and stereotypes which anthropologists have convincingly deconstructed and historicized. The concern with a thinning of connection harks back to organicist dreams of a healthy, thickly interconnected society, a set of ideas through which one can map disturbing similarities between the classics of nineteenth-century European sociology and the most virulent forms of current European "integralism" (Holmes 2000); by contrast, concerns with too much connection are clearly informed by a set of older representations of Mediterranean corruption (Gellner and Waterbury 1977) and "amoral familism" (Banfield 1958) which have long provided a convenient foil for an idealized description of a rational, civic, modern north (Herzfeld 1989; McDonald 2000).

However, deft analytical unpacking of these tropes and historicization of these discourses, although an important endeavor, only take us so far. What such critiques find it harder to account for is the extent to which discourses around society can come to make sense to people and to feed into their everyday dealings with each other. I will argue that ostensibly abstract discourses about the state of Corsican society as either overconnected or underconnected draw their experiential power from a different logic, an embodied and situated relationality which enmeshes persons in connections with other persons, places, stories, and things in powerful and often ambivalent ways. Such kinds of connections to people, places, and stories mean that one will not be stranded by the side of the road or hitchhiking in a strange place; they mean that one will be conversant with Corsican names and the likelihood or otherwise of another's tall tales; they mean that one can drive fast and sure around familiar bends while talking about something else; they mean that one will have a ready band of polyphonic singers at one's wedding in the village chapel one has helped to restore; they mean that one might have uses for a broken car. But they also mean that one has to be careful whom one tells about one's drug habits, and they mean that the promise of interaction with someone who is patently disconnected might suddenly feel like a form of thrilling release. In Crucetta, this experiential matrix was often referred to in terms of "knowing" (*connaître*).

Everyone Knows Everyone Else

As we saw in chapter 2, Corsica is often depicted as a thing "out there," impenetrable to outsiders, and one strand of this discourse presents Corsica as a dense, unfathomable skein, a thickly interconnected network in which occult relationships and criminal entanglements mirror a tangled, impenetrable vegetation—the proverbial *maquis*. This kind of depiction has its positive flip side in images of a healthy, thickly interconnected society, miles away from the disaggregation and breakdown of postmodern urban life. Such depictions are ethnographically present in Crucetta, for instance, in the commonplace statement that "here, everyone knows each other." The "here" in question might be the village, a cluster of villages, or indeed the island itself, and "here" is often expressed in opposition to an elsewhere which is usually implicitly or explicitly continental France. For instance, when I bumped into an acquaintance from Crucetta at a football match held at a stadium on a neighboring *commune,* he commented: "you know, this isn't the Parc des Princes [a famous Parisian stadium]. We all know each other here!"

It would be easy to explain (away) such ideas of everyone knowing each other, like ideas of Corsicans' link to the island, as merely metaphorical or romantic constructions. Such tropes, after all, are as old as the romantic opposition between country and city (Williams 1975), and they draw on pervasive European models of a shift from community to society, from tradition to modernity, and so on. The anthropological literature on the construction of difference to which I have referred throughout this book might prompt us to consider such statements as a form of Barthian boundary maintenance or, indeed, a way of thinking about one's own place in a broader scheme of center and periphery—like the Greek islanders in David Sutton's account who contrast their own social integration to the disintegration of the Greek mainland and, beyond that, of a purportedly more modern, European core (Sutton 1998, pp. 35–56). Such analyses help us to make sense, among other things, of the intrinsic ambivalence of such claims. The statement "we all know each other" can be a form of self-congratulation, suggesting that Corsica or Crucetta are places of warm and easy sociality, but it is just as often a critical claim, casting these places as panoptic settings in which people are always looking over your shoulder. Anthropologists have done much to illuminate the semiotics of such reversible self-stereotyping in the Mediterranean and elsewhere.

And yet, as with place, with language, or with identity, such tropes of inter-knowledge are not simply floating in the ether, but rather, they get their experiential validity from real connections and disconnections, the actual relations in which people are enmeshed in Crucetta—as well as the connections they fail to make. After all, it is evidently not the case in Crucetta, as I suggested in the first chapter, that everyone knows each other. On the contrary, Crucetta is full of moments of nescience and disconnection, of misunderstanding, and, very simply, of people being strange to one another. And yet it is precisely at such moments that this claim gets its most powerful experiential validation.

The image this brings up for me is the aftermath of a well-attended choral concert which was held in Crucetta as part of a fundraiser in December 2002. Around fifty people had been crammed for over an hour into the small chapel by the main church, listening intently to the *chorale de la Balagne,* as they intoned a succession of French, Corsican, and Italian songs. Now, people were milling around and stretching their legs on the dusty forecourt of the chapel, under the multicolored glow of the electric bunting. It was a pleasant evening for the season, and friends and acquaintances took this occasion to greet each other and comment on the music. I found myself standing next to one of the teachers at the school and, for want of anything to say, noted how surprised I had been to find that I knew the choirmaster, who happened to be an educational administrator living in a nearby town. It was quite a shock to see this man, who had always struck me as an extremely serious and indeed somewhat stiff character, singing lustily from behind an electro-acoustic guitar. My interlocutor responded to my comment with a shrug: "Well, we all know each other here." She then asked me whether I would be going down for a drink at the *salle polyvalente,* the village's multipurpose events hall, and I said I would. She, however, decided it was getting late, and with a brief good evening, started toward her car for the very short drive down to her house in the periphery of the village.

Looking around me, I couldn't see many familiar faces. None of the people there lived up in the old village—most seemed to be from the villas and farther afield—and they moved in clumps, shooting an occasional hello into the darkness over someone's shoulder. As I started to follow the flow of people who were heading down the hill toward the *salle polyvalente,* I bumped into Françoise (the one who in chapter 2 had been so keen to tell me about the mysterious goings-on in Corsica). Françoise was heading uphill with her two granddaughters, back toward the old village. "Aren't you coming for a drink?" I asked. Françoise shook her head and shrugged slightly: "No," she said, "I don't know anyone." And she started back up the hill, toward the cobbled street. Up ahead of her, two elderly women in dark, simple dresses were slowly making their way homeward in the dim orange halo of the electric lights.

When I finally made it to the *salle polyvalente,* various groups of three or four people had commandeered the small square tables, which had been neatly covered with paper tablecloths held down by white plastic clips. At the back of the room, three volunteers were filling plastic glasses with red, white, or sweet wine, pastis-and-water, or whisky. Apart from those who were sitting down, the room was rather sparsely populated, with ten or fifteen people standing by the makeshift bar in groups of two or three. I spotted the choir leader and went straight for him, as he was the only person I recognized in the room. He had just picked up a plastic glass from the bar, and I intercepted him as he moved away from one group of jocular middle-aged men. He scanned my face briefly, gave me a reserved *bonsoir,* and kept moving until he blended into another group, whose backs closed up on him, leaving me stranded, alone in the crowd. Looking around me, I noticed that I was the only person who was there alone.

One often thinks of exclusion as the fact of being left out of a community, an opposition between one element and a whole bounded set. Standing alone in the *salle polyvalente,* I certainly understood why Françoise had not come down, and I was experiencing this "we all know each other" from the outside: yes, "they" all seemed to know each other. And to cast this as an observation or an impression (let alone a trope) is to mistake the nature of the phenomenon: my position there was powerfully and affectively untenable. Swallowing the shame of being a bad ethnographer, I slunk out of the *salle polyvalente* and started walking back up toward the old village, toward the lurid orange lights and the steep cobbled streets. And yet, exclusion in the above-mentioned sense (one element versus a set) was not, on close observation, what had just happened. There was no collective experience or collective personality from which I was left out; there was no boundary maintenance, speaking literally; there was no group. The people in the *salle polyvalente* were sitting and standing in fairly self-contained bunches, and replaying the scene in hindsight, I now know that a number of the people there had no clue as to who some of the others were. People had come from other parts of Corsica or from the mainland to visit relatives, the choral group and their friends were from across the region, and so on. This was not a coherent group, but rather a polythetic set, an assemblage of people who were partially connected to one another. And as my experience of other such gatherings before and since has showed, it would have been amply sufficient, in order to make my position there tenable—and, indeed, to turn what had felt like a disheartening failure into an enjoyable evening full of ethnographic intimacy—for me to have known one or two people, for me to have been, however tenuously and partially, known.

Hyper-Transitive Knowledge

One evening, a few days after my first arrival in Crucetta, I walked into the small local bar, loaded with shopping bags. I offered a meek *bonsoir* as I stepped into the doorway. Conversation ceased abruptly, and two dozen eyes turned on me. I mumbled that I would put down my bags by the door, and proceeded to do it, uncomfortably. Luckily, at that moment, Mr. Frank, who had stayed outside to pee against a wall, came in behind me, and the atmosphere lightened. Laughter, jokes, greetings flew across the room as conversation resumed. I was with him. I had met Mr. Frank, a jovial sixty-three-year-old, a half-hour earlier, at the bench in the town of Ile Rousse from which the road to Crucetta begins. I had hitched a ride down to the town earlier that afternoon to do some shopping, and neighbors in Crucetta had assured me that I would easily be able to hitch a ride back if I sat on the aforementioned bench. Especially today, they said, since there was a fair in town, and lots of people would be driving back and forth. In this, they were right: there was indeed much traffic, but no one stopped. I had begun to despair of ever making it back to the village, when Mr. Frank appeared. He was wearing a blue cloth jacket and, somewhat incongruously, was carrying a balloon in one hand and a pizza box in the other. As we got to talking, Mr. Frank told me that he didn't have a car, because he had spent most of his life working for the state-owned train company on the French mainland and was thus entitled, he claimed, to take any train for free. Much good did this do him in Corsica, however, and he noted wryly: "Here, if you don't have a car, you're dead!" Five minutes later, Mr. Frank had snagged us a ride with the village's grocer, and as we stepped out of the car on the Place de la Mairie, he invited me for a drink in the bar, saying, "Come, I'm going to make you known." That was my first introduction to a word I was to encounter often in Crucetta, *connaître,* "to know," used intransitively. As we sat in the bar, and the rounds followed each other, Mr. Frank gave me a lecture on the importance of knowing:

> Him, there, he's the boss of the restaurant. Now, you know him. You can go eat over there, you'll pay less. If you just go like this, and you don't know anyone, they'll make you pay . . . [signed: "much more"]. And now, if you go, you can eat well, drink well. . . . A lamb, you pay 200 francs for it if you know. . . . The people, if they know you, you're protected. You say, in Crucetta, you say, I know Mr. so-and-so, Mr. so-and-so, the people, they help you. If something happens to you, they're there, they help you.

Anyone with a background either in Mediterraneanist anthropology or in French stereotypes about Corsica may feel that Mr. Frank is telling us nothing new. It is not uncommon to think of Corsica, and of the Mediterranean more generally, as a kind of paradise for Barthian transactionalists, a place where the individual's understanding and manipulation of interpersonal relations are the keys to social life. But Mr. Frank was referring to something thicker and more complicated than simply doing things through "friends of friends" (Boissevain 1974): knowing, like "belonging" in Jeannette Edwards' account of Alltown, connects more than just people.

Like a number of other European languages, but unlike English, French has two words for knowing: *connaître* and *savoir*. Whereas *savoir* could be glossed as "knowing that," *connaître* describes knowledge in the sense of acquaintance or familiarity: one knows, in this sense, a person, a story, a place, or a method.[1] In common French usage, both verbs are transitive. By contrast, in Crucetta, I often heard *connaître* used intransitively in phrases such as "here, you have to know" (*ici, il faut connaître*). Like many other features of Français régional de Corse (cf. Jaffe 1999), this intransitive use of *connaître* would probably be described as derived from Corsican. However, whatever its linguistic derivation, this intransitive version of knowing is more than a linguistic quirk: it enables people to express a particular notion of knowing as an open-ended activity. For instance, having attended my first village council meeting, I met one of the councillors who was helping to slaughter lambs in his father's cellar. He asked me what I had thought of the council meeting, in which a passionate argument had arisen over a complex issue of land rights. I answered that I felt much of it had gone over my head. He answered with a smile: "Of course, you don't know" (*Bien sur, tu connais pas*).

Connaître in this sense implies knowing people, knowing people's business, and, more generally, knowing the business of the village. As a result, the notion of intransitivity does not quite capture the spirit of this usage. It is not that *connaître* becomes a true intransitive, indicating some form of knowledge in the abstract, something immanent or objectless. Rather, this is a form of pseudo-intransitivity: since no particular object is specified, this allows for knowing to refer implicitly to a multiplicity of interconnected objects ("here, you have to know"). To mute or suppress a direct referent (knowing X) is to open up a theoretically unlimited set of connections (knowing). Far from being intransitive, then, this use of knowing could well be described as hyper-transitive: *connaître* describes an activity of proliferating connection—N + 1. And indeed, mapping—making and remaking connections in conversation with a group of friends and neighbors—was an activity which people in Crucetta appreciated in itself and were prepared to spend a great amount of time and effort doing. It would be quite common for someone who mentioned a person in passing as part of a story to be interrupted by the listeners: "Which Jean? Jean the shepherd, or Catherine's Jean?" "No, no, this is Jean the uncle of the one from the blue house!" "From Lumio?" "From the south. His wife was from Lumio." "Oh, so Jean Pietrone?" "Yes, Pietrone, I think he was called. His brother used to go hunting with my father; they called him 'growler.'" "His daughter is the one who married the old Damiani, isn't she?"

etc. Such discussions were always greeted with enthusiasm and sometimes took over from the story itself.

Being on Bad Terms: Disconnection and Lack of Connection

Whether one knew and was known was not just verbalized, but also made evident in the minutiae of everyday practice. I was often struck, for instance, by the particular attention paid in Crucetta to everyday encounters between people who know each other. Forms of greeting are fairly regular and patterned: in order of decreasing formality, people shake hands, kiss (once on each cheek), and, for the most intimate or those who are constantly in each other's company (such as friendly neighbors in the old village), verbal acknowledgment is usually sufficient for everyday, unmarked encounters. Whereas cross-gender handshakes and handshakes between women are a clear mark of formality, usually confined to a first meeting, men shake hands up to a far greater level of acquaintance and informality, and only kiss close friends and relatives. What was striking was the care that went into acknowledging people, and acknowledging them once a day. Often, at quarter past eleven, when the schoolteachers who had been working in their respective classrooms met in the playground, one or the other would ask: "Have we seen each other this morning?" If the answer was negative, they would proceed to kiss each other. Conversely, an absentminded attempt to shake hands with someone whom one had already greeted was sometimes rejected and usually incurred an amused comment. There were few other excuses for refusing a handshake: if one's hands were dirty, one could offer the wrist; if one's right hand was occupied, one could offer the left, sometimes with the formulaic apology: "it's the hand of the heart" (*c'est la main du coeur*). It was equally important to "salute" (*saluer/salutà*) people in passing, and when driving by, in which case the horn was often used. Conversely, failure to acknowledge people, even in passing, was rarely left uncommented—people would talk. Thus, the son of Pascal the schoolteacher, who was my age and spent most of the year studying on the Continent, was rather concerned that, since he had no memory for faces, he would often during his stays in Crucetta fail to recognize people, especially when he drove past them on the road. It was lucky, his parents noted, that he had a smiling and amenable face, which allowed people to believe he was recognizing them even when he wasn't.

In other words, the way one practically micro-managed one's acquaintances fed back into this common knowledge about the kind of person one was. But deeper and more enduring rifts and disconnections could also be marked in these everyday encounters between people who knew each other. On one occasion, I met Petru, Pierre-Antoine, and a group of their friends on the square, and proceeded to shake hands with all but Petru, whom I had already greeted earlier. Seeing that the two of us didn't shake, Pierre-Antoine joked: "are you enemies?" Even though this was clearly not a serious question, it suggested that the importance of marking connection stands out against the possibility of explicitly marking disconnection. Indeed, while there was a stated ideal in Crucetta that one should be "on good terms with everyone" (*esse bè incu tuttu u mondu*), in fact, many people seemed to be explicitly and publicly on bad terms with one or more other people. Even though the causes and strengths of the disputes and the contexts and contents of the (non-)relationships varied widely, there seemed to be a fairly socially acknowledged way of being on bad terms. "Being on bad terms" (*etre mal/esse male*) rarely went as far as "enmity" (*inamicizia*), which was a very serious and, some said, irreversible state; usually, bad terms were confined to a marked disconnection and were identified and referred to in terms of people not talking or, more commonly, not saluting each other.

Knowing who was on bad terms with whom was part of *connaître* more generally. Against this background, whether one person saluted or failed to salute another, or whether he went into the bar when he knew someone else was in there—all these minute events became meaningful; would be noted with a shrug, a nod, and a muttered half-comment; and remembered long afterward. I was struck, for instance, when Marie-Paule and I had a falling-out near the end of my stay, that Petru's wife, Marie-Josée, commented on the fact that we had sat at the same table during a bingo evening nearly six months earlier. And between straightforward good terms and bad terms lay a wide grey area made up, to quote one of Pierre Bourdieu's descriptions of "practice," of "ambiguous conduct that can be disowned at the slightest sign of withdrawal or refusal, . . . uncertainty about intentions that always hesitate between recklessness and distance, eagerness and indifference" (Bourdieu 1990, p. 81). *Connaître,* therefore, does not just refer to information about connections broken and remade; it is also the practical mastery of this permanently shifting field. As I began to suggest in chapter 3, knowing in this sense connected not just people, but also places, stories, objects, in heterogeneous assemblages. Knowing, in this sense, ceases to be a question of representation; it goes beyond even the common social production of a purely semantic fabric and becomes a question of belonging "forged through a variety of connections, and a diversity of attachments, which include links to pasts and persons, as well as to places" (Edwards 1998, p. 148).

The practice of being on bad terms also opens a gap between disconnection and lack of connection. For instance, Pierre-Antoine's joke was premised on everyone knowing that Petru and I were not in fact, indeed could not be, on bad terms: the humor turned on the point that someone as unconnected as myself could not possibly be on bad terms with anyone, since being on bad terms already involves knowing and being known in a way in which I clearly was not. In this sense, the explicit disconnection of being on bad terms was internal to knowing (*connaître*), just as "silence is not external to language" (Derrida 1992, p. 14)—unlike the simple lack of connection of the unknown hitchhiker by the side of the road, or the absent presence of Franco-Maghrebians in the village.

Knowledge, Closeness, and Blood

My discussion of *connaître* has so far glossed over very different kinds of connections, as people in practice in Crucetta tended to do, glibly associating, in the connections they traced, different kinds of people, places, and things across distinctions of value, identity, or domain: old people, young people, Corsicans, Continentals, supermarkets, churches, computers, donkeys. Knowing, in this general sense, was also a placeholder for a range of often very different relationships: being connected through kinship, friendship, and common experiences of different sorts all point to different depths and kinds of relations—as Edwards and Strathern put it in a commonplace English idiom, being related is not the same as relating (2000, p. 154). And yet, I might add, the two are related within the broader idiom of *connaître*.

As a token of this propensity of knowing to slide into substance, the phrase "here, everyone knows each other" was often associated with another, more specific claim to the effect that "here [and, once again, this could refer to entities of various sizes], we are all related" (*simu tutti parenti*). Anthropologists such as Georges Ravis-Giordani have taken this claim at face value, speaking of "a situation of generalised kinship" which once bound Corsican villages and made them into organic communities. But this is also a trope which feeds into a moral and metaphorical account in which Corsicans as a human group are set off from the rest of France. An instance of this can be found in the Corsican language learning method *Le Corse sans Peine* (Marchetti 1974), written in the heyday of the *riacquistu,* the rediscovery and elaboration of Corsican culture, and strongly linked to the rise of political regionalism/nationalism. The book is actively engaged in the promotion of Corsican language and culture, and it purports to give slices of dialogue representative of Corsican concerns. Lesson 5 has two people working out the very remote family ties which link them. It ends with the statement: "If you look far enough, [we Corsicans,] we're all related." A more theorized but in many senses similar account of capillary networks binding together the whole island is present in the work of Charlie Galibert, who argues that the micro-political relations observed at the level of individuals and families extend, ultimately, to the Corsican people as a whole: "It is in these internal negotiations and arguments, this translation of the administrative, the institutional, the civic, into familial passionate intensities, that one sees at play the resistance and the [ingenuity] of a people, at the very heart of the family, and by capillarity, of family groups and villages, up to the island as a whole" (Galibert 2004b, p. 161).

This propensity of knowledge and relatedness to collapse upon one another into ethnicized, indeed, biologized distinctions was evident in a controversial court case in 2002, in which two Corsican nationalists were accused of murder and the prosecution had provided evidence based on mitochondrial DNA. In the end, however, after taking expert advice, the judge ruled that the evidence was not sufficient. He commented, in court: "Here we have a factor which is specific to Corsica. It seems that on this island, everyone knows each other more or less. You are all a bunch of clones! I'm exaggerating, but it really is quite astounding. Corsicans who know nothing of their family connections, and don't know each other have the same genetic footprint, which is rather vexing" (Chemin 2002a, n.p.). The judge's comments—which predictably caused outrage among Corsican as well as Continental commentators—resonate with the discourses examined in chapter 2, in which Corsica is unknowable, unclear, because of the excessive entanglements and connections among its elements. Corsicans all "know" each other, the judge is complaining, which is why it is impossible to "know" who is who, to disentangle them from one another, even with the help of the most recent technology. Knowing each other and being related are clearly not one and the same, but the judge's statement stands as a powerful instance of the multiple connections between the two, the many ways in which, as Marilyn Strathern has argued, kinship and knowledge by turns extend and interrupt one another (Strathern 2005). As in the judge's language, the statement that "here, we all know each other" can either be taken to reflect a more fundamental point about biological relatedness, or stand in stark contrast to it, as when one doesn't know to whom one is related.

At the interface between these two possibilities, there was also in Crucetta a soft modulation, a kind of continuity between kin and other types of relation, as in the case of Virgile, an elderly gentleman who after talking at some length about a childhood friend of his, who had later become a mayor in the south of the island, mentioned as an afterthought that they were "a little bit cousins" (*un peu cousins*). Kinship was an extremely explicit and salient concern for both Corsicans and non-Corsicans in Crucetta, but it faded into other kinds of relations in a way which makes it imprudent to cast it as a separate system.

Classic accounts of Corsican kin reckoning, such as that by Ravis-Giordani (1983, pp. 343–384), describe a system of bilateral descent with strong local endogamy, which in the past used to lead to Ravis-Giordani's above-mentioned "situation of generalised kinship." Within this proliferation of connections by descent or affinity referred to as "kinship" (*parentia*), Ravis-Giordani notes that Corsicans isolate consanguinity (*u sangue*) as a more solid set of connections. Within these ties of blood, direct agnatic descent is reckoned up to the seventh generation; this line of descent is referred to as *a sterpa,* from the Latin *stirpis,* meaning "root" or "stock," which also gives *sterpà,* "to extirpate or eradicate." Ravis-Giordani finds a functional justification for the number seven, suggesting that this number corresponds to the number of ascending and descending generations one is likely to *know,* thus relating cognation back to cognition (ibid., p. 343). Collateral descent, by contrast, is reckoned on the model of Catholic canon law, with its concern for regulating the closeness of intermarriage. Children of siblings are *cucini carnali* (lit. "flesh cousins"), while their children will be *cucini di terzu* (lit. "cousins of third"), and their children *cucini di cuartu* ("cousins of fourth"). The image here is of an increasingly widening pyramid, the first layer of which is a sibling pair (hence, what in English would be "second cousins" are here "cousins of third"). This is also explicitly a story about blood and dilution. While direct descent is reckoned to the seventh generation, collateral descent is only reckoned to the fourth, which is when ties of blood are considered to be loose enough for marriage. Preferential marriage between cousins of the third and fourth degree—where "there is a little blood," but not too much—represented, for Ravis-Giordani, a looping back of alliance (*un renchainement d'alliance;* ibid., p. 344), a mechanism to constitute solid family groups, an endogamic concern with keeping blood in the family, as it were.

As we saw at the beginning of this chapter, when Ravis-Giordani turns from his ethnohistorical account of the recent past to a description of Corsica at the time of his ethnography in the 1970s, he describes a once-coherent system now stretched almost beyond recognition and partially in tatters. Given the well-known critiques of the tendency of Durkheimian functionalism to overestimate the coherence of social "systems," I remain agnostic about this narrative of change from a previously stable state. The past, after all, often has a tendency to look stable when seen from the present.

However that may be, in my own experience, Corsicans in Crucetta whom I asked to explain *parentia* did so primarily in generational terms, but without drawing any explicit distinction between ways of reckoning cognatic and collateral descent. This is a key internal distinction which gives Ravis-Giordani's account its coherence and structural effect: without this distinction, the difference between reckoning some blood relations up to the seventh degree and others only to the fourth becomes a problem in need of resolution. And this is indeed how it often emerged in conversations in Crucetta. For instance, Marie-Josée, Petru's wife, and her friend Antoinette were at pains to explain that there were carnal cousins, third cousins, and fourth cousins. "And fifth cousins?" I asked. They both replied that there was no such thing. But then, Antoinette noted, even "further than the fourth," there are some who "hold each other" (*chi si tenenu*), a phrase I had heard in other contexts to describe people who were close, who liked each other, or who looked after one another. For instance, Petru once claimed of the Franco-Maghrebians who lived in the village, with more than a touch of ambivalence, that they "held each other" in this way: they were a group, they looked after each other. This was implicitly in response to the idea that they might be disenfranchised, that one should be worried for them. So the fact that people held each other even "further than the fourth" suggested that there was something there. But then, Marie-Josée rejoined, there are some who don't hold each other even before the fourth, although this is not a good thing. "You see," she said, pointing to Antoinette with a large smile, "her grandfather was the brother of my grandmother, so that makes us *cucine di terza,* and we hold each other, too." That was the first intimation I had that they were related in this sense, but the weight of her sentence was on the second part: what she was foregrounding about their relationship was the conjoining of these two factors: being cousins and being close. Almost as an afterthought, Antoinette noted that, of course, even after the fourth, "there was blood" (*chi hè u sangue*), whether or not people held each other. I asked how far there was blood, and Antoinette replied, rather noncommittally: "Well, they used to say that blood lasted seven generations," so that an illness or deformity might lie dormant for six generations, but if it didn't reappear in the seventh, it was gone. Her tone and relative lack of interest suggested, however, that we had entered a zone of speculation.

A similar set of issues emerged in a conversation with my landlord, Xavier, and his wife. He was always keen to feed me some tidbits of Corsican sayings and particularities, and one afternoon as we sat over an aperitif, he noted, as he was discussing some distant cousins of his with whom he had had a falling-out: "Here, we say *di cuartu in cullu!*" The expression literally translates as "from the fourth into the butt," or perhaps, less literally, "from the fourth onward, up yours!" He glossed this as meaning that one should never rely on relations beyond the fourth generation: "After that," he said, "we're no longer kin [*parenti*]." His wife interjected sharply: "But that's not true! They've shown, now, that they can trace your genes over seven generations."

These accounts of kin reckoning are reminiscent in some respects of the account of English kinship by Jeannette Edwards and Marilyn Strathern. As in the English case, "social and biological claims . . . , each endlessly ramifying in themselves, serve equally to link and to truncate one another" (2000, p. 159). Kin reckoning thus appears not as a stable system, but as the mobile and disputed nexus of different kinds of relations, none of which can totally define or delimit it: on the one hand, the putatively open-ended connections of biological substance, which are only limited by various appeals to knowledgeable others ("they used to say . . . ," "they've shown . . ."); on the other, the equally open-ended relationality of cooperation, friendship, and closeness, which extend beyond kinship proper. The claim that one can be "a little bit cousins," in and of itself, stands for this continuity between kinship and other forms of relatedness, which throws a wrench into the works of orderly depictions of kinship as a self-contained system. In other words, the kind of relationality I have described as knowing (*connaître*) can both incorporate and stretch beyond kinship and other forms of relatedness.

A Problem

We have thus returned, along a different path, to the point made in the last three chapters, about the authoritative nature of ambiguities: the webs spun by knowing (*connaître*) can shift situationally from encompassing different kinds of people through multiple kinds of relation, to shrinking into the more restrictive and homogeneous networks of kinship or ethnicity. Although "we all know each other" could effortlessly and silently stretch to include Continentals, "we are all related" usually did not. Whereas the first was a general idiom about locality and thickness of relation, the latter assumed that the networks mapped were homogeneous in one important sense: all their elements (people, places, stories, objects) were Corsican, and this was indeed the principle of their connection. Importantly, it was neither one nor the other of these ways of relating, but rather the constitutive ambiguity between the two, which gave the interiorities of interknowledge their experiential conviction and resilience.

This, in turn, restates in sharpened form a problem inherent to earlier anthropological discussions of interknowledge (*interconnaissance*) as a form of village sociality (introduced in chapter 3). Indeed, in such analyses, interknowledge effectively marks an interiority, "the closed universe of the village community, in which links of *interconnaissance* powerfully insert the individual into the group" (Zonabend 1990, p. 260). This common knowledge produces the organic interpenetration of place, people, and history, "the *communitarian mental landscape* in which the community re-identifies itself" (Galibert 2004b, p. 205). Therefore, in these anthropological analyses, as in the popular English imagination as described by Marilyn Strathern, "villages are imagined as centers that remain fixed. They form a focus for long-term attachment, containing folk intermeshed in an intricate web of connections, each place a discrete unit looking outwards" (2004, p. 23; see Strathern 1981). This is not to say that such accounts necessarily turn on the fetishization of the kind of "small-scale communities of face-to-face contact" of which anthropological critics have been so suspicious. On the contrary, we can see, for instance, in Galibert's historical ethnography of the Corsican village of Sarrola Carcopino, through the letters and writings of one of its inhabitants turned colonial soldier in the late nineteenth century, that *interconnaissance* can span continents and be mediated through letters from Madagascar negotiating the marriage of a cousin back in the village (Galibert 2004b). But even in this case, this interknowledge maps an inside, an interiority which is all the more impenetrable for not being straightforwardly spatialized, a village carried within oneself to the ends of the world.

In other words, this interiority of a network in which every element belongs to every other provides a very powerful account of the content, resilience, and persuasion of what is commonly rendered as identity—rather too powerful, in fact, since it makes it difficult to see how anyone might ever "get in." This is not just a theoretical or a philosophical problem but also a pragmatic one—as in the case of Galibert, a Continental anthropologist reflecting on the question of whether and to what extent he has become an insider, a villager in Sarrola Carcopino, where he has lived intermittently for twenty-five years (Galibert 2004a, p. 114 and passim). The problem for a newcomer in Crucetta is, where to begin making connections when every connection refers you to something else? Where, in other words, does one pick up the thread? Pollock and Maitland write: "Such is the unity of all history that anyone who endeavours to tell a piece of it must feel that his first sentence tears a seamless web" (Pollock and Maitland 1898, quoted in Thornton 1988, p. 299). Such is the problem of a newcomer in Crucetta, and in many other places besides. How does one become someone who knows? How does one become known?

8

Anonymous Introduction

All of philosophy so far has been premised on the verb to be, whose definition seemed to be the philosopher's stone one should discover. One can say that, had it been premised on the verb to have, many sterile debates . . . would have been avoided.—From the principle I am, it is impossible to derive, with all the subtlety in the world, any existence besides my own; hence the negation of external reality. But if you postulate I have as the fundamental fact, the owned and the owner [*l'eu et l'ayant*] are both given as inseparable.

—TARDE 1999[1895]

Is hospitality a question asked of he who arrives . . . : what are you called? Tell me your name, what should I call you, I who call you, I who desire to call you by your name? . . . Or does hospitality begin in a welcome without a question, in a double erasure, an erasure of the question and of the name?

—DERRIDA 1997

Another Problem

Anthropologists working in Corsica have often remarked that personal introductions on the island put a strong and fairly formalized emphasis on the evocation of people and places which the interlocutors "have in common" (Ravis-Giordani

1983; Jaffe 1999, p. 58). When the two people meeting are Corsican, this tends to include questions about their villages of origin, leading, if the villages are known, to discussions of their families. By contrast, non-Corsicans, such as the many continental French people residing on or visiting the island, are not expected to have a village. In their case, introductions tend to move from their home towns, to their places of residence in Corsica, and finally to their Corsican acquaintances there; these will be examined fairly relentlessly until a commonality is found: a place or, preferably, a person that both interlocutors know. Alexandra Jaffe identifies this as a "classic Corsican encounter ritual" (Jaffe 1999, p. 58). As Georges Ravis-Giordani puts it, at the end of such introductions, "the stranger is no longer unknown, he is situated in a network, of which his interlocutors hold a few strands" (Ravis-Giordani 1983, p. 228).

These descriptions were confirmed by my own ethnographic experience in Crucetta. In my experience of such encounters, however, I noted an initially surprising point which the above literature does not mention: the one name one was not likely to hear throughout this process of evocation of people and places was one's interlocutor's. In the early stages of fieldwork, I often introduced myself by name to people I had met in bars or squares, only to find that, contrary to what I expected, no name was offered in return, and conversation simply proceeded from there. I thus came to know people for weeks, exchanging life histories, discussing important topics, and never once had them introduce themselves by name. As a result, my fieldnotes, particularly from the early days, are full of contextual designations, such as "the man with the cats," "upstairs neighbor of Jean-Marie," etc. This kind of "anonymous introduction" did not, of course, happen every time I met someone new, and a formal exchange of names was the norm in many contexts, such as when visiting someone at their home or in most settings implicitly deemed official or professional. Yet it happened enough in the early days of fieldwork for me to notice it, and in time, I stopped proffering my name as an opening gambit on first meetings with people in the bars and squares of Crucetta.

The notion of an anonymous introduction conjures up the tantalizing promise of a new anthropological object. Yet, at the risk of disappointing some readers, I am not claiming to have uncovered a specifically Corsican ritual of introduction, with standard proprieties and rules. Rather more modestly—although the conclusion will show that there is more than just modesty involved—I will use "anonymous introduction" in this chapter as a shorthand for a more loosely defined object: not a formal cultural practice but a tendency, an orientation, toward name-avoidance in initial encounters. This tendency toward name-avoidance was also present in less extreme cases, in which the interlocutor's name would eventually be mentioned, but only at the end of a conversation, as in the following example.

I was returning from a morning walk to the nearby village of Sant'Antoninu when I crossed paths with an elderly man wearing blue dungarees, a checked shirt, and a cloth cap. He was carrying a white plastic bag of the supermarket variety, and his muddy shoes spoke of a recent trip into a field. Emboldened by his friendly look, I decided to attempt a greeting in my fledgling Corsican and said, "*Salute!*" He replied in the same language, and we exchanged some pleasantries about the weather. He asked where I was heading, and I answered that I had just been on a walk and was heading back to Crucetta. He said, "Ah, so you are staying in Crucetta?" I replied rather clumsily in my struggling Corsican that I was "from Crucetta, well, no, I mean I'm not *from* there, but I live there." He gestured slightly impatiently at this, as if to say "of course you're not *from* there" and looked at me quizzically. So I explained that I was a student from England who had come to work on Corsican bilingual schooling. He clapped his hand to his mouth in genuine astonishment at this and said, rather hurriedly: "I'm sorry, I had taken you for a Corsican, because you saluted me. I thought 'He's Corsican,' so I spoke to you in Corsican." He seemed to think this had been overly familiar, but I reassured him, saying that, on the contrary, I was trying to learn Corsican so every little bit helped. I tried to launch further discussion on this topic, but he hadn't quite finished with me and asked me where in Crucetta I was staying. I told him the name of the neighborhood, Piazza à O, and he said he knew it well. I ventured the name of my friend Petru, thinking that they might know each other. My interlocutor was very pleased at this and asked for news of Petru, whom he described as a good friend. We spoke of Crucetta, Petru, and Piazza à O for a while. As we parted, my interlocutor asked me to wish Petru a good day from him. "You'll say 'Saveriu the shepherd says hello, Saveriu from Sant'Antoninu [*Saveriu di Sant'Antoninu*].'" His name, therefore, far from being an opening gambit, was the very last thing he told me, without any expectation that I would offer my name in return.

This was not an isolated case. Such offers of names often came at the end of long conversations, at parting, and in relation to a third party: "You'll tell Pascal that you met me. Didier, I'm Didier," or "Tell him that Guy—that's me—still remembers that school play we did." In none of these cases was I expected to reciprocate—nor was it easy to escape the feeling that the name was not exactly given for my benefit but rather for that of the third party to whom I became a link, as the third party had been a link between me and my interlocutor.

Conversely, to explicitly ask for someone's name on a first meeting could produce real awkwardness. This was brought home to me quite forcefully one afternoon, ten months into my time in Crucetta, as I sat with a half-dozen neighbors under the large tree in Piazza à O. My Continental neighbor Cécile had brought some iced tea and plastic glasses. I was vaguely strumming on a guitar and joining in the desultory chat, interrupted only by the scraping noise of steel chairs as one or another of us moved to follow the shade. An elderly woman from another neighborhood came up and joined us: her grey hair was pristinely curled, and her dark cloth dress simple but freshly pressed. Everyone there apart from Cécile and me were villagers who knew her well, and she was greeted in the nonchalant and minimalist way reserved for close associates: a nod, a hand put briefly on someone's shoulder. The new arrival sat by Marie-Josée and, looking straight at me, asked her something in Corsican which I could not catch. In response, Marie-Josée, also staring at me, explained to her in Corsican, although slightly more loudly, that I was a student who had come here to study the village and told her where I lived. Having been thus introduced, I now intervened in the same language: "Yes, I'm staying over there, near the path to the little cross." The new arrival noted, with kindly admiration, "and he speaks Corsican, too!" I smiled "thanks." After a while, Cécile, the only person there who did not speak Corsican, settled a little more comfortably in her chair and asked the woman in French, "Excuse me, but, what's your name?" The woman, and the rest of the company, stared at her in silence. Cécile continued, hesitantly: "Er . . . you wouldn't by any chance, um . . . be Madame Mattei?" (Mattei is the single most common patronym in Crucetta.) After another long stare, the woman finally answered, with icy dignity: "No, Madame Mattei was my mother. I *used* to be a Mattei." But she firmly did not give her name. Another tense silence. Cécile pursued: "Do you look much like her? . . . Your mother?" No answer, perhaps a vague shrug. Cécile: "And so do you . . . do you live in the village?" The woman answered "yes," as if to say "of course." Cécile then went on to explain confusedly that she had long ago briefly met a Madame Mattei, and hence was wondering whether they were the same person. Her explanation fell flat. I started a tune to change the conversation.

Beyond Self and Other

Two related anthropological traditions, which have, in different ways, animated my account throughout this book, provide ready frameworks for contextualizing such encounters. The first is the classic community studies approach, which might lead us to ask about the proprieties of introduction, hospitality, and the management of interpersonal knowledge. Like other Mediterranean locations (Pitt-Rivers 1954; Campbell 1964), Corsica has yielded careful studies of small-scale communities of face-to-face interaction (e.g., Chiva 1963; Caisson 1978; Ravis-Giordani 1983) which suggest a deft balance between an ideology of reciprocity and equality, on the one hand, and contests for power and political influence over extended kin-based networks, on the other, a context in which public displays of autonomy are the flip side of an expectation of unfailing corporate solidarity (Gil 1984). Corsican villages emerge as places in which honor is negotiated before the agonistic public of the square and through the intimate secrecy of the house, spaces in which the individual self/Other encounter harks back to confrontations between kinship groups and where, as a result, relationships have to be micro-managed: "people outside the immediate family should not necessarily be trusted, and information restricted to the smallest possible unit" (Jaffe 1999, p. 47). Twenty-first-century authors have continued to speak of "the Corsican 'method' of mistrust of the other's gaze and of discretion in regards to speech. . . . To say too much is harmful, one must not say what one knows, betray secrets; but also: one should not ask" (Galibert 2004a, pp. 6–7).

In this tradition, a general sense of reticence in initial encounters with strangers might be thought to express a tension between the principles of hospitality, which require opening to the outsider, and honor, which requires controlling public knowledge of the family to maintain reputation (e.g., Ravis-Giordani 1983, pp. 228–229, 374–378; cf. Caisson 1974). There is much to be retained from these earlier community studies, as I have argued throughout this book. And yet the question of secrecy does not quite get to the bottom of name-avoidance per se.

Certainly, introductions I witnessed in Crucetta (and, indeed, pretty much everywhere else) involve a delicate diplomacy in which the information one gives, implies, or hides is always carefully managed. As I showed in chapter 5, the crucial fact of whether one is or is not Corsican, for instance, is rarely explicitly articulated, but rather politely guessed at through implicit clues. However, names in the above cases did not constitute particularly privileged or valuable information, as was made manifest by the ease with which they could in fact be given where relevant (as in Saveriu's case)—if anything, as I will show below, they were fairly devoid of signification to an outsider. In Cécile's example, the negative reaction to a stranger asking to know one's name seems to suggest this kind of economy of secrecy (also described for other French rural locations, e.g., Zonabend 1990). And yet it is notable that the woman's proud response that she *"used to be* a Mattei" was as revealing, if not more, of family histories and her private life than a simple answer concerning her patronym would have been. This all suggests that it is not so much the content of the information which matters here, as the act of suppressing it or explicitly asking for it. Name-avoidance in these encounters was therefore not, I will argue, about the management of sensitive information, but rather about *indirectness;* the relevance of this distinction will become clearer as I proceed.

The second anthropological tradition has focused on identity and difference: this might take as its starting point the fact that one of the protagonists in each of these stories is not Corsican, and ask about boundary maintenance, cultural stereotyping, and insider/outsider relations. The occasional incidence of uncomfortable and stilted interactions, such as that in the square, described above, finds a ready explanation, particularly in the eyes of Continentals, in a broader narrative about Corsica's difference from (the rest of) France. In the popular anthropology of tourists, visitors, and some Corsicans, such moments are often understood as revelatory of something deep-seated about Corsican culture or mentality, namely, an oft-cited Corsican propensity to closedness, taciturnity, or (again) secrecy. Some go so far as to portray the island as a whole as closed and "xenophobic," as, to quote one French television program, "an island that is afraid of the Other" (see Candea 2006).

Recent anthropologists of Corsica have challenged such depictions of a closed island by making what is perhaps the quintessential anthropological move, in line with the earlier community studies accounts: stressing the relational nature of self/ Other distinctions (Desanti 1997; Desideri 1997; Galibert 2004b; see also Ravis-Giordani 1983, p. 231). While they acknowledge the passionate attachment of Corsicans to their island, these authors argue that such identities are articulated and reinforced by opposition to, and therefore in relationship with, Others. Thus, for instance, Charlie Galibert notes, quoting Cassano:

> [F]or the islander, "the frontier is sacred because it preserves the relation between identity and difference, insofar as this relation constructs-identifies a community by opposition to others, to all the others" (Cassano 1998, p. 63). For the islander, the elsewhere is already here, because the island can only exist in its relationship to the other, to the continent, to the rest of the world. (Galibert 2004b, p. 27)

This approach, too, is to a great extent compelling and has informed some of the argument of this book. And yet its emphasis on selves and Others leaves unanswered precisely the questions which are relevant to anonymous introductions: could this line ever be breached? How might an outsider become an insider? This is a problem of introduction in the etymological sense of insertion, of leading inside, as in the introduction of one thing into another—here, of one person into a collective entity or relational assemblage. In order to see how anonymous introductions might do this, we need to suspend for a moment the self/Other, me/not-me logic, which informs both the community studies approach and more recent accounts of identity and difference.

A Solution

Part of what seems uncanny, or indeed oxymoronic, about the notion of an anonymous introduction comes from the commonsense assumption that an introduction is primarily a means for two persons to learn facts about each other; it does indeed seem strange in this context to omit what should be a crucial fact, the interlocutors' names. But one could also think of introductions as events in themselves, relational events in which two persons are transformed from people who did not know each other into people who do. That this involves more or, in some cases, less than an exchange of factual information becomes particularly obvious when introductions take on an extremely formalized aspect, such as, for instance, in the admissions ceremony for fellows of King's College in Cambridge. After new fellows have sworn their allegiance in the chapel, been admitted by the provost, and signed the register, the final element of the ceremony requires the newly admitted fellows to stand in line while all the existing fellows (in recent years, over a hundred) file by and shake hands with each in turn, introducing themselves by name. It is not expected, of course, that the new fellows will remember the names which are fired at them in quick succession, nor even necessarily that the existing fellows will remember those of the new recruits. The event is rather part of a broader process which turns a person into a fellow.

This particular example, by virtue of being so radically devoid of the pragmatic function one usually assigns to introductions involving a direct exchange of names, points to a formal property of all such introductions: they first acknowledge a disconnection, in order formally and explicitly to create a connection. To return to Pollock and Maitland's formulation, such introductions go right ahead and tear the seamless web, in order to suture it back together. Introductions of the kind I described in the opening pages of this chapter do precisely the opposite. They loop in the *inconnu* (the one who is not known),[1] by working out the chain of connections that links her to her interlocutor. The initial disconnection between the interlocutors is not foregrounded nor formalized as in a direct exchange of names; it is held in abeyance until an underlying connection can be established. At the end of this process, what appears is that the interlocutors had, in fact, been connected all along. The web remains seamless, and so the problem has disappeared.

Of course, not all connections are made of the same stuff, and being connected through kinship, friendship, common experiences of different sorts, as we have seen, all point to different depths and kinds of relation. This heterogeneity of connections means that anonymous introductions are not the hub of some ever-expanding, generative, and benign principle of relationship. On the contrary, such introductions vividly bring up the different ways in which the interlocutors are situated via acquaintances, places, status, wealth, knowledge, and so forth. As the exchange progresses, the interlocutors are increasingly located, defined, and limited. But the initial bracketing of the name creates an indirectness: this mutual location is subordinated to the process of finding one or more common points of reference. This indirectness is what makes such introductions polite and also enjoyable.

Employing for a moment the distinction proposed by Gabriel Tarde in the opening quote, one might say that, rather than beginning by postulating "I am," anonymous introductions work through a whole series of "I haves" until they elicit some form of mutual possession between the two parties. Whereas, as Tarde notes, postulating "I am" turns the existence of the Other (the not-me) into a problem (who *are* you?), beginning with "I have" premises the self on a set of connections; it opens a chain of connections which are explored until some form of mutual possession is discovered. Anonymous introductions allow this mutual possession to predate and preempt the direct opposition between self and Other (for an expanded discussion of this point, see Candea 2010B).

In other words, rather than follow the commonsensical solution of explaining this anonymity by reference to some profound cultural propensity of Corsicans to secrecy, we might experimentally seek an analogy further afield. In his analysis of name-avoidance among Korowai-speakers of southern West Papua, Rupert Stasch has argued that "name utterance is avoided because to utter the other's name would be to refer to the other in a manner emphasizing that person's existence as a singular being whom the speaker apprehends as an object independent of the existing dyadic tie" (Stasch 2002, p. 347). Persons thus emerge as secondary or derivative, "metonymic extrusions of social dyads" (ibid., p. 342). I would argue that a similar logic is at play here, although one would have to replace dyads with myriads: anonymous introductions make the person secondary not to the self/Other distinction, but to a multiplicity of connections, some of which already bind the interlocutors to one another. Incidentally, this is emphatically not because Corsicans don't imagine persons to be singular beings (any more than Korowai-speakers operate with a single—relational—model of personhood; ibid., p. 355), but because in Corsica, as in (the rest of) France, West Papua, or Mongolia (Humphrey 2008), multiple models of what it is to be a person coexist.[2]

In this case, anonymous introductions allow one way of doing personhood to be bracketed in favor of another. The anonymity thus becomes a way to perpetuate a polite fiction: the fiction that everyone is already connected to everyone else, that, as one hears over and over in Crucetta, "here, everyone knows everyone else." To open by either stating one's name or asking for a name would be to puncture this fiction and state that one's interlocutor doesn't *know* and/or that he is not *known*. Anonymous introductions avoid this unpleasantness by bracketing the question of one's name and searching instead for a third term somewhere else—rather like Mr. Frank, in the previous chapter, was the third term between me and the other people in the bar. And in the process, anonymous introductions actually transform the interlocutors into persons who know—not just persons who know each other, but persons who *know* in the open-ended sense described in the previous chapter. In this sense, the fiction (that we already know each other) becomes reality. The initial indirectness is key here, since by blocking a straightforward exchange of names, by bracketing that particular version of singular personhood, it opens up what could be a simple binary into a proliferation of other connections.

N + 1

We can now track this indirectness, of which anonymous introductions give a clear and concentrated picture, in other encounters in Crucetta. Speaking of the streets and squares of "the traditional Corsican village," Ravis-Giordani paints a striking picture: "No stranger would dare enter this space without a specific reason for doing so. He could not bear the incongruity of his situation for long. This is precisely because he is not in a space which is open to all. And this space which is both common to all the neighbors and closed to foreigners is indeed the first definition of the village" (1983, p. 182). The anthropologist's description, albeit cast in ethnohistorical terms, is resonant with many an *inconnu*'s experience in Crucetta today. For a tourist or first-time visitor, passing through the smaller squares or alleys can sometimes feel like running the gauntlet: conversation usually stops at one's approach, and fixed stares follow one in and out of view. Sometimes, a curt nod or half-smile rewards an attempt at a greeting. But perhaps the most unnerving is the muttering as one leaves. An understanding of Corsican makes it no more amiable, as the words are usually: "Who/whose is that one?" (*Di quale hè què?*) I will return below to the particular syntax, which is significant, and to the kind of relationship it indexes.

During my fieldwork, I progressively shifted from being the *inconnu* who was stared at, to being one of those sitting with friends and staring at hapless tourists—at least in the neighborhood which, through the same set of processes, was becoming my own. From this later vantage point, I came to see that the same kind of indirectness was at play in this situation as in the introductions examined above. In my experience in Crucetta, when someone who was not known (an *inconnu*) entered a square, alley, or bar in which there were already two or more people, a direct question as to his or her identity was rare. It was much more usual to ask someone else present who this newcomer was. Often, the companion of the person who inquired would answer: "you know, he's the nephew of Marie-Josée," or "they're the ones who're renting at Madame Mattei's." At that point, if the person in question is still within hearing, he can complete the introduction himself ("yes, that's right, I'm back for the summer"), or merely join in the conversation. If the inquiry is met with a shrug, the newcomer may very well take this exchange as a cue to introduce himself—often in a similarly roundabout way: "I am the son of Mr. Poulain," etc. As with the anonymous introductions, these encounters are premised on indirectness. The indirectness here is of a more obvious kind: it involves asking a third party who the unknown person is, rather than confronting him with the question; however, it does the same work of looping in, by attempting to discover a preexisting connection, rather than explicitly marking a disconnection.

The indirectness is present, too, in the very expression which is used to inquire about someone's identity: *di quale hè?* literally translates as "of whom is that?" The counterparts of this question are naming expressions, such as "Ghjaseppu di Matteu" or "Marie di Ghjuvan-Pasquà," where "of" (*di*) refers to a relation. Formally, *di* is used to refer the person to her father—but it can also be used in a much looser and more contextual way, to specify someone by reference to another person or place. In asking *di quale hè?* one onlooker is asking of another, effectively, to whom can I connect this third person? To whom does he belong?

But names themselves are no end point. For names, too, refer persons to other persons. In Corsica, as elsewhere in Europe, patronyms are inherited in the male line, but first names, too, are transmitted from family members (Ravis-Giordani 1983, pp. 371–372). Many people also have nicknames (*cugnomi*), such as "the mouse," "growler," or "birdy," which are sometimes passed down the male line at the same time as patronyms, as qualifiers to distinguish between different lines bearing the same patronym. These nicknames refer persons to other persons, then, but also to events or characteristics relating to the person to whom the nickname was originally attached. The actual formation of the nickname is often a story which is told, adding yet another set of connections to the account of the person (see Ravis-Giordani 1983; Zonabend 1990). The most inventive case of naming I came across in Crucetta concerned not a person, but a dog, which famously ate the cake at a wedding celebration. It was known thereafter as "To the Happy Couple."

This returns to confirm my initial claim that anonymous introductions are not primarily concerned with the concealment of valuable information. Names in and of themselves tell one very little, given the very high level of homonymy in Crucetta and in Corsica more generally—which itself is a factor of historically high levels of local endogamy in the case of patronyms, and of practices of inter-familial name transmission in the case of first names (Ravis-Giordani 1983). It is thus not particularly pertinent to assume that names are hidden because they constitute valuable knowledge; on the contrary (were it not for the strikingly negative reaction to Cécile asking to know the woman's name, for instance), one might even object to my analysis that names are simply left out because they would be meaningless to anyone who does not already know the broader relations within which they come to mean. In this particular context, we might agree with J. S. Mill that "[o]bjects thus ticketed with proper names resemble, until we know something more about them, men and women in masks. We can distinguish them, but can conjecture nothing with respect to their real features" (Mill 1974, pp. 979–981, quoted in Bodenhorn and Von Bruck 2006). In other words, in a reversal of anthropological common sense, it is the name, not the anonymity, which could be taken to constitute a mask, whereas the unpacking of relationships between interlocutors reveals far more of substance than the name would have. What matters then is the situation which is enabled by the fact of not giving or asking for a name, not the information which is muted.

The indirectness of anonymous introductions is thus repeated and amplified in a number of other contexts: in encounters on the public square, in the very form of questions about identity, in the attributions of names and nicknames. Indirectness upon indirectness upon indirectness. Each query concerning identity is refracted into a question of connections, and each connection traced prompts a further connection: N + 1.

Arbitrary Locations and Anonymous Introductions

My account of anonymous introductions in this chapter has thus been diametrically opposed to the popular explanations with which I started: far from being evidence of Corsican closedness or secrecy, such moments of name-avoidance, I have argued, might be seen as the precise instant when a gap opens through which an outsider can start to become an insider. Perhaps, as Derrida suggests, not asking for a name is here the pinnacle of hospitality. By bracketing identity, anonymous introductions allow for connection to emerge not through difference, but before it. This form of indirectness, which obviates the self/Other opposition, reverberates in other practices of relationality in Crucetta, through which people become persons who know and who are known, while identity opens up onto belonging in a proliferating logic of N + 1. And since belonging, like identity, can produce its own ethnicized closures, the anonymous introduction is one of the ways in which, in concrete encounters, this closure can be deferred.

In order to outline this argument clearly against more familiar literature on dualism, identity, and secrecy, however, I have run the risk of overstating the case. I am in no way suggesting we forget the long tradition of self/Other dualism in the anthropology of Corsica and the Mediterranean. My analysis of anonymous introductions just burns a small hole into this broader picture, a contained space in which relationality is turned on its head, a *ligne de fuite* which completes just as it challenges the bigger picture. But it remains undoubtedly the case, as my initial example suggested, that the very same encounter which can open up a space for relationality in this way can also become a vector of schismogenesis, when people use the notion of cultural difference as a frame through which to read and objectify each other's behavioral proprieties.

This in turn, and in conclusion, poses a problem of anthropological description. Having developed an early and admittedly rather crude version of this argument when still in the field in 2003, I ran it past Jeanne, a Continental friend in the village, when she brought up the question of Corsican closedness to foreigners. Among other things, Jeanne had referred to the encounter described above and held it up, in a manner quite familiar to anthropologists, as an archetypal moment, a vignette which reveals something profound about Corsican cultural logics. Corsicans, she argued, don't come forward to greet you; on the contrary, "they observe you, they talk about you, they judge you."

The paradox will not be lost on the reader: I have been arguing that the indirectness of anonymous introductions, of encounters where someone asks a third party who someone else is, even of the form of the question itself ("*of whom* is this?") are all polite ways of obviating opposition, of looping a newcomer into an existing assemblage of people and things without marking their disconnection too starkly in the first place. They allow connections to proliferate and are the very process whereby one can slowly become someone who knows and who is known. And yet, it is this same indirectness which my friend was singling out as proof of "their" difference from "us."

The paradox is in part a problem of anthropological convention. When I described my analysis to Jeanne, I cast it in the classic anthropological idiom: I presented anonymous introductions as a Corsican cultural feature, with specific rules and rituals, to which she, as a non-Corsican, had failed to conform. As a result, Jeanne's sense of Corsican closedness was, if anything, reinforced: this may be the Corsican way of doing things, she agreed, but it's still not "real" hospitality, it's not "normal." Normal, Jeanne claimed, was to go toward the newcomer, to talk directly. She said she had often been a newcomer in villages on the French mainland, and this was what happened. So, my anthropological account only fed into the binary opposition. "The Corsican," she concluded, "isn't open. He's closed."

In other words, I was doing the opposite of an anonymous introduction. The introductions I have been describing bracket the label one should give to one's interlocutor in order to let other connections proliferate. My anthropological account of them had done precisely the opposite: it had begun by labeling anonymous introductions as a Corsican thing and thereby foreclosed various possibilities for Jeanne to relate to them. A story about ways of relating became a story about how different Corsicans were from her.

Can we imagine an anthropology which would avoid this pitfall, by modeling itself on anonymous introductions? Throughout my discussion of relationality in this book, and particularly in the last chapter and this one, I have done my best to elude one question which some will consider crucial: *where* does this type of relational knowledge operate? As one anonymous reviewer of an earlier iteration of this argument noted, it is unclear how far, ethnographically speaking, *connaître* is supposed to extend: after all, the reviewer noted, what is being described here is not uncommon to other Mediterranean island contexts. There is no straightforward answer to this question: people in Spain also ask each other "of whom are you?" (¿*de quien eres?*); *cugnomi* refer one to the *cognomen* of Roman antiquity (Salway 1994)— so perhaps this is, after all, a Mediterranean story? But there is more: Marcel Proust describes the importance of knowing in very similar terms in the fictional—and yet recognizably French—town of Combray;[3] similar plays on names to those in Crucetta have been described in the Bourguignon village of "Minot" described by Zonabend and others (Zonabend 1990); some of the naming practices discussed here are inflected by Catholicism; in some ways, Edwards and Strathern's account of English kinship is so apposite as to suggest that much of what I have been describing here could be glossed as "Euro-American" (Edwards and Strathern 2000); some might even be tempted to go further, and try to find in the similarity between this case and Stasch's account of West Papua something even more fundamental about human relationality. All of these framings and many, many more are plausible. Some are perhaps more plausible than others, but at the limit, any such zoning will be arbitrary, a matter of excluding certain elements or including others. I would argue, paraphrasing Annemarie Mol, that "the possibilities of contextualisation are endless. They can be piled up to the point where the material analysed here can be said to come from [Crucetta] and [Crucetta] alone" (Mol 2002, p. 183; see also Galibert 2004b, pp. 217–218).

Maybe putting it like this (foregrounding singularities and extensions, rather than cultural labels) would have made it clearer to Cécile how she could relate to anonymous introductions, how she was already related to them. And yet such indeterminacy goes against some of our deepest and most ingrained disciplinary instincts, which prompt us to ask, yes, but to what is this account relevant? Of what is it representative? What, in the final instance, is the entity which is being described? When all is said and done, we need to know whether really this is just a Corsican thing or a Mediterranean one, whether somehow the author imagines he has discovered something so specific and different that it only happens in one village in the north of Corsica, or whether this is just a needlessly complex and arbitrarily localized description of a plain old human universal. These questions, however, all start from the same assumption, namely, that anthropology's purpose is to give insight into entities (cultures or societies) which correspond to named human populations.

The persistence of this view in anthropology resonates with a specific and widespread conception of what anthropology is, ultimately, supposed to be: "After more than a century of existence, anthropology has only just begun to understand its proper role among the social sciences. It is, we now recognize, the systematic study of the Other, whereas all of the other social disciplines are, in one sense or another, studies of the self" (Adams 1998, p. 1). This is anthropology as a "science of alterity and of difference," which aims to "formulate questions which will allow a given culture to render more explicit to itself its own difference" (Galibert 2004b, pp. 19, 11). That the most handy way of conceptualizing difference remains the device of a "culture" mapped onto a named population explains the otherwise surprising endurance of this element of anthropological convention: despite repeated attacks on the notion of cultures as bounded wholes,[4] it remains the case that anthropological accounts are conventionally located in a context which is usually associated with a named group of people—whether defined ethnically ("among the X"), linguistically ("among Y-speakers"), specifically ("among high-caste Hindu refugees from Z"), or implicitly by reference to a geographic area ("in A").

In the Corsican case, a number of anthropologists have produced accounts of traditional Corsican culture and society,[5] while others have explored, drawing on a phenomenological and symbolist framework, the experiential intricacies of Corsican identity.[6] In both cases, the starting point of the analysis is necessarily the assumption that Corsican culture, society, or identity is a distinct object, an entity which can serve as a context for the account. The details, complexities, and specificities of these entities are elaborated; particular events, behaviors, or beliefs are explicitly or implicitly contextualized within this framework (as *Corsican* events, beliefs, or behaviors); and the framework itself is then related to other similar or broader categories, in claims that Corsican culture is part of larger Mediterranean or European ensembles, that Corsican identity is a subset of a more general phenomenology of "insularity,"[7] or that ascriptions of cultural difference mute taken-for-granted similarities (Lenclud 1996).

In other words, while anthropologists today are overwhelmingly attuned to the analytical deficiencies of holism and the dangers of essentialist visions of cultural boundedness, insofar as they take not just difference but the difference of a named group of people as a starting point for analysis, they effectively have to begin with abstracted social or cultural wholes (cf. Leach 2010). This can then be modified or muted by arguments about the fluidity or internal diversity of such cultural entities, the blurredness of their edges, or the ways in which the Other is included in the self through the relational constitution of identity. But such caveats do not in the end change the fact that any account which takes a named group of people as a meaningful context has on its horizon (however distantly) the image of "cultural packages, coherent inside and different from what is elsewhere" (Mol 2002). This is so, on a purely logical level, because some minimal form of internal coherence and difference from the outside must be assumed in the first place in order to define such entities as meaningful contexts. This epistemological stance yields to self-fulfilling prophecies about cultural coherence, such as when the anthropological literature on Corsica yields a broad consensus that, to quote Galibert, "two centuries of Frenchification have not managed to make Corsica, ethnologically speaking, into a French entity" (2004b, p. 13). To confirm or deny such a claim would require, first, a workable definition of what the boundaries of such ethnological entities might be, and second, the kind of exhaustive statistical or diffusionist tracking of cultural traits the possibility or relevance of which few anthropologists today would be prepared to endorse.

⟨ By contrast, an account—such as this one—which refuses to specify its context in terms of a named population will almost necessarily appear incomplete or inconclusive. But then, in taking that risk here, I am only emulating on an analytical level the ethnographic phenomenon I have been describing. Anonymous introductions, I have argued, bracket, mute, and ignore the question of the label one should give one's interlocutor, in order to unravel connections and make relationships appear. In refusing to label anonymous introductions as a Corsican thing, or a rural French, or Mediterranean, or European one, one might say I have replicated in my own account a feature of anonymous introductions: I have bracketed the question of identity, of the label one should give to these practices, in order to describe their "properties" (what they have, not what they are), to follow their ethnographic threads and complexities until it becomes clear that they were already, in some ways, familiar, without ever being entirely so. ⟩

This brings us back to the beginning: the ethnographic phenomenon of anonymous introductions mirrors the methodological fiction, in the first chapter, of arbitrary locations. To arbitrarily select Crucetta, not as an already determined entity whose contours were to be mapped, but as a placeholder, an anonymity, a holding-in-abeyance, allowed the account to pursue a different way of thinking about relationality, just as the holding-in-abeyance of the unknown person's name allows her to become known, to have already been known. The unasked question of Crucetta's coherence as a village or an anthropological place was what opened the account to an examination of the constant making and unmaking of coherence in the village, the interplay of categories and boundaries. The unasked question of someone's name is what enables the *inconnu* to become someone who was already known—someone who is related and unrelated in a number of specific and traceable ways.

These two processes mirror each other, and we can thus, perhaps, obviate the problem of "the impossible relation between the 'anthropological' method based on listening/observation and the Corsican 'method' of mistrust of the other's gaze and of discretion in regards to speech" (Galibert 2004a, p. 6). The parallel between the anthropological account and local ways of knowing emerges at the moment when we let go of the anthropological labeling which makes this "local"[8] way of knowing the expression of a named cultural Other, a *Corsican* way of knowing. This is a situated, momentary intervention, not the negation of difference (as if really what we all are were exhausted by some other category, such as French, European, or human). It is just an unasked question, in the wake of which a multitude of connections and disconnections, of differences and similarities flood into the account, and one finds oneself once again in the familiar world in which "nothing is absolutely universal, not because something is relatively particular, but because 'everything' is relational" (Viveiros de Castro 2003, p. 11).

But that would be too neat an ending, so here is a final disturbance. This parallel between anthropological and local (arbitrarily located) methods is, of course, not perfect. No such parallels are. This one breaks down when it becomes clear that this book has also been a journey from the unknowable (Corsica as mystery and essence) to the merely unknown (all that has not been described or accounted for in the pages of this book). And this is also where I finally part company with Galibert, who retains a taste for the ineffable something of Corsica: "Big voice of the island, murmur of the leaves, hiccup of foam on the seventh wave; each graft of smell or light onto my senses repeats: you are not from here, what could you understand" (Galibert 2004a, p. 141). By contrast, my account has stayed with a more pedestrian project of explanation: "To explain is not a mysterious cognitive feat, but a very practical world-building enterprise that consists in connecting entities to other entities, that is, in tracing a network" (Latour 2005, p. 103).

Where this method parts company also with that of people in Crucetta is in the unidirectionality of this reduction of the unknowable to the unknown and the single-mindedness of this commitment to making it—always partially, of course—known. People in Crucetta, too, are doing this, through anonymous introductions, as well as through everyday situated interventions which puncture the ineffable totalities of personhood, culture, society, community. They, however, are also doing more than I am when I write as an anthropologist: they are also rebuilding these ineffable totalities, not just as totalities, but as ineffable (Galibert 2004a, p. 130). This is why there is, perhaps, after all, a slightly hollow ring, to the "real constructivist" claim that we are to take seriously the entities which people attempt to build, rather than glibly deconstructing them from the heights of the ivory tower (Latour 2005, p. 98). Certainly, redescribing entities as heterogeneous networks does not describe them away, any more than describing a building site makes a building fall down. And yet this redescription, when it puts entities back together, omits one element: the ineffable itself. To the romantic or the poet, this may smack of disenchantment. Be that as it may, the excitement of tracing connections has its own enchantment, which my colleagues in Cambridge share with my friends in Piazza à O. Disenchanted or not, the kind of exercise in which I have been engaging here remains necessarily partial, questions breeding questions, without ever coming to rest at the stopping point of the ineffable. Marilyn Strathern calls it anthropology (2004), Max Weber calls it science: a form of questioning "that in reality never comes, and never can come to an end" (1998, p. 138). This project (and that is the mark both of its limitation and of its value) overlaps only partially with what people in Crucetta do, since they have both questions and answers.

Notes

Prologue

1. This point is made explicitly by Henare, Holbraad, and Wastell 2006.

1. Arbitrary Location

1. In 1851, for instance, a councilor (presumably from Pietra) lodged a formal complaint against the mayor's administration, and particularly against his allowing the schoolmaster and schoolmistress to remove their schools (which in those days were held simply in rented rooms), "contrary to all propriety," from Pietra to Casale. An official inquiry took place, which ascertained the facts and judged that, by moving to Casale, the teachers had made themselves unable "to provide instruction to all the children of the *commune* and particularly to supervise them, as is their Duty." As a result, the council voted to withhold the two teachers' payment for the year 1852. The girls' school, and the schoolmistress's pay, were only reestablished in 1855. The fact that Casale is at most a mile and a half away from Pietra suggests that the issues at stake went beyond the children's physical ability to attend class.

2. This document was filed in the school archives.

3. One might say, following Alain Badiou, that in each case, a multiplicity is "counted as one": "Since the One is not, every 'one-effect' [*effet d'un*] is the result of an operation, the 'counting-as-one'" (Badiou 1988, p. 539).

4. See also Galibert's counter to Strathern's critique of the association between village and community (Galibert 2004a, pp. 80–81). The village is a community, despite everything, for Galibert, because of the ineffable link which he claims unites the individual Corsican person, the village, and the whole island, all concentric and mutually implicated

figures of oneness. The island as a whole, whose coherence in the end trumps contingency, remains the guiding light of Galibert's accounts, whereas it is only one among many actors in mine.

2. Mystery

1. Blanqui 1995[1838]; Mottet 1980[1836]; Abbé Gaudin 1997[1787]; Réalier-Dumas 2000[1819].

2. Bourde 1999[1887]; Clémenceau 1999[1908]; Glavany 1998; Forni 1999; Blanqui 1995[1838].

3. The young Kabyles will very quickly become good laborers, even quicker than the Europeans, for their primitive natures are the most receptive; they have a great vacuum to fill; they absorb knowledge almost without effort, unconsciously, as a sponge absorbs water. It is a virgin land where fecundity arrives almost spontaneously. They assimilate languages, arts, formulas, with a marvelous promptness. (Rambaud 1892, quoted in Silverstein 2004, p. 55)

4. The famous French *ethnologue* Marcel Griaule, then, is merely echoing the master of French comparative sociology when he writes: "Ethnography is suspicious, too, of itself—for it is a white science, i.e., stained with prejudices" (Marcel Griaule, quoted in Clifford 1981, p. 550).

5. The year in which *An Account* was published was the same year in which Genoa handed the rebel island to France. Boswell later asked to be the royal commissioner of the short-lived Anglo-Corsican kingdom, but was turned down (Brady 1965, pp. 176–177).

6. Boswell, on the other hand, was explicitly defending a cause and "erecting [a] monument to liberty" (Boswell 1768, p. xiv). He trusts that his readers "will readily make allowance for the enthusiasm of one who has been among the brave islanders, when their patriotic virtue is at its height, and who has felt as it were a communication of their spirit" (ibid., p. 9). And yet, the exception confirms the rule. Boswell isn't just partial, he *identifies and apologizes for* his partiality. Under closer scrutiny, such a position, far from challenging the claims to positivism and objectivity, validates and reinstates them.

7. When I enter into verbal communication with one or more of my fellows, . . . this relation is the relation of one social element with other social elements, considered individually. By contrast, when I observe, listen to or study my natural environment, rocks, water, plants even, each object of my thought is a hermetically sealed world of elements which may indeed know or possess each other intimately, like members of a social group, but which I can only embrace globally and from the outside. (Tarde 1999[1895], pp. 90–91; my translation)

For a more extensive discussion of Gabriel Tarde, see Candea (2009, 2010A, 2010B).

3. Place

1. According to the Department of the Physical Sciences of the Environment based at the University of Corte. http://spe.univ-corse.fr/expe_feux/html/pr%E9sentation.html. (Accessed 10/09/2009).

2. Ibid.

3. http://spe.univ-corse.fr/filippiweb. (Accessed 10/09/2009).

4. http://spe.univ-corse.fr/expe_feux/html/convention.html. (Accessed 10/09/2009).

5. Ibid.

6. http://www.unita-naziunale.org/portail/u_focu_basta.htm. (Accessed 10/09/2009).

7. For a rather different attempt to bring theories of distributed/extended cognition into dialogue with ethnography, see Pedersen (2006).

4. Things

1. This is a clipped version of Piazza à l'Olmu, "the square with the elm." In French, the square is known as La Place de l'Ormeau and often just as La Place.

5. People

1. No more specific authorship is available. The following quotations are drawn from the appendix to the ECRI's *Second Report on France,* which the authors introduce in the following manner:

> In the course of the confidential dialogue process between the French governmental author-
> ities and ECRI on the draft text on France prepared by ECRI, a number of comments of
> the French governmental authorities were taken into account by ECRI, and integrated
> into the report. However, following this dialogue, the French governmental authorities
> expressly requested that the following observations on the part of the authorities of France
> be reproduced as an appendix to ECRI's report.

2. In recognition of the high mobility of much of the population of the island, *residence* is further defined as a fixed and stable residence coinciding with the "centre of material and family interests," thereby excluding the large population of Continental part-time residents, but not members of the Corsican diaspora (who can claim nationality through descent).

3. This is, in my experience, the most common etymological exegesis, although I was once told of a variant whereby it referred to the pointy hats of the Continental policemen who hunted Corsican bandits in the nineteenth century. The hats, seen at a distance over the tangled scrubland of the *maquis,* betrayed the approach of the lawmen. Again, the symbolic associations here are obvious.

4. A crucial shade of meaning between the terms *Arabe* and *Maghrébin* is often over-looked: the latter, built on *le Maghreb* (from Al-Maghrib, the land of the setting sun), is in effect a geographic designation for the descendants of all the people to whom French colonial parlance had applied the terms "native" (*indigene*) or "Muslim" (*musulman*). "Arab" and "Berber" are two further subdivisions of this category, subdivisions with complex histories and volatile political correlates. The contested histories of these distinctions are at the center of some of the most pressing political debates about Franco-Maghrebians in France today (Silverstein 2004). Yet many Corsicans and Continentals seem unaware of this distinction and treat *Arabe* and *Maghrébin* as synonyms.

5. *A techja* means "sick of it," "had enough." The website, although fairly lighthearted, presents itself in part as a reply to continental French stereotypes of the island and islanders.

6. Languages

1. Jensen noted, based on fieldwork in the mid-1990s, "The older generation especially exhibit linguistic insecurity *vis-à-vis* the constructed Corsican written and read aloud in the media. It is said that the language is 'unnatural,' not for 'ordinary people.' Others point to the inconvenience that since the news in Corsican is translated by Corsican linguists, the language used is 'academic' and 'ridiculous'" (Jensen 1999, p. 89). In Crucetta, barely a decade later, I came across no instances of this kind of dismissive critique of "constructed" Corsican as unnatural, academic, or ridiculous. While such opinions may very well have existed, of course, the claims to speaking only "a dialect of Corsican" were made in a way which implied a rather more uncritical acceptance of the existence of a "proper" Corsican standard.

2. It is interesting to note that Grégoire, a figure of evil in the regionalist pantheon, is exalted as a precursor, for other reasons, by French anti-racists, although the historical accuracy of this categorization has been questioned (e.g., Lloyd 1994).

3. *S'ancrer pour mieux s'ouvrir.* The phrase originated in some official publication and became a byword among teachers and administrators

4. This is a problem faced by any French person with a "foreign"-sounding name. The solution is, metaphorically speaking, to spread the foreign name as "flatly" as possible on a French-language canvas. I find that I now have the deeply ingrained habit of spelling out my name to interlocutors ("Candea, c-a-n-d-e-a").

5. And, indeed, some place names, such as Bastia, were almost always "Gallicized" in French speech; in those cases, Corsicanized pronunciation became quite a marked statement.

6. I am grateful to Alexandra Jaffe for clarifying this point.

7. This is much like the *a pa pa* described by Cowan for Greece (Cowan 1990, p. 116). Herzfeld (personal communication) noted that *po po po* is also sometimes used in Greece to express surprise at the magnitude of a phenomenon. Interestingly, *po po po* also became a characteristic interjection in *pataouète,* the lingua franca drawing on French, Spanish, Italian, Maltese, and Corsican, which was associated with French settlers in Algeria around the turn of the twentieth century (Prochaska 1990).

8. That my final sentence in this exchange was, in fact, rather incorrect raises a number of interesting issues. It amounted to a literal translation of the French phrase "je ne faisais pas attention," in which the original French syntax was preserved. More "standard" Corsican would be "un era mica attentu." As such, my sentence could probably be taken as an example of what Jaffe calls "Gallicised Corsican" (Jaffe 1999, p. 115).

7. Knowing

1. Belmonte comments on this distinction in his famous Neapolitan ethnography *The Broken Fountain:* "The Italian verb translated in this instance as 'to know,' *conoscere,* refers to 'that knowledge that issues directly from the involvement of the person in the world,' as opposed to *sapere,* 'that knowledge that is objectively separable from the central core of one's subjectivity'" (Belmonte 1989, p. xvii).

8. Anonymous Introduction

1. The French word *inconnu* is the best term here since it simply denotes "one who is not known," without the additional connotations carried, in English, by words such as "stranger," "foreigner," or "outsider."

2. Anthropologists have profusely shown the importance, in other Corsican contexts, of binary and indeed agonistic self/Other encounters (Ravis-Giordani 1983, pp. 129–157, 206–231; Galibert 2004b, p. 158).

3. In Combray, to see "a person whom nobody knew" was as improbable as to meet a character from Greek mythology, and within living memory, each time one of these stupendous apparitions had been reported in the Rue du Saint-Esprit or in the Square, it had invariably turned out, after judicious and apposite research, that the fabulous monster was reduced to the dimensions of "a person whom somebody knew," either personally or by proxy, and who enjoyed official status as a relative of the Combray family. . . . In Combray, everything and everybody, both animals and people, were so well known to everybody else that if my aunt happened to notice down in the street a dog "that she didn't know," she could not take her mind off it and would devote to this incomprehensible event all her powers of induction and her empty hours. (Proust 1982, p. 44)

4. Abu-Lughod 1991; Gupta and Ferguson 1992; Malkki 1995, to name but a few.

5. See, for instance, Alsmark 1979; Caisson 1978; Lenclud 1979; Olivesi 1983; Ravis-Giordani 1983; Tiévant and Desideri 1986.

6. Desideri 1997; Galibert 2004b; Meisterheim 1999. For an excellent overview of Francophone work on Corsica, see Galibert 2005.

7. Galibert 2004b; Meisterheim 1999.

8. The arbitrary location (be it Crucetta or another) allows us to say "local" without "smuggling back in assumptions about small-scale societies and face-to-face communities that we thought we had left behind" (Gupta and Ferguson 1997, p. 75).

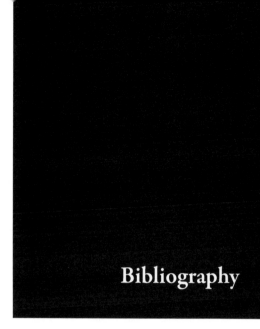

Bibliography

Abbé Gaudin. 1997[1787]. *Voyage en Corse, et vues politiques sur l'amélioration de cette isle; Suivi de quelques Pièces relatives à la Corse, & de plusieurs Anecdotes sur le caractère & les vertus de ses habitans.* Nimes: Lacour.

Abu-Lughod, L. 1991. "Writing against Culture." In R. C. Fox, ed., *Recapturing Anthropology.* Santa Fe, N.M.: School of American Research Press, 137–162.

Actes du Colloque Statistiques "Ethniques." 2006. Paris: Centres d'analyse stratégique. Available at www.strategie.gouv.fr/IMG/pdf/ActesStatistiquesethniquesvers13-11.pdf.

Adams, W. Y. 1998. *The Philosophical Roots of Anthropology.* Stanford, Calif.: CSLI Publications.

Ager, D. E. 1999. *Identity, Insecurity and Image: France and Language.* Clevedon, United Kingdom: Multilingual Matters.

Alsmark, G. 1979. *Herdar på Korsika.* Lund: LiberLäromedel.

Anderson, A. 2001. *The Powers of Distance: Cosmopolitanism and the Cultivation of Detachment.* Princeton, N.J.: Princeton University Press.

Anderson, B. 1991. *Imagined Communities: Reflections on the Origin and Spread of Nationalism.* London: Verso.

Andreani, J.-L. 1999. *Comprendre la Corse.* Paris: Gallimard.

Antonetti, P. 1973. *Histoire de la Corse.* Paris: Laffont.

Appadurai, A. 1986. "Introduction: Commodities and the Politics of Value." In A. Appadurai, ed., *The Social Life of Things: Commodities in Cultural Perspective.* Cambridge: Cambridge University Press, 3–63.

———. 1988. "Introduction: Place and Voice in Anthropological Theory." *Cultural Anthropology* 3(1): 16–20.

Ardener, E. 1989. "'Remote Areas': Some Theoretical Considerations." In M. Chapman, ed., *Edwin Ardener: The Voice of Prophecy and Other Essays*. Oxford: Basil Blackwell, 211–224.

Associu per a Cunsulta Naziunale. 2002. Available at www.cunsulta.com.

Badiou, A. 1988. *L'être et l'événement*. Paris: Seuil.

Balbi, J.-H. 1989. "Identité Culturelle." *Cahiers de l'Institut du Développement des Îles Mediterranéennes* 1: 115–119.

Balibar, E., and I. Wallerstein, eds. 1991. *Race, Nation, Class: Ambiguous Identities*. New York: Verso.

Banfield, E. C. 1958. *The Moral Basis of a Backward Society*. Glencoe, Ill.: Free Press.

Barth, F., ed. 1969. *Ethnic Groups and Boundaries*. London: George Allen and Unwin.

Bashkow, I. 2004. "A Neo-Boasian Conception of Cultural Boundaries." *American Anthropologist* 106(3): 443–458.

Bauman, Z. 1999. *Modernity and Ambivalence*. Ithaca, N.Y.: Cornell University Press.

Baumann, G. 1996. *Contesting Culture: Discourses of Identity in Multi-ethnic London*. Cambridge: Cambridge University Press.

———. 1999. *The Multicultural Riddle: Rethinking National, Ethnic and Religious Identities*. London: Routledge.

Belmonte, T. 1989. *The Broken Fountain*. New York: Columbia University Press.

Bernabéu-Casanova, E. 1997. *Le Nationalisme Corse: Genèse, succès et échec*. Paris: L'Harmattan.

Bianchi, D. 2002. *Les Couteaux Corses*. Paris: Crépin-Leblond.

Biggi, M., and A. Meisterheim. 1997. "Utopie et planification." In *Catalogue de l'exposition Mesure de l'île*. Corte: Musée d'Anthropologie de la Corse, 25–36.

Blanqui, A. J. 1995[1838]. "Rapport sur l'etat économique et moral de la Corse." In J. M. Goulemot, P. Lidsky, and D. Masseau, eds., *Le Voyage en France: Anthologie des voyageurs français et étrangers en France aux XIXe et XXe siècles (1815–1914)*, Paris: Robert Laffont, 465–489.

Blu, K. I. 1996. "'Where Do You Stay At?': Home Place and Community among the Lumbee." In S. Feld and K. H. Basso, eds., *Senses of Place*. Santa Fe, N.M.: School of American Research Press, 197–227.

Bodenhorn, B., and G. Von Bruck. 2006. "'Entangled in Histories': An Introduction to the Anthropology of Names and Naming." In G. Von Bruck and B. Bodenhorn, eds., *The Anthropology of Names and Naming*. Cambridge: Cambridge University Press, 1–30.

Boissevain, J. 1974. *Friends of Friends*. Oxford: Blackwell.

———. 1975. "Introduction." In J. Boissevain and J. Friedl, eds., *Beyond the Community: Social Process in Europe*. The Hague: Department of Education Science of the Netherlands.

Boissevain, J., ed. 1996. *Coping with Tourists: European Reactions to Mass Tourism*. Oxford: Berghahn.

Boswell, J. 1768. *An Account of Corsica*. Glasgow: Foulis.

Bourde, P. 1999[1887]. "En Corse: L'esprit de clan, les moeurs politiques, les vendettas, le banditisme." In G.-X. Culioli, ed., *La Corse aux rapports*. Ajaccio: DCL.

Bourdieu, P. 1980. "L'Identité et la représentation: Eléments pour une reflexion critique sur l'idée de région." *Actes de la Recherche en Sciences Sociale* 35: 63–72.

———. 1990. *The Logic of Practice*. Cambridge: Polity.

Bowen, J. R. 2006. *Why the French Don't Like Headscarves: Islam, the State and Public Space.* Princeton, N.J.: Princeton University Press.

Brady, F. 1965. *Boswell's Political Career.* New Haven, Conn.: Yale University Press.

Briggs, C. L. 1996. "The Politics of Discursive Authority in Research on the 'Invention of Tradition.'" *Cultural Anthropology* 11(4): 435–469.

Caisson, M. 1974. "L'hospitalité comme relation d'ambivalence." *Études Corses* 2: 115–127.

———. 1978. *Pieve e paesi: Communautés rurales corses.* Paris: Centre National de la Recherche Scientifique.

Campbell, J. K. 1964. *Honour, Family and Patronage: A Study of Institutions and Moral Values in a Greek Mountain Community.* Oxford: Clarendon.

Candea, M. 2006. "Resisting Victimhood in Corsica." *History and Anthropology* 17(4): 369–384.

———. 2007. "Arbitrary Locations: In Defence of the Bounded Field-Site." *Journal of the Royal Anthropological Institute* 13: 167–184.

———. 2008. "Fire and Identity as Matters of Concern in Corsica." *Anthropological Theory* 8(2).

———. 2009. "Arbitrary Locations: In Defence of the Bounded Field-site (with a New Afterword)." In M.-A. Falzon, ed., *Multi-sited Ethnography: Theory, Praxis and Locality in Contemporary Research.* Aldershot: Ashgate, 25–46.

———. 2010A. "Introduction: Revisiting Tarde's House." In M. Candea, ed., *The Social after Gabriel Tarde: Debates and Assessments.* London: Routledge.

———. 2010B. "Anonymous Introductions: Identity and Belonging in Corsica." *Journal of the Royal Anthropological Institute.* 16: 119–137.

———. Forthcoming A. "'Our Division of the Universe': Making a Space for the Non-political in Anthropology of Politics." *Current Anthropology.*

———. Forthcoming B. "'I Fell in Love with Carlos the Meerkat': Engagement and Detachment in Human–Animal Relations." *American Ethnologist.*

Carrington, D. 1962. *This Corsica: A Complete Guide.* London: Hammond.

Casanova, G. 1980. *Pour une Corse Française: Paroles pour une île.* Paris: Albatros.

Cassano, F. 1998. *La pensée meridienne.* La Tour d'Aigues: L'aube.

Chapman, M. 1978. *The Gaelic Vision in Scottish Culture.* London: Croom Helm.

———. 1992. "Fieldwork, Language and Locality in Europe, from the North." In J. D. Pina-Cabral, ed., *Europe Observed.* London: Macmillan, 39–55.

Chartier, E., and R. Larvor. 2004. *La France éclatée? Régionalisme, autonomisme, indépendantisme.* Brest: Coop Breizh.

Chemin, A. 2002a. "Les Traces ADN utilisées dans les enquêtes butent sur une spécificité Corse." *Le Monde,* 15 November.

———. 2002b. "Les contours d'un 'peuple corse' virtuel sur www.cunsulta.com." *Le Monde,* 26 November.

———. 2003. "Les premières 'cartes d'identité corses' seront distribuées le 8 mai." *Le Monde,* 26 April.

Chiorboli, J. 1991. *La Langue des Corses: Grammaire et Glottopolitique.* Rouen: University of Rouen.

Chiva, I. 1958. "Causes sociologiques du sous-développement régional: L'exemple Corse." *Cahiers internationaux de Sociologie* 24: 141–147.

———. 1963. "Social Organisation, Traditional Economy and Customary Law in Corsica: Outline of a Plan of Analysis." In J. Pitt-Rivers, ed., *Mediterranean Countrymen.* Paris: Mouton.

Clark, A., and D. J. Chalmers. 1998. "The Extended Mind." *Analysis* 58: 10–23.

Clémenceau, G. B. 1999[1908]. "Rapport Clémenceau." In G.-X. Culioli, ed., *La Corse aux rapports.* Ajaccio: DCL.

Clifford, J. 1980. "Review Essays: Orientalism (Edward W. Said)." *History and Theory* 19(2): 204–223.

———. 1981. "On Ethnographic Surrealism." *Comparative Studies in Society and History* 23(4): 539–564.

———. 1986. "Introduction: Partial Truths." In J. Clifford and G. Marcus, eds., *Writing Culture: The Poetics and Politics of Ethnography.* Berkeley: University of California Press, 1–26.

———. 1988. *The Predicament of Culture: Twentieth Century Ethnography, Literature, and Art.* Cambridge, Mass.: Harvard University Press.

Clifford, J., and G. Marcus, eds. 1986. *Writing Culture: The Poetics and Politics of Ethnography.* Berkeley: University of California Press.

Cole, J. 1977. "Anthropology Comes Part Way Home: Community Studies in Europe." *Annual Review of Anthropology* 6: 349–378.

———. 1997. *The New Racism in Europe: A Sicilian Ethnography.* Cambridge: Cambridge University Press.

Colombani, J. 1973. "Les institutions politiques et administratives de la Corse sous la Monarchie Française (1768–1789)." *Études Corses* 1: 235–237.

Colonna, F. 1997. "Educating Conformity in French Colonial Algeria." In F. Cooper and A. Stoler, eds., *Tensions of Empire: Colonial Cultures in a Bourgeois World.* Berkeley: University of California Press, 346–370.

Colonna d'Istria, R. 1997. *La Corse au XXe siècle: Histoire des Heurs et Malheurs d'une province Française.* Paris: France-Empire.

Conseil Constitutionnel. 1991. "Décision no. 91-290 DC." Available at www.conseil-constitutionnel.fr/conseil-constitutionnel/francais/les-decisions/depuis-1958/decisions-par-date/1991/91-290-dc/decision-n-91-290-dc-du-09-mai-1991.8758.html. (Accessed 10/09/2009).

Cowan, J. K. 1990. *Dance and the Body Politic in Northern Greece.* Princeton, N.J.: Princeton University Press.

Crang, M. 1999. "Knowing, Tourism and Practices of Vision." In D. Crouch, ed., *Leisure/ Tourism Geographies: Practices and Geographical Knowledge.* London: Routledge, 238–256.

Culioli, G.-X. 1990. *Le Complexe Corse.* Paris: Gallimard.

———. 2003. "Pétition." Available at www.corsica.ch/wwwboard/messages/33.html.

Culioli, G.-X., ed. 1999. *La Corse aux rapports.* Ajaccio: DCL.

Cuq, H., and X. De Roux. 1997. *Rapport d'information déposé en application de l'article 145 du Règlement par la mission d'information commune sur la Corse: Auditions,* vol. 2. Paris: Assemblée Nationale.

Daston, L., and P. Galison. 2007. *Objectivity.* Cambridge, Mass.: Zone.

De Francheschi, J. 1986. *Recherches sur la Nature et la répartition de la propriété foncière en Corse de la fin d l'ancien régime jusqu'au milieu du 19ème siècle.* Ajaccio: Cyrnos et Méditerranée.

De La Rocca, J. 1857. *La Corse et son Avenir.* Paris: Plon.

De Lemps. 1843. *Panorama de la Corse ou histoire abrégée de cette île, et Description des moeurs et Usages de ses habitants.* Paris: Siriou.

DeCerteau, M., D. Julia, and J. Revel, eds. 1974. *Une politique de la langue: La Révolution Française et les patois: L'Enquête de Grégoire.* Paris: Gallimard.

Deleuze, G., and F. Guattari. 1980. *Capitalisme et schizophrénie II: Mille Plateaux.* Paris: Minuit.

Derrida, J. 1992. "Force of Law: The Mystical Foundation of Authority." In D. Cornell, M. Rosenfeld, and D. Carlson, eds., *Deconstruction and the Possibility of Justice.* London: Routledge.

———. 1997. *De l'hospitalité (Anne Dufourmantelle invite Jacques Derrida à répondre).* Paris: Calmann-Levy.

Desanti, D. 1997. "Effacer la Mer: Une reflexion sur l'identité Corse." *Esprit* 5: 148–155.

Desideri, L. 1997. "L'Autre scene pour avoir lieu." In L. Desideri and M. Caisson, eds., *Cahiers d'Anthropologie,* vol. 5: *La Griffe des Légendes: Corse, mythes et lieux.* Ajaccio: Musée de la Corse/Collectivité territoriale de Corse.

Di Meglio, A. 2003. "L'Avènement de l'Enseignement du Corse." In J. Fusina, ed., *Histoire de l'école en Corse.* Ajaccio: Albiana, 507–546.

Dumont, L. 2006. *Introduction to Two Theories of Social Anthropology: Descent Groups and Marriage Alliance.* Oxford: Berghahn.

Durkheim, E. 1964. *The Rules of Sociological Method.* New York: Free Press.

———. 1984. *The Division of Labour in Society.* London: Macmillan.

———. 1988. *Les Règles de la methode sociologique.* Paris: Champs Flammarion.

Éducation Nationale. 2001. "Langues et Cultures Régionales." *Bulletin Officiel de l'Éducation Nationale* 33 (Encart). Available at www.education.gouv.fr/bo/2001/33/encart.htm.

Edwards, J. 1998. "The Need for 'a Bit of History': Place and Past in English Identity." In N. Lovell, ed., *Locality and Belonging.* London: Routledge, 147–167.

Edwards, J., and M. Strathern. 2000. "Including Our Own." In J. Carsten, ed., *Cultures of Relatedness: New Approaches to the Study of Kinship.* Cambridge: Cambridge University Press.

European Commission against Racism and Intolerance. 2000. "Second Report on France." Available at http://hudoc.ecri.coe.int/XMLEcri/ENGLISH/Cycle_02/02_CbC_eng/02-cbc-france-eng.pdf.

Evans-Pritchard, E. E. 1940. *The Nuer: A Description of the Modes of Livelihood and Political Institutions of a Nilotic People.* Oxford: Oxford University Press.

———. 1976. "Some Reminiscences and Reflections on Fieldwork." In Evans-Pritchard, *Witchcraft, Oracles and Magic among the Azande.* Oxford: Clarendon, 240–254.

Fabian, J. 1983. *Time and the Other: How Anthropology Makes Its Object.* New York: Columbia University Press.

Filippi, P. 1992. "Le Français Régional de Corse." Ph.D. thesis, University of Corsica.

Fischer, E. F. 1999. "Cultural Logic and Maya Identity: Rethinking Constructivism and Essentialism." *Current Anthropology* 40(4): 473–499.

Follorou, J. 1999. *Corse: l'Etat bafoué.* Paris: Stock.

Forni, R. 1999. "Rapport fait au nom de la commission d'enquête sur le fonctionnement des forces de sécurité en Corse" (Documents d'information de l'Assemblée nationale, no. 1918). Paris: Assemblée Nationale. Available at www.ladocumentationfrancaise.fr/rapports-publics/994001751/index.shtml. (Accessed 10/09/2009).

Foucault, M. 1976. *Histoire de la Sexualité,* vol. 1: *La Volonté de Savoir.* Paris: Gallimard.

———. 1979. "What Is an Author?" In J. V. Harari, ed., *Textual Strategies.* Ithaca, N.Y.: Cornell University Press.

———. 1994. "De l'amitié comme mode de vie." In D. Defert and F. Ewald, eds., *Michel Foucault: Dits et Écrits 1954–1988,* vol. 4. Paris: Gallimard, 163–167.

Frake, C. O. 1996. "Pleasant Places, Past Times and Sheltered Identity in Rural East Anglia." In S. Feld and K. F. Basso, eds., *Senses of Place.* Santa Fe, N.M.: School of American Research Press, 229–257.

Franklin, A. 2003. *Tourism: An Introduction.* London: Sage.

Friedman, J. 1997. "Global Crises, the Struggle for Cultural Identity and Intellectual Porkbarrelling: Cosmopolitans versus Locals, Ethnics and Nationals in an Era of Dehegemonisation." In P. Werbner and T. Modood, eds., *Debating Cultural Hybridity: Multi-Cultural Identities and the Politics of Anti-Racism.* London: Zed, 70–89.

Galibert, C. 2004a. *Guide non Touristique d'un village Corse.* Ajaccio: Albiana.

———. 2004b. *La Corse: Une île et le monde.* Paris: Presses Universitaires de France.

———. 2005. "L'épistémè ethno-anthropologique corse: De l'observation distanciée à la tentation d'une ethnologie de l'acteur." Available at www.espacestemps.net/document 1185.html. (Accessed 10/09/2009).

Geertz, C. 1973. *The Interpretation of Cultures: Selected Essays.* New York: Basic.

———. 1984. "Anti Anti-relativism." *American Anthropologist* 86: 263–278.

———. 1988. *Works and Lives: The Anthropologist as Author.* Stanford, Calif.: Stanford University Press.

Gell, A. 1995. "The Language of the Forest: Landscape and Ponological Iconism in Umeda." In E. Hirsch and M. O'Hanlon, eds., *The Anthropology of Landscape: Perspectives on Place and Space.* Oxford: Clarendon, 232–254.

———. 1998. *Art and Agency: An Anthropological Theory.* Oxford: Oxford University Press.

Gellner, E. 1983. *Nations and Nationalism.* Oxford: Blackwell.

Gellner, E., and J. Waterbury, eds. 1977. *Patrons and Clients.* London: Duckworth.

Gerth, H. H., and C. W. Mills, eds. 1948. *From Max Weber: Essays in Sociology.* London: Routledge and Kegan Paul.

Gil, J. 1984. *La Corse: Entre la liberté et la terreur.* Paris: Différence.

Glavany, J. 1998. "Rapport fait au nom de la commission d'enquête sur l'utilisation des fonds publics et la gestion des services publics en Corse." Paris: Assemblée Nationale. Available at www.assemblee-nationale.fr/11/dossiers/corse.asp. (Accessed 10/09/2009).

Graziani, A., and D. Taddei. 2002. "La Période révolutionnaire à Île-Rousse, Monticello et Santa-Reparata." In A. d. H. e. G. d. Monticello, ed., *Vingt chapitres de l'histoire de Monticello.* Ajaccio: Albiana, 147–169.

Green, S. 2005. *Notes from the Balkans.* Princeton, N.J.: Princeton University Press.

Grillo, R. D. 1985. *Ideologies and Institutions in Urban France: The Representation of Immigrants.* Cambridge: Cambridge University Press.

———. 2003. "Cultural Essentialism and Cultural Anxiety." *Anthropological Theory* 3(2): 157–173.

Grillo, R. D., ed. 1980. *"Nation" and "State" in Europe: Anthropological Perspectives.* London: Academic.

Guide du Routard: Corse. 2003. Paris: Hachette Tourisme.

Gupta, A., and J. Ferguson. 1992. "Beyond 'Culture': Space, Identity and the Politics of Difference." *Cultural Anthropology* 7(1): 6–23.

———. 1997. "Discipline and Practice: The 'Field' as Site, Method and Location in Anthropology." In A. Gupta and J. Ferguson, eds., *Anthropological Locations: Boundaries and Grounds of a Field Science.* Berkeley: University of California Press, 1–46.

Hall, T. E. 1968. "The Development of Enlightenment Interest in Eighteenth-Century Corsica." *Studies on Voltaire* 64: 165–185.

Handler, R. 1984. *Nationalism and the Politics of Culture in Quebec.* Madison: University of Wisconsin Press.

Handler, R., and J. Linnekin. 1984. "Tradition, Genuine and Spurious." *Journal of American Folklore* 97: 274–290.

Harrison, S. 2003. "Cultural Difference as Denied Resemblance: Reconsidering Nationalism and Ethnicity." *Comparative Studies in Society and History* 45(2): 343–361.

Henare, A., M. Holbraad, and S. Wastell, eds. 2006. *Thinking through Things: Theorising Artifacts Ethnographically.* Cambridge: Cambridge University Press.

Herzfeld, M. 1985. *The Poetics of Manhood: Contest and Identity in a Cretan Mountain Village.* Princeton, N.J.: Princeton University Press.

———. 1987. "'As in Your Own House': Hospitality, Ethnography, and the Stereotype of Mediterranean Society." In D. Gilmore, ed., *Honor and Shame and the Unity of the Mediterranean.* Washington, D.C.: American Anthropological Association, 75–89.

———. 1989. *Anthropology through the Looking-Glass: Critical Ethnography in the Margins of Europe.* Cambridge: Cambridge University Press.

———. 1997. *Cultural Intimacy: Social Poetics and the Nation-State.* London: Routledge.

Hewitt, R. 2005. *White Backlash and the Politics of Multiculturalism.* Cambridge: Cambridge University Press.

Hirsch, E. 1995. "Introduction." In E. Hirsch and M. O'Hanlon, eds., *The Anthropology of Landscape: Perspectives on Place and Space.* Oxford: Clarendon, 1–30.

Hobsbawm, E. J., and T. Ranger, eds. 1983. *The Invention of Tradition.* Cambridge: Cambridge University Press.

Holmes, D. R. 2000. *Integral Europe: Fast-Capitalism, Multiculturalism, Neofascism.* Princeton, N.J.: Princeton University Press.

Hossay, P. 2004. "Recognizing Corsica: The Drama of Recognition in Nationalist Mobilization." *Ethnic and Racial Studies* 27(3): 403–430.

Humphrey, C. 2008. "Reassembling Individual Subjects: Events and Decisions in Troubled Times." *Anthropological Theory* 8(4): 357–380.

Huntington, S. P. 1993. "The Clash of Civilizations?" *Foreign Affairs* 72(3): 22–49.

Hutchins, E. 1996. "Learning to Navigate." In S. Chaiklin and J. Lave, eds., *Understanding Practice.* Cambridge: Cambridge University Press, 35–63.

Ingold, T. 1993. "The Temporality of the Landscape." *World Archaeology* 25(2): 152–174.

———. 1994. "Introduction to Social Life." In T. Ingold, ed., *Companion Encyclopedia of Anthropology: Humanity, Culture and Social Life.* London: Routledge.

Irvine, J. T., and S. Gal. 2000. "Language Ideology and Linguistic Differentiation." In P. V. Kroskrity, ed., *Regimes of Language: Ideologies, Polities, and Identities.* Santa Fe, N.M.: School of American Research Press, 35–83.

Jaffe, A. 1996. "The Second Annual Corsican Spelling Contest: Orthography and Ideology." *American Ethnologist* 23(4): 816–835.

———. 1997. "Narrating the 'I' versus Narrating the 'Isle': Life Histories and the Problem of Representation on Corsica." In D. Reed-Danahay, ed., *Auto/Ethnography.* Oxford: Berg, 145–166.

———. 1999. *Ideologies in Action: Language Politics on Corsica.* Berlin: Mouton de Gruyter.

———. 2005. "La polynomie dans une école bilingue corse: Bilans et defis." *Marges Linguistiques* 10: 282–300.

———. 2007. "Minority Language Movements." In M. Heller, ed., *Bilingualism: A Social Approach.* Basingstoke: Palgrave, 50–70.

Jehasse, O. 1986. *Corsica Classica.* Ajaccio: La Marge.

Jensen, J. B. 1999. "Politics of Language and Language of Politics: Corsican Language Activism and Conflicts between Internal and External Representations of National Identity." *Folk* 41: 77–98.

Kahn, J. S. 2003. "Anthropology as Cosmopolitan Practice?" *Anthropological Theory* 3(4): 403–415.

Karsenti, B. 2006. *Politique de l'Esprit: Auguste Comte et la naissance de la science sociale.* Paris: Hermann.

Kuper, A. 1994. "Culture, Identity and the Project of a Cosmopolitan Anthropology." *Man* 29(3): 537–554.

———. 2005. *The Reinvention of Primitive Society: Transformations of a Myth.* London: Routledge.

Labro, M. 1977. *La question corse.* Paris: Entente.

Larsen, J., and M. Haldrup. 2006. "Material Cultures of Tourism." *Leisure Studies* 25(3): 275–289.

Latour, B. 1993. *We Have Never Been Modern.* London: Harvester Wheatsheaf.

———. 2002. "Gabriel Tarde and the End of the Social." In P. Joyce, ed., *The Social in Question: New Bearings in History and the Social Sciences.* London: Routledge, 117–132.

———. 2004. *Politics of Nature: How to Bring the Sciences into Democracy.* Cambridge, Mass.: Harvard University Press.

———. 2005. *Reassembling the Social: An Introduction to Actor-Network-Theory.* Oxford: Oxford University Press.

Lave, J. 1996. "The Practice of Learning." In S. Chaiklin and J. Lave, eds., *Understanding Practice: Perspectives on Activity and Context.* Cambridge: Cambridge University Press, 3–32.

Laville, A. 1999. *Un crime politique en Corse: Claude Erignac, le préfet assassiné.* Paris: Cherche Midi.

Leach, E. R. 1964. *Political Systems of Highland Burma.* London: Bell.

Leach, J. 2010. "Intervening with the Social? Ethnographic Practice and Tarde's Image of Relations between Subjects." In M. Candea, ed., *The Social after Gabriel Tarde: Debates and Assessments.* London: Routledge.

Lefevre, M. 2000. *Geopolitique de la Corse: Le modèle républicain en question.* Paris: L'Harmattan.

Lenclud, G. 1979. "Des feux introuvables: L'organisation familiale dans un village de la Corse traditionnelle." *Études Rurales* 76: 7–50.

———. 1996. "The Factual and the Normative in Ethnography: Do Cultural Differences Derive from Description?" *Anthropology Today* 12(1): 7–11.

Linnekin, J. 1991. "Cultural Invention and the Dilemma of Authenticity." *American Anthropologist* 93(2): 446–449.

Lloyd, C. 1994. "Universalism and Difference: The Crisis of Anti-Racism in the UK and France." In A. Rattansi and S. Westwood, eds., *Racism, Modernity and Identity: On the Western Front.* Cambridge: Polity, 222–244.

———. 2000. "Interpreting Racist Violence in France." In T. Allen and J. Eade, eds., *Divided Europeans: Understanding Ethnicities in Conflict.* The Hague: Kluwer Law International, 285–301.

Loughlin, J. P. 1989. *Regionalism and Ethnic Nationalism in France: A Case Study of Corsica.* Florence: European University Institute.

MacDonald, S. 1993. "Identity Complexes in Western Europe: Social Anthropological Perspectives." In S. MacDonald, ed., *Inside European Identities: Ethnography in Western Europe.* Oxford: Berg, 1–26.

Malinowski, B. 1972. "Phatic Communion." In J. Laver and S. Hutcheson, eds., *Communication in Face to Face Interaction.* Middlesex: Penguin, 146–152.

Malkki, L. H. 1995. *Purity and Exile: Violence, Memory and National Cosmology among Hutu Refugees in Tanzania.* Chicago: University of Chicago Press.

Marcellesi, J.-B. 1989. "Corse et Théorie Sociolinguistique: Reflets Croisés." In G. Ravis-Giordani, ed., *L'île Miroir: Actes du Colloque d'Aix en Provence, 27–28 novembre 1987.* Ajaccio: La Marge.

Marchetti, P. 1974. *Le Corse sans Peine.* Paris: Assimil.

———. 1989. *La Corsophonie: Un idiome à la mer.* Paris: Albatros.

Marchetti, P., and D. A. Geronimi. 1971. *Intricciate è Cambiarine.* Nogent-sur-Marne: Beaulieu.

Marcus, G. 1995. "Ethnography in/of the World System: The Emergence of Multi-Sited Ethnography." *Annual Review of Anthropology* 24: 95–117.

Marcus, G., ed. 1999. *Ethnography through Thick and Thin.* Princeton, N.J.: Princeton University Press.

Marcus, G. E., and M. M. J. Fischer. 1986. *Anthropology as Cultural Critique: An Experimental Moment in the Human Sciences.* Chicago: Chicago University Press.

Masson-Maret, H. 1991. *La Personnalité Corse: Étude Ethnopsychologique.* Ajaccio: La Marge.

McDonald, M. E. 1989. *We Are Not French.* Cambridge: Cambridge University Press.

———. 1993. "The Construction of Difference: An Anthropological Approach to Stereotypes." In S. MacDonald, ed., *Inside European Identities: Ethnography in Western Europe.* Oxford: Berg, 219–236.

———. 2000. "Accountability, Anthropology and the European Commission." In M. Strathern, ed., *Audit Cultures: Anthropological Studies in Accountability, Audit and the Academy.* London: Routledge.

McKechnie, R. 1993. "Becoming Celtic in Corsica." In S. MacDonald, ed., *Inside European Identities: Ethnography in Western Europe.* Oxford: Berg, 118–145.

Meisterheim, A. 1999. *L'île laboratoire.* Ajaccio: Piazzola.

Mill, J. S. 1974. *A System of Logic,* vol. 7. London: Longmans.

Mitchell, T. 1988. *Colonising Egypt.* Berkeley: University of California Press.

Mol, A. 2002. *The Body Multiple: Ontology in Medical Practice.* Durham, N.C.: Duke University Press.

Montesquieu, C. 1787. *Oeuvres,* vol. 2. London: T. Evans.

Mottet. 1980[1836]. "Rapport Mottet." In X. Versini, ed., *Le Vie quotidienne en Corse au temps de Mérimée.* Paris: Hachette.

Narayan, K. 1993. "How Native Is a 'Native' Anthropologist?" *American Anthropologist* 95(3): 671–686.

Navaro-Yashin, Y. 2002. *Faces of the State: Secularism and Public Life in Turkey.* Princeton, N.J.: Princeton University Press.

———. 2007. "Make-Believe Papers, Legal Forms and the Counterfeit." *Anthropological Theory* 7(1): 79–98.

Noer, A. 1988. *Le Centralisme dans la Politique Linguistique: La Corse, un exemple de Minorité Nationale.* Copenhagen: Romansk Institut, Copenhagen University.

Olivesi, C. 1983. "Le Système politique corse: Le clan." *Cuntrasti* 1: 13–24.

Ozouf, M., and J. Ozouf. 2001. *La République des instituteurs.* Paris: Seuil.

Pedersen, M. A. 2006. "Talismans of Thought: Shamanist Ontologies and Extended Cognition in Northern Mongolia." In A. Henare, M. Holbraad, and S. Wastell, eds., *Thinking through Things: Theorising Artifacts Ethnographically.* Cambridge: Cambridge University Press, 141–166.

Pellegrinetti, J.-P. 2005. "Langue et identité: L'exemple du Corse durant la troisième république." *Cahiers de la Mediterranée* 66. Available at cdlm.revues.org/index116 .html. (Accessed 10/09/2009).

Physical Sciences of the Environment Department, University of Corte. 2009. "Plate-Forme expérimentale de terrain." Available at http://spe.univ- corse.fr/expe_feux/html/pr%E9sentation.html. (Accessed 10/09/2009).

Pitt-Rivers, J. A. 1954. *The People of the Sierra.* London: Weidenfeld and Nicolson.

Poggioli, P. 1999. *Corse: Chroniques d'une île déchirée, 1996–1999.* Paris: L'Harmattan.

Pollock, F., and F. W. Maitland. 1898. *The History of English Law before the Times of Edward I.* Cambridge: Cambridge University Press.

Pratt, M. L. 1986. "Fieldwork in Common Places." In J. Clifford and G. Marcus, eds., *Writing Culture: The Poetics and Politics of Ethnography.* Berkeley: University of California Press, 27–50.

Préfecture de Corse. 2003. "Site de la Préfecture et des services de l'Etat en Corse." Available at www.corse.pref.gouv.fr. (Accessed 10/09/2009).

Prochaska, D. 1990. *Making Algeria French: Colonialism in Bône, 1870–1920.* Cambridge: Cambridge University Press.

Proust, M. 1982. *A Search for Lost Time: Swann's Way,* trans. James Grieve. Canberra: Australian National University Press.

Rabinow, P. 1989. *French Modern: Norms and Forms of the Social Environment.* Cambridge, Mass.: MIT Press.

Radio Corsica Frequenza Mora. 2003. "News." 1 September.

Rattansi, A. 1995. "'Western' Racisms, Ethnicities and Identities in a 'Postmodern' Frame." In A. Rattansi and S. Westwood, eds., *Racism, Modernity and Identity: On the Western Front.* Cambridge: Polity, 15–86.

Ravis-Giordani, G. 1983. *Bergers Corses.* Aix-en-Provence: Edisud.

Réalier-Dumas, M. 2000[1819]. *Mémoire sur la Corse.* Nimes: Lacour.

Reed-Danahay, D. 1996. *Education and Identity in Rural France: The Politics of Schooling.* Cambridge: Cambridge University Press.

Rey, A., ed. 1993. *Dictionnaire Historique de la Langue Française.* Paris: Dictionnaires le Robert.

Rousseau, J.-J. 1953. "Part I of the Constitutional Project for Corsica." In F. Watkins, ed., *Rousseau: Political Writings.* London: Nelson, 279–320.

Said, E. W. 1979. *Orientalism*. New York: Vintage.

Salini, D. 1996. *Musiques Traditionnelles de Corse*. Ajaccio: A essagera/Squadra di u Finuselu.

Salway, B. 1994. "What's in a Name? A Survey of Roman Onomastic Practice from c. 700 B.C. to A.D. 700." *Journal of Roman Studies* 84: 124–145.

Sanguinetti, A. 1979. *Procès des Jacobins*. Paris: Grasset and Fasquelle.

Schneider, D. M. 1968. *American Kinship: A Cultural Account*. Englewood Cliffs, N.J.: Prentice-Hall.

Schneider, J. 1998. *Italy's "Southern Question": Orientalism in One Country*. Oxford: Berg.

Sheller, M., and J. Urry, eds. 2004. *Tourism Mobilities: Places to Play, Places in Play*. London: Routledge.

Shore, C. 1993. "Inventing the 'People's Europe': Critical Approaches to European Community 'Cultural Policy.'" *Man* 28(4): 779–800.

Silverman, M. 1992. *Deconstructing the Nation: Immigration, Racism, and Citizenship in Modern France*. London: Routledge.

Silverstein, P. A. 2004. *Algeria in France: Transpolitics, Race and Nation*. Bloomington: Indiana University Press.

Simi, P. 1963. "Le climat de la Corse." *Bulletin de la Société de Géographie* 76: 1–122.

———. 1979. "Cadre Naturel." In *Encyclopédies Régionales*. Paris: Bonneton, 213–287.

Smith, A. L. 2006. *Colonial Memory and Postcolonial Europe: Maltese Settlers in Algeria and France*. Bloomington: Indiana University Press.

Stasch, R. 2002. "Joking Avoidance: A Korowai Pragmatics of Being Two." *American Ethnologist* 29(2): 335–365.

Stolcke, V. 1995. "Talking Culture: New Boundaries, New Rhetorics of Exclusion in Europe." *Current Anthropology* 36(1): 1–24.

———. 1997. "The 'Nature' of Nationality." In V. Bader, ed., *Citizenship and Exclusion*. London: Macmillan, 61–80.

Strathern, M. 1981. *Kinship at the Core: An Anthropology of Elmdon, a Village in North-West Essex in the Nineteen-Sixties*. Cambridge: Cambridge University Press.

———. 1995. "The Nice Thing about Culture Is That Everyone Has It." In M. Strathern, ed., *Shifting Contexts: Transformations in Anthropological Knowledge*. London: Routledge, 153–176.

———. 1999. *Property, Substance and Effect: Anthropological Essays on Persons and Things*. London: Athlone.

———. 2004. *Partial Connections*. Savage, Md.: Rowman and Littlefield.

———. 2005. *Kinship, Law and the Unexpected: Relatives Are Always a Surprise*. Cambridge: Cambridge University Press.

Sutton, D. E. 1998. *Memories Cast in Stone: The Relevance of the Past in Everyday Life*. Oxford: Berg.

Sykes, K. 2007. "Subjectivity, Visual Technology, and Public Culture: Watching the Ethnographic Film, *Malanggan Labadama* in New Ireland." *Sociological Review* 55(1): 42–56.

Taguieff, P.-A. 1987. *La Force du Préjugé*. Paris: Découverte.

Tarde, G. 1999[1895]. *Monadologie et Sociologie*. Le Plessis: Synthélabo.

———. 2000[1899]. *Social Laws: An Outline of Sociology*. Kitchener: Batoche.

Taussig, M. 1992. "Culture of Terror—Space of Death: Roger Casement's Putumayo Report and the Explanation of Torture." In N. B. Dirks, ed., *Colonialism and Culture*. Ann Arbor: University of Michigan Press, 135–173.

Taylor, C. 1994. "The Politics of Recognition." In A. Gutmann, ed., *Multiculturalism: Examining the Politics of Recognition.* Princeton, N.J.: Princeton University Press.

Thiers, Ghj. 1989. *Papiers d'identité.* Levie: Albiana.

Thiesse, A.-M. 1997. *Ils apprenaient la France: L'exaltation des régions dans le discours patriotique.* Paris: Maison des Sciences de l'Homme.

Thomas, N. 1990. "Sanitation and Seeing: The Creation of State Power in Early Colonial Fiji." *Comparative Studies in Society and History* 32(1): 149–170.

Thornton, R. J. 1988. "The Rhetoric of Ethnographic Holism." *Cultural Anthropology* 3(3): 285–303.

Thrift, N. J. 2004. "Intensities of Feeling: Towards a Spatial Politics of Affect." *Geografiska Annaler,* ser. B, *Human Geography* 86(1): 57–78.

Tiévant, C., and L. Desideri. 1986. *Almanach de la mémoire et des coutumes: Corse.* Paris: Albin Michel.

Turner, T. 1993. "Anthropology and Multiculturalism: What Is Anthropology That Multiculturalists Should Be Mindful of It?" *Cultural Anthropology* 8: 411–429.

Urla, J. 1988. "Ethnic Protest and Social Planning: A Look at Basque Language Revival." *Cultural Anthropology* 3: 379–394.

Verdoni, D. 1999. "L'insularité, approche herméneutique de la variation." In A. Meisterheim, ed., *L'île Laboratoire.* Ajaccio: Piazzola, 436–442.

Viveiros de Castro, E. 2003. *And.* Manchester: Manchester University Press.

Waldren, J. 1996. *Insiders and Outsiders: Paradise and Reality in Mallorca.* Oxford: Berghahn.

Weber, E. 1976. *Peasants into Frenchmen: The Modernisation of Rural France 1870–1914.* Stanford, Calif.: Stanford University Press.

Weber, M. 1998. "Science as a Vocation." In H. H. Gerth and C. W. Mills, eds., *From Max Weber: Essays in Sociology.* London: Routledge, 129–156.

Werbner, P. 1997. "Essentialising Essentialism, Essentialising Silence: Ambivalence and Multiplicity in the Constructions of Racism and Ethnicity." In P. Werbner and T. Modood, eds., *Debating Cultural Hybridity: Multi-Cultural Identities and the Politics of Anti-Racism.* London: Zed.

Wilk, R. 1995. "Learning to Be Local in Belize: Global Systems of Common Difference." In D. Miller, ed., *Worlds Apart: Modernity through the Prism of the Local.* London: Routledge, 110–133.

Williams, R. 1975. *The Country and the City.* St. Albans: Paladin.

Willis, F. R. 1980. "Development Planning in Eighteenth-Century France: Corsica's *Plan Terrier.*" *French Historical Studies* 11(3): 328–351.

Wilson, S. 1988. *Feuding, Conflict and Banditry in Nineteenth-Century Corsica.* Cambridge: Cambridge University Press.

Zonabend, F. 1990. "Jeux de noms: Les noms de personne à Minot." In T. Jolas, M.-C. Pingaud, Y. Verdier, and F. Zonabend, eds., *Une campagne voisine.* Paris: Maison des Sciences de l'Homme, 241–280.

Index

NEW ANTHROPOLOGIES OF EUROPE

Daphne Berdahl, Matti Bunzl, and Michael Herzfeld, founding editors

MATEI CANDEA is a lecturer in social anthropology at Durham University. He is editor of *The Social after Gabriel Tarde: Debates and Assessments*, a reconsideration of the work of the nineteenth-century French sociologist and philosopher.